Pilgrim Band

"Tom Bandy's magnificent book takes its readers on a spiritual journey in the three stages: foundation, journey, and spirit, and develops a groundbreaking blueprint for shaping Christian community in the twenty-first century under the title 'pilgrim band.' A pilgrim band is 'a mobile, adaptable, and purposeful partnership holding one another accountable for spiritual growth and holistic health.' This new form of a spiritual community replaces traditional forms of Christianity and realizes itself—following Paul Tillich—as a religion of the concrete Spirit in everyday life and in mutual mentoring on the journey through time."

—**Christian Danz**, Institute for Systematic Theology and Religious Studies, University of Vienna

"Thomas Bandy has his finger on the pulse of the moment. It will be needed even more in the future. International forces of political domination, economic inequality, and social isolation are not going anywhere. Rather than criticize them by rehashing old debates, hope should be placed in smaller unexpected communities leading to genuine human flourishing. Local bands may not look familiar but refreshing alternatives to institutional breakdowns are just what the world needs."

—**Benjamin J. Chicka**, Senior Lecturer of Philosophy and Religion, Curry College

"With prophetic punch and poetic precision, Tom Bandy maps the migration from religious institutions to spiritual pilgrimage. His 'pilgrim band' concept isn't just another church growth strategy. It's a GPS for discipleship in a world of spiritual nomads. Blending ancient pathways with digital highways, Bandy shows how mutual mentoring creates liminal spaces where Spirit moves, and transfiguration happens. A must-read for anyone thirsting for authentic companionship in our twenty-first-century culture with our twenty-second-century kids."

—**Leonard Sweet**, author of *Designer Jesus*

"*Pilgrim Band* is a profound and timely reflection on the future of faith in a rapidly changing world. Bandy masterfully weaves personal insight, theological depth, and cultural analysis to offer a compelling vision of spiritual mentorship and companionship that promises to bring hope in a time of anxiety and chaos. A powerful resource for seekers, mentors, or those who are curious about an approach to the life of faith that is both new and ancient."

—**Thomas Barlow**, Gerald L. Schlessman Professor in Methodist Studies, Iliff School of Theology

"Bandy provides an analysis that highlights the perennial human need to feel connected with the sacred. He describes how, as our inner compass seeks guidance and growth, we often find a resonance with someone who becomes our mentor. Together, and often with others in similar relationships (our Pilgrim Band), we move as one toward a deeper harmony. He suggests it is this, not the institutional church, that underlies the significance and inevitability of worship."

—**Sharon P. Burch**, Board Chair, Interfaith Counseling Center

Pilgrim Band

Our *Shared* Quest for Meaning and Purpose

Thomas G. Bandy

WIPF & STOCK · Eugene, Oregon

PILGRIM BAND
Our Shared Quest for Meaning and Purpose

Copyright © 2025 Thomas G. Bandy. All rights reserved. Except for brief quotations in critical publications or reviews, no part of this book may be reproduced in any manner without prior written permission from the publisher. Write: Permissions, Wipf and Stock Publishers, 199 W. 8th Ave., Suite 3, Eugene, OR 97401.

Wipf & Stock
An Imprint of Wipf and Stock Publishers
199 W. 8th Ave., Suite 3
Eugene, OR 97401

www.wipfandstock.com

PAPERBACK ISBN: 979-8-3852-3717-3
HARDCOVER ISBN: 979-8-3852-3718-0
EBOOK ISBN: 979-8-3852-3719-7

VERSION NUMBER 03/20/25

Scripture quotes are from New Revised Standard Version Bible, copyright © 1989 National Council of the Churches of Christ in the United States of America. Used by permission. All rights reserved worldwide.

Where noted, Scripture quotes are from Revised Standard Version of the Bible, copyright © 1946, 1952, AND 1971 the Division of Christian Education of the National Council of the Churches of Christ in the United States of America. Used by permission. All rights reserved.

For my beloved wife and lifelong companion.

And for my precious family:
past, present, and future.

Contents

Preface | ix
Introduction | xi

Foundation
The Ancient Way | 3
Seekers and Travelers | 12
Anxiety and Hope | 21
The Incentive for Pilgrimage | 35

Journey
Me? Mentor? Maybe? | 47
Heartbursts | 65
First Steps | 81
Walk with Me | 93
Talk with Me | 104
Walk Together | 114
Talk Together | 129
Trek Together | 142
Transitions | 158

Spirit
On Being Spiritually Present | 167
On Faithfulness | 180
On the *Pilgrim Band* | 195

Bibliography | 205

Preface

This book has been a work in progress over two decades. My career has required me to function in many ways: teacher, tutor, congregational clergy, denominational officer, consultant, non-profit CEO, for-profit president, leadership coach, author, editor, publisher, and lots of smaller tasks in between roles. I have had the good fortune to be married to my best friend all that time, to sustain international friendships across different sectors, and to build cross-cultural relationships around the world.

In all those functions and transitions, I always asked myself the question everyone asks of themselves: *What will I do now?* But as time passed, I began to ask a different question. *What am I really doing?* The rationale for the first question is clear enough. Earn a living, shape a lifestyle, raise a family, fulfill ambition. The rationale for the second question is more profound but harder to define.

Is there a purposefulness that links all the disparate activities of one's life into a single trajectory? Not a *chosen* career that can be changed as circumstances demand, but a *given* pattern of anticipation and expectation that is continuous through all circumstances? We are conscious of the former, but often unconscious of the latter. Yet it is this thread of purposefulness that brings meaning to life.

I think that more and more people are trying to answer this second question. Or perhaps it is better to say we are trying to *face up* to this question. It is a challenging, disconcerting, and uncomfortable question because there is a corollary to it. If we face up to what we have *really* been doing with our lives, we are forced to decide what we *should* be doing with our lives. If, somehow, we have gone "off track" in our living, how do we realign our lives with our destiny?

PREFACE

This is not just a moral dilemma but a spiritual one. It is the difference between resignation and hope, and between resentment and love. It seeks the reunion of freedom and limitation, long separated by the radical individualism and self-centeredness of modernity and the authoritarian demands of institutions. It involves the recovery of the lost concept of "soul" and the rediscovery of the connection between "soul" and "Spirit."

I am very grateful to the many mentors who have influenced my life, some known and some unknown, and particularly to those companions from the international Tillich societies and inter-faith organizations who have included me in their *pilgrim bands*.

Tom Bandy, November 2024

Introduction

Twenty years ago, at the peak of my international speaking tours, I participated in four gatherings prescient for the future of Western spirituality.

- The first was a meeting with an ecumenical group from South Africa, in which we discussed their perceived need for a "New Reformation" to reestablish the dogmas and practices of classic Protestantism.
- The second was a conference hosted by leading Christian evangelicals in California in which church growth experts and mega-church pastors strategized a radical transformation of declining congregations.
- The third was a seminar associated with Claremont School of Theology connecting church renewal with process theology (later to become popularized as "Progressive Christianity").
- The fourth was an event held in the cricket stadium in Perth, Australia, in which we talked about systemic change, cultural heritages, and spiritual life.

Each event had its own cultural context. But each context participated in larger, global crises including racial and ethnic tension, economic disparity, environmental catastrophe, political polarization, radicalized religion, and self-centered secularization.

The fourth event had the greatest, lasting impact on my quest for meaning and sense of purpose. The first three reflected the church's preoccupation with itself and the future of the institution. The fourth led me to reflect on cultural diversity, the power of heritage and history, and the future of the Christian movement. Indeed, it led me to reflect on the activity of the Spirit in history, which is to say, my history, your history, and our histories.

INTRODUCTION

Every five centuries or so the Christian movement seems to experience a major socio-cultural-spiritual reboot.[1] Any number of ethnic and linguistic, liturgical and dogmatic, educational and organizational changes may occur. The measure of credibility for church leadership shifts. The priorities of mission and the measurable outcomes of "successful" mission may shift dramatically.

We remember, for example, revolutionary changes that occurred as apostolic mission shifted to Constantinian orthodoxy, the dramatic effects of the schism that divided the Western and Eastern church traditions, the Anglican revision and the Protestant Reformation, the emergence of modern denominationalism, and most recently the post-Christendom institutional decline and rise of personal spiritualities.

Every reboot feels like chaos. In part, this is because religious change is often accompanied by (although not necessarily caused by) political and economic crises precipitated by climate changes, pandemics, economic volatility, wars, population migrations, and so on. Overall anxiety about loss of control over hearts and minds, as well as attitudes and behavior patterns, usually generates a heady brew of religion and politics. Eventually, religion and politics disentangle themselves. Why? I think the answer is that chaos precipitates a quest for meaning and purpose. While this is a *personal* need, it is not an *individual* journey. It is a shared journey because meaning and purpose emerge from a sense of our common humanity as it is touched by the immanence of God. The catchall term for this link between the finite and the infinite is "spirituality."

"Spirituality" can be described in unlimited ways, but it is always a combination of "reach" and "depth." The "reach" of spirituality is that it emerges from the empathy human beings have with each other across the spectrum of suffering and joy. The "depth" of spirituality is that it connects not only with ultimate mystery but with the felt touch of the Holy. It is an incarnational experience that binds people together in hope.

There really is a difference between "religion" and "spirituality." While religion may be *progressive*, spirituality is not. Spirituality is *regenerative*. Spirit does not reject, judge, or build on the past. It restores, revives, and replenishes the present. Moreover, while religion can be *manipulated* within history, spirituality *influences* the course of history. Spirituality is what infuses, empowers, and shapes life. Religion is an expression, but not the substance, of Spirit. And in times of chaos, we turn instinctively to the

1. Tickle, *Great Emergence*.

INTRODUCTION

original source of meaning and purpose rather than cling to controlling institutions or follow popular trends.

While every reboot of the Christian *movement* has its own historical context, I think there are three consistent outcomes.

First, the primary method of spiritual growth and faith formation changes. Just as the impact of the printing press and the rise of nation states transformed the Christian movement in the fifteenth century, so now the impact of the internet and the rise of lifestyle networks transforms the Christian movement once again. The maturation process no longer depends on stability, physical presence, the ability to read, and a standardized regimen. Today it relies on mobility, virtual as well as physical presence, the ability to converse, and a flexible process of action and reflection.

Curriculum to conversation. Catechism to companionship. Classroom to coffeehouse. As the Sunday-centric link between preaching and Christian education declines, it is being replaced by a daily (even moment-to-moment) link between mentoring and media. Chaos reveals that knowledge is not enough. Facts can be cleverly interpreted, distorted or invented in a multitude of ways for hidden agendas. What is needed is wisdom, that penetrating discernment of truth based on inward integrity and outward perspicacity. This is the essence of mentoring.

In the Christian movement, this shift in the method of maturation does not mean that teaching and textbooks, preaching and curricula, will disappear. Their function becomes more specialized. They support and expand the core mentoring relationship. On the one hand they become more *motivational*. They do not intend to inform so much as to inspire and to encourage. On the other hand, they become more *intensive*. They do not survey broad topics but offer deep dives into ultimate concerns.

Portability is crucial to relevance. Life is changing so quickly, cultural contexts are mingling so creatively, and challenges are emerging so unexpectedly, that education must be "on-demand." We don't consult our lecture notes. We do connect with a blogger. We can't take time off for graduate school to listen to an expert. We must make time for significant conversation with an expert along the roads we travel.

Second, the primary network of personal support and social action changes. We are no longer controlled by hierarchies, corporations, or even congregations, but we are influenced by influencers. In the fourth century the source of inspiration and energy that shaped Christian attitudes, convictions, and habits shifted from the apostolic tradition to state-controlled

Christendom. In the ninth century it shifted from the state to the diocesan hierarchy. In the fifteenth century it shifted from the hierarchy to the local congregation or kirk. In the nineteenth century it shifted from the congregation to the denomination. And today it is shifting from the congregation and denomination to what I call the *Pilgrim Band*.

Chaos inspires panic, and panic provokes the old orders to clamp down and control. Nevertheless, the locus of decision-making changes and our assumptions about who can do what, how, where, when, and in what order of priority change. The same is true today. There is a great deal of panic about the decline of the church, and great efforts to control Christian thought and behavior by policy or persecution. Yet the Christian movement is alive and well . . . just taking new forms.

The *pilgrim band* is a mobile, adaptable, and purposeful partnership holding one another accountable for spiritual growth and holistic health. It is a small, fluid group with high trust based on shared values and convictions rather than institutional rules and traditions. It is united by a common vision for a better world. It pursues a holy destination, but with utmost patience and flexibility, pausing frequently to help others along the way. Each partner practices a lifestyle of humility and curiosity, communion and conversation, compassion and service wherever they are, whatever they do, among whoever they're with.

Today this shift might be described as the difference between a "committee" and a "true team." This is an organizational shift that impacts all public sectors and is the organizational boundary between modernity and postmodernity. The committee has great responsibility but limited authority. It has the power to implement only what is commanded but must get approval for the plan and defer final evaluation to a higher authority. The *pilgrim band* is a true team, which we might say embodies the "entrepreneurial spirit" of postmodernity, and has real power to discern, design, implement, and evaluate its work without seeking outside approval or validation.

The *pilgrim band* is an intimate relationship both physical and virtual. It often begins with a mentor, but mentoring soon becomes mutual. Their resources are "devotional" in the broadest sense and span all media (blog, image, music, video). Yet the *pilgrim band* will pause for rest and reflection, or divert from its path to serve others, or change careers, or alter their plans in unexpected ways. They require resources that open their minds to new ideas and help them explore depth dimensions.

INTRODUCTION

In the Christian movement, this shift in the primary network of activity does not mean that denominations, diocese, and congregations will cease to exist. Instead, they consolidate. They become useful resources, albeit not necessarily the only resources. They can define boundaries for action but cannot prescribe any specific action. In short, congregations and denominations are no longer *primary*, but (at best) *secondary* to Christian activity.

Third, the nature and preparation for professional careers and Christian vocations changes. Previous generations were faced with workplace questions: *What do you want to do? How will you measure success?* Emerging generations are faced with lifestyle questions: *Who do you want to be? How will you measure fulfillment?* Similarly, Christians in the days of Christendom were asked task-oriented questions: *What does God call you to do? What church does God call you to serve?* But Christians in these post-Christendom days are faced with relational questions: *Who does God want you to become? With whom does God call you to live?*

This generational attitude shift is more than just an anti-institutional rejection of "religion" in favor of vague individual "spiritualities." It springs from the intuition that career and calling are not discerned by exploring external opportunities but by discerning internal values and convictions. Moreover, this is more than just renewed interest in spiritual life because it is not motivated by a desire to *step away* from busy-ness of living, but a desire to *step into* the purposefulness of living. It is, as my greatest influencer Paul Tillich might say, an obsession with a "religion of the concrete spirit."[2] This is more than an interest in spiritual presence. It is a passion to *be* spiritually present in daily living.

This means that the boundaries between what is considered "secular" and "sacred" have disappeared. Spirituality penetrates every occupation and public sector, for-profit and non-profit, and is often most vividly revealed in organizations beyond the church and events other than Sunday worship. This has also generated renewed interest in demographic and lifestyle research. While the former tracks traditional data for age, race, income, etc., the latter tracks changing attitudes and habits of behavior. Together these help spiritual travelers interpret hopes and anxieties and find the "traveling companions" for the *pilgrim band*.

---

2. Tillich, "Significance of the History of Religions," 90–91; and *Systematic Theology* vol. 3.

INTRODUCTION

This book attempts to explain how all three of these transformations are unfolding today, and how they are changing the very nature of the Christian movement as radically as similar shifts did in the past.

- The first chapters lay a foundation to understand the growing interest in mentoring and the companionship of the *pilgrim band*. We explore the varieties of seekers today, and the motivations for spiritual travelers.

- In the middle chapters, I try to provide a kind of "manual" for the practice of mutual mentoring and describe the conversations and interactions of the journey of the *pilgrim band*.

- In the final chapters, I offer a broader perspective on the praxis of being spiritually present in life and the goal of aligning one's inner life and outward activity with greater purpose.

The Christian movement is changing because religion in general is rediscovering its original reach and depth. Religion itself is changing because Spirit is being revealed through cultural forms in new and unexpected ways.

Foundation

As far as we can discern, the sole purpose of human existence is to kindle a light in the darkness of mere being. —CARL JUNG[1]

---

1. Jung, *Memories, Dreams, Reflections*, 382.

The Ancient Way

ANCIENT AND POSTMODERN PEOPLE have similar assumptions about education, which makes the ancient way of mentoring and the conversational intimacy of a small group very appealing to emerging generations. These assumptions are very different from the past few centuries... and from the regimented and classroom educational systems of the parents and grandparents of these emerging generations.

The *purpose* of education is different. Ancient people knew that the point of education was to shape a lifestyle that would help individuals live in harmony with the world and contribute to the well-being of the community in which they lived. Modern people assume that the point of education is to sharpen skills that will help individuals control the world around them and achieve personal success.

Therefore, the *method* of education is different. Ancient civilizations understood that the best way to achieve the goal of education was to connect inquiring minds with wise people. This was an intimate relationship that combined reflection and action. Inquiring minds learned through dialogue that allowed each party to both ask and answer questions. Mentees learned through observation and imitation of the intentional and daring, and spontaneous and mundane, behaviors of their role models. Modern people understand that the best way to achieve their goals for education is for experts to lecture groups, download information, and correct mistakes. The behavior of the teacher outside of the classroom is irrelevant.

Modern education still tends to be highly individualistic. Yes, students might be in a classroom, but it is a classroom filled with *individuals*, many of whom are competing for attention, grades, and scholarships. The most common experience of collaborative learning is that the pace and depth of insight is determined by the slowest and least motivated classmate. The quick and the earnest can go faster and farther if they do it by themselves.

The ancient way is the mutual mentoring of a band of like-minded, highly motivated brothers and/or sisters. We see glimpses of the ancient way as far back as the first dynasties of Egypt, whose wisdom was later incorporated in the Old Testament book of Proverbs. We see glimpses of this in the relationships between prophets like Elijah and Elisha, and missionaries like Paul and his traveling companions. We see this among ancient Greek philosophers: Socrates to Plato, to Aristotle, to Alexander. We see it in their philosophical schools and their friendship circles.

The ancient way was not just one to one mentoring, but also *mutual* mentoring. The archetype was the symposium. This was a banquet of intimate friends, or, in the case of Alexander and his companions, a mobile feast, in which there was food and drink, music and art, conversation and discussion, plotting and debate, occasional confrontation and constant reconciliation. The symposium was open to all dimensions of knowing: analysis and synthesis, practical and theoretical, worldly and unworldly, cultural and spiritual.

We see it again among the Stoics of later antiquity and among the early medieval monastic orders and later schools of artists and literati of the Renaissance. We see it in late antiquity and the early Middle Ages in pilgrimages to holy places and hostels for purposeful travelers. And we also see it in Eastern cultures in Buddhism and the Tao of Confucius. To some extent it persisted in pre-twentieth-century British and German educational systems and lingers in European post-doctoral programs. But it has been largely absent in American mass production schemes of public schools and undergraduate universities.

I think the best way to contrast the ancient and modern ways of education is to say that modern people are trained to use knowledge, while ancient people were trained to absorb knowledge. Knowledge for modern people is data that can be manipulated in an infinite number of morally neutral ways, but knowledge for ancient people is wisdom that must be lived in morally sensitive ways.

Having grown up in modern ways, postmodern people (Gen X, Gen Y, and Gen Z) are learning to appreciate ancient ways. Indeed, since the modern way has led to what might be described as chronic unhappiness—or perhaps, better stated, chronic obsession with obtaining happiness that remains forever elusive—increasing numbers of Baby Boomers are changing their expectations too. Modern people can never get enough. The world is constantly slipping out of control. We find ourselves alone in an uncaring universe and in conflict with humanity and nature.

Emerging generations are "postmodern" precisely because they recognize this dead end and seek another way. If desire can never be fulfilled, then it is time to curb our desire. If we cannot manipulate the world to achieve happiness, perhaps we need to change ourselves and redefine happiness. The only thing over which we really have any power is our own state of mind, attitudes and perspectives, habits, and behavior patterns.

In a sense, postmodern generations have rediscovered what the Stoics already knew. It is normal for the world to be out of our control. To imagine it can be otherwise is abnormal and dysfunctional. You cannot *obtain* happiness, but perhaps you can *attain* it, by ceasing to pursue desires and focusing on pursuing peace. A good paraphrase of the advice of Marcus Aurelius is this: "Happiness is a by-product of thinking and acting in ways that are just, generous, resolute, purposeful, and free."[1]

Note that he says happiness is a "by-product," rather than an end. It is something you attain without having sought it. Happiness is realized in passing as one strives for a virtuous life. Moreover, that journey starts with "thinking" rather than "doing." The inner work of visualization and self-control, practiced intentionally and sacrificially, will eventually lead to actions that are just and generous. The "why" and "what for" are more relevant to happiness than "how to."

We live in an era of radical individualism that prizes self-sufficiency and believes in the principle of the survival of the fittest. Education is a competition and conforms to the economics of capitalism. It is a youth culture in which energy and imagination are valued more than reflection and experience. The older you get, the more useless you become.

Emerging generations are beginning to realize that many of the economic, social, and ecological crises of the postmodern era are precisely the result of this very Western, Caucasian, male, affluent, and pseudo-scientific attitude toward happiness. Instead of acquiring astronomical debt enrolling in institutions to learn from academic experts, perhaps we should use our mobility to find and follow wise practitioners.

---

1. Torode, *Meditations*, 71. A more literal translation by Staniforth reads: "Nothing can be good for a man unless it helps to make him just, self-disciplined, courageous, and independent." Staniforth, *Marcus Aurelius Meditations*, 121.

The postmodern challenge is that we are often stymied by the very first step. We are like Diogenes, the fourth-century BCE cynic who carried a lamp during the day looking for an honest man. We are surfing through social media hoping to find a wise person; or searching dating websites hoping to find a compatible partner; or dropping in and out of churches and social service agencies seeking a credible spiritual leader.

The postmodern breakthrough is the realization that you don't really need Marcus Aurelius to form a mentoring relationship. You can experience one to one mentoring, and even participate in a *pilgrim band*, in any career path. You just need to walk through life *thinking and acting in ways that are just, generous, resolute, purposeful, and free*. Find the courage to explore your humanity and lay yourself open to divinity. Look around with humility for travelers ahead of you and listen to their wisdom. Look around with compassion for travelers behind you to share your wisdom. You may become that wiser person who can mentor someone traveling behind you. You may not be perfectly just, generous, resolute, purposeful, and free . . . but you may be more experienced in the attempt than another and capable of helping them find their way.

The *attainment* of happiness will not ultimately be achieved by reading books, attending classes, completing graduate degrees, or obtaining certifications and ordinations. Nor can it be generated by modern definitions of success (wealth, power, prestige, etc.). It can only be accomplished in the ancient way:

- A one to one connection between a wise person and an inquiring mind.
- The priority of authentic relationships over the manipulation of data.
- The primacy of community over individuality.
- The reunion of knowledge and lifestyle.
- Alignment of one's mind, heart, and purpose with a greater good.

This ancient and postmodern way is counterintuitive to the modern mind. And the modern world, and institutional forms of education, are not designed to do it. *Mentoring* has little to do with *teaching* and everything to do with *influencing*.

First, mentoring is all about *experience*, not success. Mentors speak from the "school of hard knocks" and from the "school of hard-fought victories" that have occurred in their personal lives. This is one reason why the ancients (and Eastern and Aboriginal cultures) have revered older people. However, in our world, young people have often experienced a lifetime of pain and hope in just a few short years, and it is entirely possible that young people may be able to speak from experience even more powerfully than seniors.

Mentoring is about *discernment*, not about expertise. One does not have to have professional training in therapy or advanced degrees in any specific subject. Expertise may be helpful in certain situations, and mentors frequently seek specialized training to bond with, communicate with, or advise individuals facing unique challenges. Yet it is the experience of coping with life and discerning hope that is more important.

Mentoring is all about *insight*, not information. Mentors synthesize information and make intuitive leaps beyond the data to discern root causes and underlying assumptions. They "see" the hidden potential in people and events, or the self-destructive habits and recurring themes behind behavior. They are keen observers who are never quite sure what they are looking for . . . until they find it.

Mentoring is more about *synthesis* than analysis. Taking things apart and sorting things out misses the point. Human beings are always more than their constituent biological systems or psychological states. Analysis is content with reality and discovering how it works. Synthesis is restless with reality and searches for the reasons why life is what it is. Mentors help people discover or uncover truth that lies behind, or beyond, reality.

Mentoring is about sharing *wisdom*, not about providing explanations. Mentors explore motivation and purposefulness, which together form the *intentionality* that the individual brings to living. They help travelers cope with the mystery of gratuitous evil and adapt to the mystery of unexpected miracles, maintaining a sense of direction amid ambiguity. Pat answers, repetitive dogmas, aphorisms, and moralizations are foreign to the mentor. No conversation is ever quite finished; no explanation is ever quite sufficient; no perspective is ever quite complete. There is a truth, but it cannot be contained in words. An individual life can align with truth without ever fully grasping it.

Mentoring is rooted in *self-discipline*, not academic disciplines. Every field of study has its own procedures about work but demands much less rigor for the lifestyle of the worker. The most careful researchers can live the most careless lives. The most learned teachers can be the most eccentric and amoral individuals. So long as you perform well, you can live as you like.

Mentors demonstrate how to lead an ordered life. They control their passions, proceed judiciously in their actions, practice spiritual habits, exercise body and mind, and take responsibility for relationships. Self-discipline allows them to channel their energy toward others, and they are not easily distracted by their own personal needs and problems.

Therefore, mentoring is more about *selflessness* than self-awareness. It is all about surrender. Mentors move beyond self-discipline to self-forgetfulness. They try to "get out of themselves" so that they can better understand the seeker who is lost, or the traveler who is looking, or the Spirit that moves among us all. The ego gets in their way, which is why they try so hard to tame it (self-discipline) and to get beyond it (self-forgetfulness). Their humility is part of their credibility.

Now we get to the heart of the difficulty modern people have with mentoring. Mentoring is not really about self-actualization, achieving autonomy, or unleashing individuality. Starting with the Renaissance and extending through the Enlightenment, modern Western people have defined the ego—the individual—as the center of the universe. It is simply incomprehensible that anyone might deny personal survival, individual accomplishment, or private satisfaction as the ultimate motivation and goal of living.

Modern Western people prefer professionals who can help you take control of all the aspects of your life (career, marriage, family, or leisure). They compartmentalize lifestyle so that you can manage life and become a success. Mentors help you stake all that for a higher purpose. Modern people prefer therapists who can help you resolve tensions, lower stress, and lead a balanced life. Mentors help you live with tensions, explore truths that may raise your stress, and embrace an unbalanced life that tips in the direction of God.

I think it quite possible for mentoring to occur within any religious or philosophical tradition. But I find the Christian perspective to be especially fruitful because it removes the hidden elitism often associated with the "guru" revealing spiritual secrets to a "follower." Mentoring in the Christian perspective broadens the possibilities for helping one another find meaning and purpose. Mentoring occurs in a small community of earnest, disciplined, accountable seekers.

In many philosophical and mystical traditions, mentoring occurs in the context of divine transcendence. Stoicism, for example, is profound, but it is also very abstract. The light of reason, universal order, the laws of nature, and the pursuit of virtue are framed by a transcendent perspective of the sublime that is dispassionate and unreachable. It takes ascetic courage and rigorous self-denial to be a Stoic—or an adherent to any kind of philosophy of life—in the real world. Mysticism is profound, but very esoteric. Enlightenment and serenity are hard to attain and difficult to sustain and not readily transferrable to the average person.

In the Christian perspective, mentoring occurs in the context of divine immanence. Set aside all the doctrines and dogmas and rituals. The essence of Christianity is "God-with-Us," or, as *pilgrim band*s often discover, "God-among-Us." It is about incarnation. As we shall see, incarnation can be experienced in many ways. But the immanence of God provides both encouragement and acceptance. We do not have to be *immensely* courageous to lead a spiritual life. We just need to be *more* courageous because God is alongside to encourage and strengthen us. We do not have to punish ourselves for every failure in pursuing a spiritual life. We can accept acceptance as a gift from God.

Christian *education* has been described as helping people live in imitation of Christ. This implies aligning one's lifestyle with the model, message, and mission of the historical Jesus. But over time the quest for the historical Jesus has been subjugated to the dogmas, doctrines, ideologies, and perspectives of the institutional church. Christian *mentoring* assumes that the historical Jesus is not only beyond our reach but also irrelevant to our quest. The experience, model, message, purpose, ministry, and companionship of *God incarnate* today are central. Beyond any institutional dogma or perspective, there is a divine immanence that is always mysterious but can still be discerned and heard if you are willing to stop, look, and listen. It will never be fully understood, but it can be touched, tasted, smelled, and incorporated in our lifestyles. Christian mentors not only point toward classical ideals of virtue, truth, beauty, and freedom. They point toward Christian ideals of forgiveness, the goodness of creation, the bonds of community, and the depths of love.

The goal of mentoring is to shape integrity, discern purpose, and (coincidentally) attain happiness along the way. A good paraphrase of Marcus Aurelius reads: "The way to peace is to be content with yourself, honor the light of reason within, live in harmony with others, and be grateful to the gods for the universe and your role in it."[2] The goal of explicitly Christian

---

2. Torode, *Meditations*, 48. A more literal translation by Staniforth reads: "A respect and esteem for your own understanding will keep you at peace with yourself, at one with

mentoring is similar. The way to peace is to be true to yourself, honor the light of hope within and beyond you, live in harmony with creation and God's purpose, and be grateful to God for ultimate acceptance.

I think mentors in all religious traditions and philosophies of life believe that "the truth is out there," and the truth is "in here," and that the two are internally connected. But I think the *pilgrim band* also believes that the truth is alongside us in the journey toward enlightenment. It is the experience of incarnation that makes spirituality possible for ordinary people. It is not just something attainable only by gurus and saints, priests or prophets, or heroes and heroines. You can do it. I can do it. We can do it not just because God is above us or inside us, but because God is beside us.

This book focuses on the mystery of incarnation, divine immanence, the touch of the Holy, or (in the common language of all those seeking meaning and purpose in life) Spirit. It focuses on what it means to live in a way that is transparent to that mystery and motivated by that mystery. The dogmas and doctrines, rituals and practices, and institutional expectations of churches are secondary at best. In a sense, mutual mentoring as I see it in the twenty-first century is much like mutual mentoring in the second century. The mystery of incarnation—and all the intimations of hope and love revealed through incarnation—is what is most urgent for seekers and spiritual travelers today.

A Personal Reflection

The world has changed so much, and so fast, that it is difficult for anyone's memory to take it all in. Numerous memoirs have been written trying to describe "the way it was," but emerging generations often find these reminiscences hard to believe. *The World of Yesterday* by Stefan Zweig is his personal memoir of life in Vienna in the last days of the Hapsburg Empire, written in the context of the Nazi Anschluss that caused him to flee Austria. He finished the manuscript (in Brazil) and sent it to his publisher (in Stockholm) in 1942, and shortly thereafter he and his wife committed suicide.

The book has always impressed me. Partly this is because it describes a very different method of education, the last gasp of which I shared. But it is also because the same depression and despair that he felt as a refugee is rising today among emerging generations struggling to fulfill their potential and

---

mankind, and in harmony with the gods." Staniforth, *Marcus Aurelius Meditations*, 95.

older generations struggling to cope with globalization, urbanization, and digitalization. We are all "refugees" from systems that have let us down.

The world of yesterday for me gave me access to mentoring in my schooling and church. My Spanish teacher introduced me to the Christian existentialism of Miguel de Unamuno (*The Tragic Sense of Life*). My minister spent hours with me discussing Paul Tillich (*Shaking the Foundations* and *Systematic Theology*). My own *pilgrim band* explored the Bible. And my music education taught me to ad lib with a jazz band. Later I enjoyed the intimacy of British scholars in St. Mary's College (St. Andrew's University, Scotland), the ecumenical dialogue with faculty and students at Princeton Seminary, and the European-style doctoral tutoring of Toronto. I wrote my dissertation in philosophical theology with a fountain pen!

In 1997 Neil Howe and William Strauss developed a theory in *The Fourth Turning* about generational change. They argued that generational change caused cultural shifts about every twenty years, and that every eighty years or so there is a major crisis. They predicted the next one would occur sometime in the middle of the twenty-first century in a confrontation between aging Boomers and emerging Millennials.[3] The theory is controversial among rigorous social scientists, but very influential among observers of culture. The crisis includes the decline of liberal arts education and religious institutions and the rise of applied science and business education and personal spiritualities.

In my experience of emerging culture, Baby Boomers are feeling more like refugees and Millennials are feeling more like pilgrims. The demographic boundaries are not precise. Some Millennials are manufacturing mythological histories, and many Boomers are exploring new worlds. The general trend, I think, is that today there are fewer *seekers* and more *travelers*. That is, spirituality is less a matter of curiosity and more a matter of urgency.

All along the way, my journey has been shaped by influential encounters rather than by programs or preachers. The experiences and techniques of mentoring have carried over into the rest of my life. My career in coaching and consulting has taken me across continents, cultures, generations, and lifestyles, and especially among the "spiritual but not religious." And everywhere there is a restlessness for a *different* way, a *better* way, and a yearning to discover (or rediscover) meaning and purpose in life.

---

3. Strauss and Howe, *Fourth Turning*, 272–302.

Seekers and Travelers

THE DIFFERENCE BETWEEN RELIGION and spirituality today is simply this. In religion, we say *I believe in God*. In spirituality, we exclaim *Oh, my God!* The bridge between statement and exclamation is what might be described as "personal religion." It is a broad spectrum of spiritual ideas, attitudes, and behavior patterns, prompted not only by alienation from religious institutions and traditions but also by the blurring of once well-defined boundaries between sectors (health, education, social service, business, entertainment, military, government, etc.) and disciplines (theoretical and applied sciences, ecology, psychology, pop culture, self-help literature, etc.). It may be broad and ill defined, but it is the fastest growing "religious" movement in Western culture, and it is permeating and transforming Protestant, Evangelical, and Catholic memberships.

While it is difficult to define "personal religion," I think two seminal authors capture the essence and urgency of this diverse movement. Evelyn Underhill introduced the average person to contemplative literature in the midst of post–World War I cynicism about institutional religion. She was the first widely read lay person to focus on the "inner life," by which she meant "all that conditions the relation of the individual soul with God; the deepening and expansion of the spiritual sense; in fact, the heart of personal religion."[1]

Paul Tillich crossed boundaries between theology, existential philosophy, and depth psychology and linked religion and culture as two sides of the same coin. He wrote that "religion is the substance of culture, culture is the form of religion."[2] In sermons popularized in the midst of post–World War II secular skepticism about God he articulated what

1. Underhill, *Concerning the Inner Life*, 1.
2. Tillich, *Theology of Culture*, 42.

many had already intuited, that there were hidden depths in daily life, including "the feeling for the inexhaustible mystery of life, the grip of an ultimate meaning in existence, and the invincible power of an unconditional devotion."[3] Religion could no longer be contained by institutional dogmas solely interpreted by professional clergy. It was within everyday life and could be interpreted by any individual.

It is in the expansion and diversity of spirituality that mentoring has regained the importance it once had in ancient times. My experience over three decades of consulting with churches and non-profits, coaching clergy and other spiritual leaders, and discovering the thirst for mentoring that is often revealed in airports and bus stops, coffee shops and pubs, health clinics and social agencies, more than in religious institutions or on Sunday mornings, has led me to define five stages in the development of personal religion.[4]

Spiritual Dilettantes

They have thrived in the relative peace, economic prosperity, and climate of opportunity that America has enjoyed in the latter half of the twentieth century. They publicly claim memberships in multiple religious organizations and privately practice church non-participation. They revisit religion at life-cycle events in their extended families. Religion is something of a hobby in which they non-contextually collect ideas from various faiths. They dabble in religion insofar as it satisfies their curiosity and assuages their personal discomforts. Their spirituality is often dismissed as shallow, self-serving, and materialistic, but there is a depth and urgency that lies beneath the surface. The context of their quest for God is shaped by a pervasive or chronic depression. Life-cycle events of birth, maturity, marriage, or death pique their anxieties over emptiness and meaninglessness. They long to discover patterns of meaning or mythologies that explain personal behavioral traits or world events.

---

3. Tillich, *Shaking of the Foundations*, 181.

4. These categories were defined in my article "Tillich and the Rise of Personal Religions," 145–49.

Divining Spiritualists

This is a somewhat smaller but growing population. Some disparage religion and look for the magical in life. They gravitate to new religious movements, aboriginal practices, psychic communications, and supernatural phenomena. Others manipulate religion to anticipate or control spiritual energies through direct or personal relationships with God, often using mediums like crystals or objects of nature, Bibles or crucifixes. Both try to access hidden knowledge through personal enlightenment. They resemble ancient Gnostics, but without the self-denial. They may be very liberal or very conservative. They are prone to believe conspiracy theories. Many claim to be members of a local religious organization but frequently quarrel with traditional dogma or denominational policy. The context of their quest for God is shaped by a pervasive sense of dread of the ominous unknown. Their preoccupation with the supernatural is often driven by anxieties about fate and death.

Seriously Experimenting

Many of these have opted out of the religious organizations altogether or are people who have grown up with no formal religious experience whatever. Their pragmatism makes them suspicious of abstractions and dogmas. For them church participation is an eccentric habit that is only occasionally useful to promote generational harmony or political policies. They are often associated with students, professionals, or entrepreneurs in corporate or retail business, influencers in sports or entertainment sectors, and struggling middle-class households keen on self-help literature and addiction intervention. They invest significant time, energy, and money exploring spiritualities. They are active seekers but are unclear about what they seek. They invest a lot of time searching for God but are hesitant to commit to any specific faith or spiritual discipline. Despite strong egos, they chronically second guess themselves, which often results in frequent changes in personal relationships, careers, and religious preferences. The context of their quest for God is shaped by a sense of estrangement from the meaning of life and their failure to build authentic relationships.

Rationally Reserved

I often find people in this group on the boards of religious and non-profit organizations and among professionals in public sectors for education, health, and social service, as well as government and legal services. They are products of the Enlightenment, confident in education, and committed rationalists. They are skeptical of supernaturalism and confident that there is an explanation for every seeming miracle. While they may have liberal or conservative ideologies, they believe that education, dialogue, and progress will achieve peace, happiness, and prosperity. Religion must be reasonable and shaped around what they assume are sophisticated tastes. God's presence is felt through responsible human behavior.

Some understand religion as a form of psychotherapy that seeks wholeness, guarantees acceptance, and perceives religious figures as archetypes. If they still participate in a religious institution, they prefer small gatherings because they resemble therapy groups. Others understand religion as cosmic harmony that reveals the order of the universe, honors creation, and reconciles enemies. If they still participate in a religious institution, they prefer larger gatherings that resemble schools with parallel programs in both applied and theoretical science. They are often passionate to "make a difference," but tend to be low risk-takers. The context of their quest for God is often shaped by a pervasive sense of guilt, inadequacy, or failure. Their ideals of truth, goodness, and beauty contrast with flawed relationships, global crises, and chronic injustice. They may be less comfortable with political ideologies and prophetic preaching and more comfortable with holistic "life" philosophers.

Radically Committed

This last category of personal religionists is relatively small. These people merge theory and practice to choose counter-cultural lifestyles that show contempt for the current world order and desire for a utopian future. For them, social service is a mystical experience, and mysticism is the ground for moral activism. Although religion is "personal," they tend to travel in small groups that share an affinity with some aesthetic or cause in the pursuit of a high ideal. They can go to paradoxical extremes of self-expression and communal accountability, freedom and obedience.

Some personalize religion *internally* and are highly committed to meditation, holistic health, naturalistic recreations, globe-trotting cultural immersion, and visual or performing arts. They are more appreciative of Catholic and Orthodox monasticism and mysticism than Protestant principles and polities. Others personalize religion *externally* and are highly committed to activism, social or political reform, action/reflection learning, and empathy with marginalized groups. They are appreciative of Protestant protest although not necessarily Protestant preaching. Both groups gravitate to church buildings converted to community centers and spiritual leaders who are heroic figures.

The context of their quest for God is often shaped by a sense of shame and abiding anger. The shame arises from experiences of personal abuse or dehumanizing oppression and empathy with homelessness and social genocide. The anger arises from experiences of emotional or economic repression, helplessness in political processes, and agony amid environmental destruction. Religion is "personal" because the threat of non-being is personal and survival urgent. The planet is at risk. Perhaps even more importantly, their soul is at risk. They often resonate with Paul Tillich's concept of "the courage to be"[5] and have a sense of urgency for the life of the Spirit.

I want to stress that all five groups of personal religionists are present *within* religious organizations as well as *beyond* religious organizations. This is why the popular demographic description of "Nones" is largely irrelevant to the expression of personal religion. Priests and pastors are increasingly shocked by liturgical idiosyncrasies and doctrinal liberties taken by people who otherwise appear to be loyal church members. Few people in America are truly devoid of spiritual interest. The "secular city" predicted in 1965 has turned out to be a bubbling cauldron of spiritualities.[6]

These five stages of spirituality represent a progressive shift from "seeker" to "traveler." Initially, religion is "personalized" to suit one's aesthetic tastes and lifestyle preferences. Spirituality *accommodates* to life. Gradually, religion becomes intensely "personal," touching on our most

---

5. Tillich, *Courage to Be*.

6. It is interesting to compare two seminal books by Harvey Cox. *The Secular City: Secularization and Urbanization in Theological Perspective*, published in 1965, discussed the irrelevance of the institutional church (and perhaps of God) in emerging secular culture. *Fire from Heaven: The Rise of Pentecostal Spirituality and the Reshaping of Religion in the 21st Century*, published in 1994, discussed the global Pentecostal movement and re-emerging spirituality in a post-secular world.

profound emotions, shaping our most intimate relationships, challenging our hidden philosophical assumptions, and disrupting our lifestyle habits. Life begins to *accommodate* to spirituality. While participants in the early stages of personal religion might be considered "spiritual seekers," participants in the later stages of personal religion might better be described as "spiritual travelers." The more "personal" religion becomes, the more their spiritual quest gains momentum and urgency.

Whatever the stage of personal religion, a person may be simultaneously mentor and mentee. The further down the road of spiritual life, the more you may be able to help those who are coming behind you. And the more you need to seek the guidance of those who are ahead of you. Nevertheless, it is difficult for those in the first stages (i.e., those *spiritual dilettantes* or *divining spiritualists*) to be effective mentors, and the more important it becomes for them to seek mentoring. Mentoring has a "been-there-done-that" quality. Mentors have personally experienced the stages of the spiritual journey. They know what it means to seek comfort, explore points of view, ask questions, struggle with faith, and experience transformation. They feel it. They have suffered because of it, but also, they have overcome suffering with insight and growth.

Ironically, religious people (clergy or lay) who have grown to thrive in organized religion are often least able to mentor others. They may teach, preach, manage, and care for members, but membership is still very demographically homogeneous, and leaders lack sensitivity to the cultural diversity of the surrounding communities. Similarly, leaders of religious organizations often lack empathy with the large numbers of people today with no Christian memory or experience with the church institution. This lack of empathy often leads them to miss or misunderstand the existential anxieties, spiritual needs, and religious questions that shape spiritualities.

Moreover, many clergy and stalwart laity may have traveled in the opposite direction through the stages of spirituality. Growing up in a religious institution, they started out as *radically committed*, then increasingly questioned the content of faith to become *rationally reserved*, then became dissatisfied with the forms of religion to become *seriously experimenting*. It is often at this stage that they drop out of membership altogether to explore eclectic and sometimes bizarre beliefs and practices and ultimately push religion to the margins of lifestyle.

Whatever direction the spiritual journey takes, the tipping point between the *irrelevance* of God and the *transcendence* of God is the experience of the *immanence* of God. This represents the key to the authenticity of mentoring and maximizes the impact of mentoring. This may be symbolized and expressed in different ways in different religious traditions, but in the Christian context typical of the West this means the experience of incarnation (not the dogmas attached to Christ, and not the historical accuracy of the life of Jesus).

The *experience* of incarnation may not be easily expressed in words, at least not in prose. Perhaps it might be expressed in artistic forms (poetry, song, images, and drama), but it cannot be contained in any generalized formula. If the mentor refers to the Bible, it is often to the Psalms, the Song of Songs, and the Gospels rather than the rituals of the Old Testament or the theological formulations of the New Testament. The spiritual journey, therefore, is more like a quest than a possession.

The immanence of God motivates, infuses, and guides the mentoring relationship. More than this, divine immanence inspires and shapes *mutual* mentoring relationships. God may be discovered in solitude, but incarnation does not encourage solitariness. To paraphrase Jesus: Where two or three are gathered in my name, *it is precisely there, in the midst of them, that I am to be found*. The spiritual journey is best pursued in the company of others who share the quest for meaning and purpose.

Following the death of Jesus, and among the stories of his later appearances, two stand out as paradigms for future Christian practice. One story is associated with the disciples miraculously speaking in tongues (Pentecost) and gathering believers to form the Jerusalem church.[7] That is the story ultimately embraced by the institutions of Christendom. The other story, however, recalls the journey of a companionship of disciples traveling to Emmaus.[8] They are in deep conversation about the significance of Jesus for themselves and the world when he joins their conversation incognito. This may be just a humble "symposium" over lunch at an inn, but they suddenly discern the immanence of God in the wine and the bread. This is the story ultimately embraced by pilgrims in the pre-Christendom and post-Christendom age. The immanence of God does not cause them to settle down and sink roots but get up and go. It does not lead to indoctrination through which they become well informed, but to conversation in which their hearts are strangely warmed.

---

7. Acts 2:1–47.
8. Luke 24:13–32.

A Personal Reflection

All my life I have worked among the religious. It began with an incarnational experience that saved my life and sanity as an adolescent, continued among churches of all traditions and across all demographic boundaries, and continues still among that growing population of seekers and travelers alienated from religious institutions.

Part of that journey included the church growth movement that began in the mid-1970s and largely ended in the early 2000s. I joined that conversation in 1997 with my first book. *Kicking Habits* explored the corporate addictions that blocked churches from transformation.[9] Indeed, as the age of church consultation declined over the next ten years, it became clear that despite the best education and coaching, most churches would not or could not change.

Of course, there are exceptions. The church, as an institution, will not disappear. But participation will continue to decline. Everywhere I go, the top reasons for non-participation in the church are the same: distrust of religious institutions, lack of credibility among religious leaders, obsession with money and the preservation of sacred cows, and the pressure from every direction (conservative and liberal) to conform.

The alternatives to the religious establishment, however, are as many as there are individual seekers. Personal, or personalized, religion has become the fastest growing spiritual movement today. This is most visible outside of America, but America is rapidly catching up. The different categories of seekers and spiritual travelers became clearer to me on two speaking tours in Australia.[10] I remember walking in Brisbane observing urban art and reflecting on the forms of culture and diversity of religious expression, and, later, being struck by the anomaly of speaking to a large crowd of seekers and travelers at the cricket stadium in Perth. I began to observe the phenomenon I came to describe as the "pilgrim band."

The depth of mentoring and the accountability of the *pilgrim band* is not for everyone . . . especially among the spiritual dilettantes, divining spiritualists, and rationally reserved. Those who value radical individualism and/or dogmatic certainties avoid it. Those who are seriously

---

9. Bandy, *Kicking Habits*.

10. Some of this is captured in my book *Talisman: Global Positioning for the Soul.* (There are two editions, from 2006 and 2017.)

experimenting or radically committed welcome it, but unfortunately many are avoiding or stepping away from religious institutions to find it.

There was a time when I led seminars studying the creeds, tracing church history, and explaining the sacraments. All good stuff . . . but less and less effective helping people experience and explore the immanence of God. Today mentoring often begins with a casual conversation along a transportation corridor. I recall checking into a hotel in a Canadian city where I was to begin a church consultation. The individual at the desk asked what brought me into town. I gestured toward a nearby church and explained. *They* then asked, with only mild curiosity and no hostility: *Soooo, what the hell do they do up there anyway?* Now *that* was a conversation!

Anxiety and Hope

Mentoring relationships never begin with conversations about theology. They always begin with conversations about anxiety. The methodology is not to begin with answers and then proceed to questions, but to begin with questions and then together search for answers. Doubt is a prerequisite of faith, but it is also the first step toward hope. In the old Christendom world, church members prioritized witness over listening. They might pretend to listen, but in fact they assumed that they already knew the questions and had already prepared the right answers. In the post-Christendom world, spiritual travelers genuinely listen for the anxieties that drive any person's quest for meaning and purpose and respond out of their experiences with God rather than dogmatic pronouncements about God.

Another way of saying this is that mentoring is not really a conversation about faith but rather a conversation about hope. The goal of mutual mentoring is not love (a friendship between mentor and mentee and future participation in a community of faith). That is the goal of Christian education. The goal of mentoring is hope (discovering a reason not to despair and keep on living). Mentoring is about building relationships and continuing dialogue, not about doctrinal agreements and institutional memberships. Mentoring is not a church growth strategy but a personal growth process. You are generating a sense of the presence of God in an individual's struggle with existential ambiguity. The goal of mentoring is not to instill *certainties* about life but rather to generate courage to face life.

Uncovering the Depths of Anxiety

Our quests for meaning and purpose arise out of our sense of the impermanence or transitoriness of life. It is not just worry about this or that problem, but anxiety about *the fundamental* problem of existence. The deepest anxieties have to do with the inevitability of death and seeming futility of life, the fragility of relationships and loss of love, rejection and estrangement, guilt and shame, gratuitous evil and unexplainable grace. The deepest anxiety is the fear that, after all is said and done, in spite of what we may have accomplished, one's life has no significance.

The Spanish existentialist Miguel de Unamuno described this as the *tragic sense of life*. It is rooted in the inner contradictions of body, brain, and heart inherent in being human. The human being is flesh and bone, mind and rationality, passion and feeling. Humans experience suffering, explain suffering, but then strive to rise above suffering. This is not mere pessimism, nor is it vague idealism, but a constant struggle for hope. He wrote:

> And the soul, my soul at least, longs for something else, not absorption, not quietude, not peace, not appeasement; it longs ever to approach and never to arrive, it longs for a never-ending longing, for an eternal hope which is eternally renewed but never wholly fulfilled. . . . Our life is a hope which is continually converting itself into memory and memory in its turn begets hope. Give us leave to live![1]

Steeped in Spanish culture, Unamuno identified Don Quixote as the epitome of the tragic spirit (the one who tilted with windmills, befriended earthy Sancho Panza, and saw a princess in the dairy maid Dulcinea). In Anglo-American culture, we might recognize the tragic heroes of Shakespeare.

There may be those who claim this does not matter. Enjoy life while you can. Accept the reality that you are on your own, for a limited time, and do the best you can for the sake of future generations who will soon forget you. In my experience, however, listening to unrehearsed conversations and observing the spontaneous behavior of the multiplying lifestyle diversity of the world, I think it is difficult to sustain such indifference.

- First, it is impossible to be indifferent to relationships, whether those relationships are with people or nature. The moment we identify with someone or something beyond ourselves and begin to care about their well-being or the well-being of the environment, we begin to worry about loneliness, loss, and fate.
- Second, it is impossible to separate reason from reality. The moment we admit that there is truth beyond our opinions, and there is a logic

---

1. Unamuno, *Tragic Sense of Life*, 256.

to the universe that is remarkably parallel to the logic of our minds, we begin to worry about missing the best that life has to offer and recognize personal flaws that limit our aspirations for fulfillment and joy.

- Third, it is impossible to separate morality from justice. The minute we admit that there are inalienable human rights we begin to worry about alienated people. There is a sense of justice beyond personal preferences and cultural mores, and laws only work if they point to a higher good.

Perhaps another way of saying this is that no matter how we live through the passage of time, it is impossible to ignore the timelessness of events that shape our lives. Love, beauty, ecstasy, harmony, and potentiality intrude on our day-to-day experiences to alert us to something beyond ourselves.

Existential philosophy and depth psychology have combined to explore the existential anxieties that drive the quest for God. One of my influencers helped me identify six fundamental anxieties. Over the years I have expanded these to eight to recognize the increasing diversity of our world. Each set of existential anxieties is related to a sense of a larger threat to life and well-being.[2]

Life Threats	Existential Anxieties	Real Life Situations
Depression	Emptiness	Lost . . . looking for direction.
	Meaninglessness	Flawed . . . looking for perfection.
Dread	Fate	Trapped . . . looking for deliverance.
	Death	Aging . . . looking for renewal.
Anger	Guilt	Broken . . . looking for healing.
	Shame	Abused . . . looking for vindication.
Abandonment	Estrangement	Lonely . . . looking for relationship.
	Displacement	Discarded . . . looking for compassion.

---

2. The insights of Paul Tillich that have had such an influence on my own quest for God and interpreting incarnation. For a further discussion of this chart see my book *Spiritual Leadership*, 6–21.

Certain anxieties are elevated in different phases of life or become acute in particular traumatic circumstances. These anxieties unconsciously shape our lifestyles by influencing the attitudes and habits that seem "natural" to us. And they become more conscious as we incorporate them in our plans, careers, and goals. They influence our preferences for religious fellowship, worship style, and education.

Emptiness and Meaninglessness

An abiding sense of depression is often associated with Baby Boomers as their careers peak and their families become empty nests. But chronic depression has become increasingly significant in the materialism of culture. Our search for meaning and purpose is often motivated by the feeling we have lost our way, or lost our identities, in a lifetime of pursuing ambition and growing wealth. We are reminded of the many personal flaws and relational failures that have accumulated over the years. Our spiritual pilgrimage is often prompted by a desire to regain direction in our lives and retrieve something of our original innocence. We long for a spiritual guide to navigate the ambiguities of living and a model of perfection to which we can aspire to imitate.

Fate and Death

An abiding sense of dread is often associated with Baby Busters (Gen X) as they juggle dual careers and family obligations and wrestle with economic uncertainty and social unrest. But an undercurrent of dread has become increasingly significant in the environmental crisis of culture. Our search for meaning and purpose is often motivated by feeling trapped by circumstances or bad habits, and the sense that time is slipping away, and opportunities are diminishing. Our spiritual pilgrimage is prompted by an urgent need for deliverance and hope for a second chance. We long for a hero to rescue us and a renewal of life.

Guilt and Shame

An abiding sense of anger is often associated with Millennials (Gen Y) as they react to broken promises and personal abuses. But a not-so-hidden ferment of anger has become increasingly significant in the polarizations and conflicts of cultures. Our search for meaning and purpose is motivated by the guilt and shame of both receiving and causing abuse. We are both victims and victimizers in a seemingly endless cycle of dehumanization. Our search for meaning and purpose is often motivated by guilt and shame, and the intuition that both our lives and society itself are broken. Our spiritual pilgrimage is prompted by desire for holistic healing and ultimate justice. We long for heroes who can heal holistically and vindicate our lives.

Estrangement and Displacement

An abiding fear of abandonment is often associated with seniors as they are parted from loved ones, disappear into assisted living, and are forgotten by colleagues. But in a world of constant movement and technological innovation there is a growing fear among all generations of being left behind. Our search for meaning and purpose is motivated by estrangement from human contact and displacement from familiar contexts. Our spiritual pilgrimage is prompted by a sense of loneliness and isolation. We long for authentic friendships and the embrace of compassion.

If you really pay attention to the unrehearsed words and spontaneous behaviors of the people around you, you begin to sense the real-life situations in which they find themselves at any given time. You get a sense of their life struggles, and therefore more clarity about their life aspirations, and the dreams or hopes that stir their interest in spirituality. Certain issues dominate our unconscious and conscious behavior, shape our relationships and goals, and predispose us to do *this* rather than *that*. At any given time, we are preoccupied with our sense of being lost, flawed, trapped, broken, abused, lonely, discarded, or impending death. We search for the courage to face these realities, and to do that we look for mentors and role models that can show us or guide us to do it.

The discovery of meaning and purpose is about discerning the substance and significance of one's life, and not just the attitudes and habits that shape our living. This can only be done if our point of reference shifts to something beyond the self toward a greater mystery that cannot be "owned," "contained," or "understood" by the individual ego. That shift does not begin with religious belief, but with the recognition of—or facing up to—the existential fears and anxieties that shape our lives.

The truth is that life is not tidy, logical, and manageable. Try as we might, "balanced living" is, and always will be, beyond our abilities to sustain. Life as we live it is a chaotic semblance of order. The routines of living are constantly interrupted by both gratuitous evil and unexplainable good. The Old Testament character Job is the paradigm of human existence. Tormented with gratuitous evil and questioning why he ever felt entitled to the good life he once had, he seeks the origins of meaning and purpose. He wants to know the real substance and significance of his life.

The "whirlwind" that sweeps Job out of his self-pity and self-absorption is a good metaphor for the Holy. Once we leave the relative security of our ego, life is apt to be turned upside down and inside out. What results is not clarity about personality type or tools to manage relationships, but awareness of the transcendent source of meaning and purpose, substance, and significance of life. God speaks to us out of the whirlwind reminding us that life began when "the morning stars sang together, and all the heavenly beings shouted for joy."[3] And we should be attentive to God's grace "as to a lamp shining in a dark place, until the morning star rises in our hearts."[4]

What is it about a "mentor" that first and foremost attracts the attention of a spiritual traveler? It is not their knowledge or professional status. It is their courage. Travelers are inspired to face the existential anxieties of their lives because they see someone who has already had the courage to face the whirlwind . . . and not only survived . . . but thrived.

Mutual mentoring begins with mutual empathy. It reduces the appearance of superiority and deepens trust. Travelers will only allow themselves to become vulnerable if the mentor does that first. Mentors help travelers confront their most urgent anxieties. This is not merely an exchange of ideas. It is no mere philosophical or theological discussion because more is at stake here than just their *thinking*. What is really at stake here is their *being*. It is only in the bold affirmation of their *being*, and the honest confrontation of *non-being*, that opens people to the possibility of hope. That is why I always say that this first step in the mentoring journey is so unsettling and daring. The courage of the mentor to be radically honest can be transferred to the traveler. The mentor is a catalyst for hope.

---

3. Job 38:1–11 NRSV.
4. 2 Pet 1:19 NRSV.

Experiencing the *Presence* of God

To experience genuine hope, and not just indulge in wishful thinking, the whirlwind of the Holy must become concentrated in the experience of the Holy One. This is the essential paradox of incarnation. St. Paul expresses this from the point of view of Christian faith: "In him all the fullness of God was pleased to dwell."[5] From the point of view of the seeker or spiritual traveler it would be more accurate to say that *wherever the fullness of God is revealed in any person or cultural form*, there is Christ. The idea of "God-among-Us" significantly broadens the potential of mentoring.

Mentors may talk about Jesus the Christ, but as an experience rather than as a theology. Incarnation is the infinite mystery that gives hope to all people. The incarnational experience cannot be contained by any religion, concept, or definition, nor even by a name like "Jesus." There is a reason why the ancient identification of God was expressed as Yahweh (YHWH). It was not a name, but an evocation of the mysterious, awesome splendor of the Holy One that can never be fully understood. God is the eternal *I Am*. Yet God is also the personal *I Am*.

If there is a "theology" of mentoring, it is not a theology of the past nor of the future, but a theology of the present. It is not about what God did for us, nor what God might do to us, but about "God-with-Us," or "God-among-Us." Evangelism in the Christendom world began with retelling the story of the historical Jesus. Indeed, scholars engaged in considerable research and debate about the truth of the historical Jesus. "Debate" is the key word. There are too many gaps, ambiguities, and contradictions in the timeline that are filled in by the dogmatic biases or ideological agendas of whichever scholar, church, or evangelist is trying to persuade seekers to become a Christian disciple.

Mentoring in the post-Christendom world does not begin with the *story* of Jesus, but rather with the *stories about* Jesus . . . the diverse interactions Jesus had with people in a wide variety of life situations. It is about how people uniquely experienced Jesus in the context of threats to life and anxieties about living. In a theology of the present, Christ is presented as "God-with-Us," but Jesus is experienced as "God-among-Us." It is the story of face-to-face encounters with the Holy One who is among us, but who defies any human attempt to contain or control the experience.

---

5. Col 1:19 NRSV.

The face-to-face encounter with the Holy One is epitomized in the story of the transfiguration of Jesus.[6] Jesus is "transfigured" (literally "re-shaped" or "transformed" into something beautiful and elevated) on the mountaintop before the very eyes of the disciples. He appears in dazzling white in conversation with the great heroes of the Old Testament Moses and Elijah. The immediate reaction of the disciples is to attempt to build a physical dwelling (church? dogma? institution?) in which to contain or control the Holy. Instead, they just receive a divine command to *listen*.

The Eastern Orthodox Church has better understood the centrality of this story for the experience of incarnation than the Western Roman or Protestant traditions. Images of the transfiguration adorn many Orthodox churches, and many churches are named for the transfiguration. The Western church has tended to focus on the Gethsemane stories of crucifixion and resurrection. This tendency has led Western theology to focus on the past and the future of grace, and less on the present experiences of grace. Perhaps this is why the tradition of spiritual leadership in the West has emphasized preaching, while the tradition of spiritual leadership in the East has emphasized mentoring.

Mentors tell the *stories* of Jesus because the Gospels do not piece together a chronological history but rather present a collage of stories that describe the multiple ways incarnation was experienced in the presence of Jesus. Among the stories of Jesus, mentors can also describe their own personal stories with Jesus ("God-among-Us"). This is plural, because in the lifetime of any person there can be multiple stories ... different experiences of incarnation that address the changing existential anxieties that dominate stages in lifestyle.

Our situation today is quite like the pre-Christian world. It is a bubbling cauldron of spirituality ... of myth and misconception, of yearning and prejudice, and of misinformation and miscommunication. Who is one to believe? Who has enough credibility to be trusted? Spiritual travelers connect with a mentor because of the mentor's life experience and not merely because of his or her theological acumen or biblical knowledge. A seeker's interest in Matthew, Mark, Luke, and John is *secondary* to their interest in your own face-to-face, transformative encounters with the Holy One. When mentors tell their own stories of incarnation, the Gospel stories intersect with your life. The mentor creates an environment or opportunity for the seeker and traveler to experience incarnation in his or her own way ...

---

6. Matt 17:1–8.

which may not exactly conform to the experience of the mentor today and which is not limited to the ways people experienced Jesus in the past.

Mentoring conversation moves one along to unpack the life story of the traveler. This is not psychotherapy (although therapy can be helpful), and the mentor is not a psychotherapist. The mentor helps the traveler explore his or her story. The questions asked by a mentor of an individual are not unlike the basic questions scholars asked about the historical Jesus. Who are you? Where did you come from? How were you born? What have you done? What do you say? Who are your friends? Where have you lived? Where have you gone? What will happen to you in the end? These questions are no longer about Jesus. They are about you.

*Pilgrim band*s move us along to unpack our life stories as they are entangled with the stories of our companions and with our joint experiences of changing cultures around us. Who are we? Where did we come from? How has our community been shaped? What have we done? What do others say? What does God say? Who are our friends? Who could become our friends? Where are we going? What will happen to us in the end?

The stories about Jesus reveal that he meant different things to different people, at different times, in different places. In other words, God is incarnate in different ways. In the same way, travelers today experience incarnation in different ways related to their anxieties and yearnings. The immanence of God may be experienced by one person or another, at one time or another, in at least eight different ways.

- The empty and lost experience Christ as Guide.
- The hopeless and flawed experience Christ as Perfect Human.
- The addicted and trapped experience Christ as New Creation.
- The aging and dying experience Christ as Promise Keeper.
- The guilty and broken experience Christ as Healer.
- The shamed and abused experience Christ as Vindicator.
- The displaced and discarded experience Christ as Rescuer.
- The estranged and lonely experience Christ as Companion.

One or two of these yearnings may be acute at any given time. The others are latent, but still present. Some may be chronic conditions. However, these eight experiences are the very stuff of existence and content of grace. Starting from our first wail when we are born, and ending with our last breath when we die, and however many seconds and moments lie in between, this is what shapes our existence. We may experience this grace at different times, with different intensities, but these are at least eight basic ways seekers and travelers experience "God-among-Us" in the situations of life. The immanence of God lies behind, but has never been contained, by the doctrines and explanations of different church traditions. Indeed, even as the experience of incarnation is revealed through various forms of religion, it shatters every religion that tries to own it.

Mentors not only have the courage to face up to existential anxieties, but they have experienced grace that helps them endure, persevere, and (to some extent) overcome anxiety. In other words, they can authentically talk about hope. The incarnational experiences of Christ as role model and guide generate hope that overcomes the threat of depression that underlies whatever we say or do. The experiences of Christ as promise keeper and agent of transformation generates hope that overcomes the dread of the unknown that lies ahead. The experiences of Christ as healer and vindicator overcomes the anger that arises from brokenness and abuse. The experience of Christ as rescuer and companion overcomes the sense of abandonment that is caused by feeling left behind.

Incarnation is the intersection of spiritual yearning and divine grace. Human beings "reach up." We reach beyond ourselves, and God "reaches down." The divine enters our personal life history.

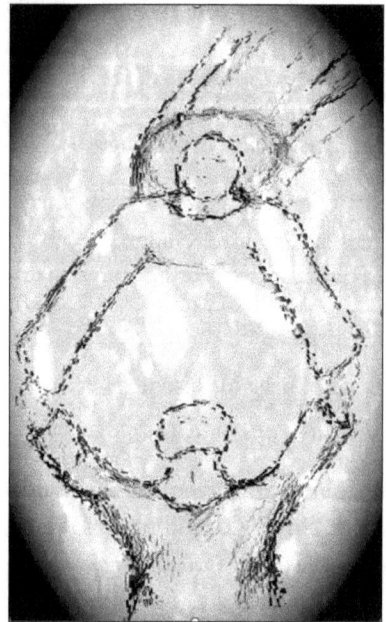

My daughter drew this picture as a child. I first used this picture in my book *Talisman: Global Positioning for the Soul*. It expresses the way we experience, however fleetingly, the immanence of God. This picture is deliberately unsophisticated, unprofessional, and perhaps even "child-like" in its presentation. That is how travelers begin to awaken their sensitivity to "God-among-Us." It may be a memory forgotten, or a hope never really explored, or a redemption never fully appreciated. The very fact of survival means that the traveler is *still here*, and *still seeking*. Being is more powerful than non-being.

We have an intuition that there is something more to life that is yet to come. Help the traveler start with his or her memories of spiritual yearning, and then explore if, when, and how that yearning is addressed by God. That intersection may not be an "embrace." Perhaps it was only a touch of the fingertips, a brush with the Holy, or a fragrance of hope. Build on this to expand the awareness of the traveler of the immanence of God in his or her own personal history.

We may temporarily avoid facing existential anxieties by affluence, good luck, or simple denial, but our mortality will always break through the static created by our egos. Mentoring is really a process of helping another person navigate all the sidetracks, barriers, and negative behaviors that block our experience with the Holy. Only then can an individual discover meaning and purpose for their lives. God has not just begun to mess with your life today. God has been messing with your life since the moment you were conceived. A person may not have known it, and perhaps only recently become vaguely and disturbingly aware of it. He or she may have recognized God's nearness and later forgotten, doubted, or rejected it. They may not remember anything remotely like God's nearness. Mentors guide the awakening of an individual to a deeper and benevolent mystery that is above, below, behind, before, beside, and within them.

Christians specifically identified Jesus the Christ as the fullness of God, but seekers and spiritual travelers identify any experience of the fullness of the Holy as incarnation. In the same way, Christians describe the outcome of one's experience with Jesus as a "calling" to become his disciple. But seekers and spiritual travelers describe the outcome of one's experience with the Holy more as a "beckoning." One is invited and encouraged into a new way of life. Christians picture an immanent God knocking on the door of your heart, waiting for you to invite Spirit in. Seekers and spiritual travelers sense that they are standing on the threshold of a new life and the hand of the Holy One is beckoning them to enter.

The *pilgrim band* seeks the immanence of God. They look for the fullness of God, fully experienced, as God is inclined to connect with their peculiarly small and paradoxically important lives. There are two reasons why the institutional church, with all its programs and liturgies, is often deemed irrelevant by travelers.

1. The institutional church filters the glory of God through layers upon layers of rationalized traditions. It is like a parent admonishing a child never to look directly at the sun, and then manufacturing ever darker sunglasses and ever thicker suntan lotions to avoid God's startling power.
2. The institutional church breaks the power of God into little, consumable pieces. It is like a corporation that doesn't want to give it all away in a single sale. Buy the basic package, and then each additional experience of grace will require an additional subscription.

Travelers in the *pilgrim band*, however, are eager to experience the whole thing. Of course, it may be harder to do than they anticipate. It may have implications that they can't imagine. Experiencing God incarnate may blow them away, overturn their ship, and wash them ashore on a different career path, in a different location, with different companions, and nothing but the clothes on their back, *but that is okay!* Such is the starvation postmodern people feel after a steady diet of institutional religion.

Just as I use the word "Christian" in the more mystical and non-dogmatic sense of "one who has experienced incarnation," so also, I think of the Christian "way" in the more existential and non-institutional sense of "one who travels a particular path" that is both transparent and faithful to incarnational experience. Any spiritual traveler along the "way" can become catalysts for others to experience incarnation. Travelers who are farther "down the road" deliberately pause and "double back" to walk with less experienced spiritual travelers who are journeying behind them.

Anyone can be a mentor in some way to another. Not only the wealthy, educated, cultured, and privileged classes of society can reasonably hope to find mentors that can shape their lives and guide them toward their destinies. Now the poor, uneducated, vulgar, and underprivileged can hope for the same. Not only professional, intellectual, certified, and salaried people can legitimately mentor inquirers or seekers toward abundant life. Now amateur, illiterate, unsophisticated, and unpaid volunteers can do the same. Anyone, regardless of any demographic marker of age, race, ethnicity, gender, family structure, occupation, income, or religion can join a *pilgrim band*.

In the words of Marcus Aurelius, the mentor's companionship and conversation help fellow travelers *act in ways that are just, generous, resolute, purposeful, and free*. In the words of St. Paul, mentors help others follow the Christian "Way" to model the "fruits of the Spirit": "love, joy, peace, patience, kindness, generosity, faithfulness, gentleness, and self-control."[7] They are there to encourage and reprove, evoking the best from the hearts of believers, and sometimes provoking them to work harder, walk faster, or serve better. Most of all, they are there to prevent sidetracks, urging travelers on the "way" to endure and persist, maintaining a straight course connecting their experience of incarnation, through compassion for other people, to joy in unity with God.

A Personal Reflection

Sometimes the mentor becomes the mentee. I had been working in Portland, Oregon, and was sitting in the aisle seat of a plane heading for Chicago. As usual, I was buried in a book. I forget the name of the book, but it was related to culture and spirituality. A quite elderly gentleman sitting in the window seat asked me what I thought of the book. He asked in such a gentle, non-confrontational, way—and yet with such obvious curiosity—that I overcame my habitual introversion, and we talked. It was another influential encounter that lasted only a few hours but had significance for a lifetime.

I discovered that he had been speaking at a university in Portland about his experience of the Holocaust. He explained that he had been the "Barber of Auschwitz." And he was one of very few Polish Jews who survived simply because of the coincidence that the camp guards needed a barber. Indeed, he was on his way home to Chicago where he owned a barber shop. A quiet, ordinary man, with extraordinary wisdom, he was occasionally asked to speak to students. He was returning home after speaking at a university convocation. So, we talked about the absence of God, the search for meaning, and unexpected callings. I listened. I learned.

His story—and the simple honesty with which he shared it—encouraged me to share my story with more honesty than I might usually reveal to a stranger. We talked about trauma and the lifelong struggle with Post Traumatic Stress Disorder. We never came to any "agreement" about religion. We didn't even agree on the existence of God. But there was no such expectation in the first place. What united us was compassion for the sufferers and seekers coping with the ambiguities of life and the anxieties of existence. We both wondered whether anything we said in public

---

7. Gal 5:22–25 NRSV.

speaking had any real impact, yet in this shared moment we each came away with more hope for the future.

Anxiety is something that we do in secret. We don't readily share it with even our closest friends, much less strangers on a plane, and we are loathe to admit it to ourselves. We are often embarrassed by it. Perhaps we are ashamed by it. And so, we pretend to a confidence that isn't really there. That is why influential encounters can be so liberating. Mentoring takes us beyond pretense to honesty, and in the very act of sharing generates authentic hope. I profited enormously from a timely conversation that lasted about two hours on a plane. Amazing. His name was Ben Scheinkopf and he died in 2017 at the age of ninety-eight.

Mentoring never begins with formulating answers to the questions of seekers. It begins with listening to the anxieties of travelers. Influential encounters like this launch us into a greater quest to find meaning and purpose for our lives.

The Incentive for Pilgrimage

WHY IS A SEARCH for meaning and purpose such a priority for a human being? What motivates a seeker to leave everything behind, or set everything aside, to become a traveler? Why do *pilgrim bands* come together? In 1406, Richard Alkerton offered this advice: "He that would be a pilgrim ought first to pay his debts, afterwards set his house in governance... and then array himself... take leave of his neighbors... and simply go forth."[1] What is the incentive that motivates so many postmodern people to turn away from stability and familiarity, not only to explore spirituality, but to do so in companionship with others?

The term "compunction" is little used today, but in the Middle Ages it was one of the most important concepts in monastic theology. "Compunction" has a different connotation than the most common modern word related to it, "compulsion." Compulsion suggests manipulation or an unhealthy need we are desperate to satisfy. Compunction suggests an inner drivenness to achieve and a healthy (albeit extreme) desire to satisfy. If the word "compunction" is used in modernity it usually refers to the absence of scruples and lack of remorse for bad behavior. But in ancient times it referred to the presence of conscience and the need for healing.

The best description of the emotion of compunction that I have ever read is offered by Jean LeClercq (OSB) quoting from St. Gregory the Great:

> In its profane use, the word compunction is a medical term, designating attacks of acute pain, of physical illness. But it has been used especially in the Christian vocabulary in a sense which, without losing contact with its origins, is nevertheless richer and loftier. Compunction becomes pain of the spirit, a suffering resulting simultaneously from two causes: the existence of sin and our

---

1. Sumption, *Pilgrimage*, 168.

> tendency toward sin . . . and the existence of our desire for God and even our very possession of God.
>
> St. Gregory, more than others, accentuated this last aspect: an obscure possession, awareness of which does not last and consequently gives rise to regret at seeing it disappear and a desire to find it again. The "compunction of the heart," "of the soul" . . . Compunction is an act of God in us, an act by which God awakens us, a shock, a blow, a "sting," a sort of burn. God goads us as if with a spear; he "presses" us with insistence, as if to pierce us. The love of the world lulls; but, as if by a thunder stroke, the attention of the soul is recalled to God.[2]

I think that describes the motivation of postmodern spiritual travelers nicely. We are motivated by a sense of loss, of something wonderful glimpsed and waiting to be recovered again. This is the nature of "sin" in its ancient sense. It is not any specific guilt for a bad deed, but a deeper sense of separation from an eternal good. And into this longing God offers hope. This awakening of the soul is a mysterious act of God. It does not come as a comforting insight to ponder, but as a shock that goads us to get moving.

The reason this awakening of the soul is such a shock to our system, blow to our ego, sting of remorse, scalding of our complacency, or burning away of our illusions is that we become aware of the existential anxieties that dominate our lives. I described these the anxieties in an earlier chapter: emptiness and meaninglessness, fate and death, guilt and shame, estrangement and displacement. It's not just the remembrance of things we have done wrong and people we have hurt, but the awareness that the limitations and frailties of existence make it inevitable that we will do wrong things that we do not really want to do and hurt the very people that we really want to love.

There is also a reason this awakening of the soul elicits new hope for the future. We become open to the possibilities of incarnational experience. I also described the immanence of God as teacher and guide, promise keeper and transformer, healer and vindicator, and rescuer and gatherer. And this is not just renewed optimism in life, but the victory of the Power of Being over Non-Being, the reunion of soul and Spirit, the recovery of lost perfection.

One reason the awakening of the soul comes as such a shock is that modern people resist the notion that there is a soul to awaken. The

---

2. LeClercq, *Love of Learning*, 38–39.

pragmatism and rationalization that emerged in the age of Enlightenment has become another "ism" in the modern era: material*ism* and rational*ism*. We have come to believe that the individual can, and should, be all-important and self-sufficient. This complacency has been shattered by a series of global and personal crises. Climate change, the extinction of species, hunger and homelessness, war and genocide have called into question our assumptions about progress. Prejudice and poverty, the widening gap between the powerful and powerless, the artificial limits forced on emerging generations blocking imagination and ambition, physical and mental and sexual abuse, have called into question our assumptions about entitlement.

I like to say that a thoroughly "modern" person does not know they have a soul until someone tries to steal it. This usually occurs through an experience of extreme trauma. This may be "global trauma" over the willful destruction of the environment, or "personal trauma" through extreme victimization by another person or life-threatening persecution by a remorseless outside authority. The experience of utter powerlessness undermines self-esteem or self-respect. It results in an unwanted but irresistible form of slavery. The tragedy is perpetuated because victims often become, in turn, victimizers of other victims. More and more people today (particularly younger generations) carry a chronic sense of anger that colors their view of reality. What is the essential value in one's existence that cannot be taken away?

This is the context for the awakening of the soul. It is not that God has created these crises, but that Spirit is using these crises to reveal what we have long denied. We remember that we have a soul . . . and just in time! One is being abused without even realizing it. For one's soul is shrinking to the point of near despair. I understand that science has determined that trauma can change the structure of the brain so that the "left brain" and the "right brain" no longer communicate. One's analytical powers are separated from one's emotional expressions. It is called "dissociation." Society "doubles down" on materialism and rationalism as if nothing is happening . . . unless we experience an awakening of the soul.

It is at this point that we feel the greatest urgency for a mentoring relationship. Initially, this is a one to one relationship because it involves such honesty and vulnerability. One's trust can extend to one person. That alone can be an act of courage. Initially, the awakening of the soul causes us to turn inward. We like to call it "meditation" or "mindfulness," but since this is often vague and unguided it is little more than poetic brooding. There is a question that dominates our conscious thoughts and unconscious anxieties: *Why am I here?*

The first question on the spiritual journey, and often the question that begins the journey, concerns the foundation or origin of personal identity. Why am I (myself, in person) here? There is an identity that is deeper than any demographic statistic. It is the human soul that cannot be contained by, or limited to, age, gender, race, nationality, family, language, occupation, education, economic class, or genetic code. We know there is more to me than meets the eye.

The question becomes more urgent as the average human lifespan increases. Despite the genuine threats of pandemic, global warming, and nuclear war, human beings are finding ways to prolong life. Indeed, the priority to prolong life has exceeded the need to simply survive. There are improved cosmetics, better medical procedures, advanced health care, techniques in genetic engineering, and artificially enhanced bodies. The potential for artificial intelligence has become so alarming that scientists are starting to lobby for a moratorium in research and development. The global population is predicted to decrease in the years to come, for the first time in history, because people are living longer and there is no need for more of them. Yet the longer we live, the more we change. We live not just one "lifetime," but several "lifetimes." Am I still the same person I once was?

In your lifetime you participate in a multitude of different plans and proposals, sign any number of contracts, accept all kinds of job descriptions, and enter innumerable formal and informal relationships. Yet if all of these could be written down, every document would have the same "boilerplate" language. "Boilerplate" originated in the nineteenth century when steel plates were affixed to machinery to identify ownership. Today "boilerplate" language is a standardized, uniform text that precedes any agreement, defines any collaboration, or underwrites any commitment. It is the seal of ownership.

The metaphor can be extended to all the "lifetimes" we experience as individuals, and all things we accumulate and relationships we generate over time, and all the trials, tribulations, and indignities we endure in our lives. There is something we "own" that cannot be bought or sold, traded, or given away, stolen, or taken even if we seem unable to hold onto it. It is as solid as steel and welded onto every aspect of our lives. "Boilerplate" is an existential foundation that remains consistent in substance even when it is expressed in different forms.

There is a second element to this initial question. *Why am I here* (in this location and this time)? Why would I assume that this is an accident? We waste a great deal of energy wishing we were someplace else or living in some previous time. We waste even more energy trying to escape into virtual reality or preparing for some post-apocalyptic future. What if one's presence in the here and now is no accident, but intentional? Focus on today. Focus on this moment. Is there a point to one's existence here and now?

"Focus" is encouraged by our connections with cultures, publics, and events. We cannot allow ourselves to "disassociate" from reality no matter how glorious or painful that might be. When an adult becomes a parent, for example, life often comes into focus. A family that we love depends upon us. When we experience other cultures, volunteer in social service, engage in peacekeeping or peacemaking, rescue another entity from extinction, or otherwise "get out of ourselves" and "into life," we begin to focus. We get the point of our existence.

This inner journey goes nowhere unless it is guided. It is not accomplished through poetic brooding. Our vague claims to meditation and mindfulness are excuses to cover up our irresolution and hidden cowardice. The inner journey is not accomplished through institutional education, nor is it accomplished by frenetic activism. We need a guide. This is the role of mentoring.

Eventually, the awakening of the soul turns outward. The first question (*Why am I here?*) raises even more questions. *Where am I going? Where should I be going?* The first question leads us to explore cultural history extending from the past and into the future. It is not just my history, but your history, and ultimately about *our* histories. The second question leads us even further to explore human destiny. And this is not just my destiny, or your destiny, but our shared destiny as human beings. These are moral questions, but they raise spiritual issues.

Because these questions take us out of ourselves and into the world, the *character* of mentoring changes. Mentoring that was once "stationary" becomes "mobile." Mentoring that relied on one, single, lasting connection becomes mutual mentoring that includes several, evolving, and changing connections. The historical model for this, perhaps, is the shift *out* from the walls of the monastery and *onto* the road of pilgrimage. We move beyond the confines of self-consciousness and into the cultural diversity of the world. Spirit moves not only in our self-awareness, but in our other-awareness.

As mentoring becomes mobile, the nature of mentoring relationships changes. One might say it is less "professional" and more "amateur," not in the sense that it is any less profound, but that the hidden hierarchy of mentoring disappears. The historical model, perhaps, is the shift from relying on the wisdom of the abbot and the imposed discipline of the monastery to relying on the shared wisdom of ordinary people with whom we travel down the road. Mentoring becomes *mutual*, and discipline becomes adaptable to the circumstances of culture.

The more flexible the method of travel becomes, and the more complex the route of travel seems, the more vital it becomes to have clarity about the destination. Otherwise, travel becomes tourism. The destination in the quest to find meaning and purpose in life is difficult to describe in any literal sense. The moment one settles down in the most beautiful places, or forms perfect relationships, or discovers final answers, the next moment our souls are stirred with restlessness again. The places and the relationships are not perfect, and the answer is not, after all, final. So, the destination of our quest is often described in poetic, metaphorical, or utopian images. Ancient pilgrims, after all, were not really traveling to Jerusalem, but to what they envisioned as the "New Jerusalem."

As we become more serious in our spiritual travels, and more urgent about the destination, another question emerges. *What company should I keep?* It is at this point that the trust of a one to one relationship between mentor and mentee is expanded.

We have many friends and colleagues, but the *pilgrim band* assumes considerable trust among participants. As mentoring becomes mutual, sometimes we invite someone to join us and sometimes we are invited to join others. There are many practical and personal considerations, but when spiritual travelers consider the company they might keep, they should consider three things.

- With whom can I celebrate life? The *pilgrim band* is a joy to be with. This is about the deeper "joy" in relationships that goes beyond likes and dislikes, friends and strangers, happiness and sorrow. These are the relationships that matter and for which you will stake your reputation and sacrifice your personal well-being.

- With whom can I be completely honest? The *pilgrim band* is an experience of vulnerability. Secrets will be shared, and confidentiality must be maintained. Crazy ideas and raw emotions can be critiqued but are never judged. Imaginations can run wild yet be objectively evaluated.

- With whom can I travel safely? The *pilgrim band* protects one another. They help each other resist manipulation, endure abuse, survive conflicts, and overcome obstacles. They carry each other's burdens and heal each other's wounds.

As the inward journey transitions into an outward journey, so also mentoring transitions into mutual mentoring. Just as you seek mentors from others, so also you become a mentor to others.

Pilgrimage is not so much *planned* as *precipitated*. And the best mentoring relationships are often accidental (or providential) rather than designed (or programmatic). Seekers do not enroll in a mentoring class but join a road trip. If you have come this far reading this book, you know that there is a great deal of mental preparation, sacrificial participation, and disciplined perspiration in a mentoring relationship, but the bond itself is often surprising and the flow of conversation unpredictable. The reason mentoring relationships are described as a covenant rather than a contract is that it is not a twosome but a threesome: you, me, and the Spirit.

We do not just passively ponder whether or not it would be helpful and then advertise for a mentoring relationship. Instead, we fall into the relationship and only later wonder why. Whether as mentor or mentee, we are *compelled* or *driven* or *beckoned* into the relationship. Sometimes it is even something we were trying to avoid, but fleeing from one mentoring relationship we find ourselves in another. We cannot escape. So, we enter the relationship as a journey into the unknown. Only later, as the journey unfolds, do we begin to ponder why we are in it at all.

In the quest for meaning and purpose, meditation leads to mentoring, and mentoring leads to pilgrimage. You cannot do it alone. You cannot depend on just one person. You cannot find it standing still. And you cannot get there without God. Our experience of God-with-Us responds to the existential anxieties that drive an individual's quest for God. Spirit inspires courage for the present but elicits hope for the future. The person God wants me to be may not be the person I already am and may not even comfortably match the expectations of the people I am currently with. On the other hand, surrendering to God's re-creation will perfect who I am and satisfy me in ways I cannot even imagine now.

Sometimes this is an "Aha!" moment as the spiritual traveler breaks with past assumptions and embraces surprising possibilities. Sometimes this comes incrementally as a "dawning realization" as the traveler gradually accepts a new point of view. Either way, it is important to understand that meaning and purpose are not revealed in absolute clarity *from above* but are discerned with considerable ambiguity *from below*. Cultural context shapes our interpretation of our past, present, and future. It cannot be helped. It is a condition of existence.

It may seem like Spirit confronts you, illuminates you, or transforms you, but in fact all these experiences are filtered through the forms of culture and conditions of existence we face. We see ourselves indirectly, as reflections in the mirror of reality. The Spirit "beckons" to you from a distance, as an indistinct version of yourself waving from afar.

A Personal Reflection

I have a passion for medieval history in both Western and Eastern traditions. Clearly, it inspires my understanding of the nature of pilgrimage. It is common today to scoff at pilgrimage. We tend to assume that Chaucer's parody of its popularity in the late fourteenth century is, in fact, the reality of how faithful Christians pursued it. *The Canterbury Tales* tell a series of stories as travelers journeyed from London to Canterbury. They are funny. But like all good comedy the stories reveal a pathos—and yearning—beneath all the ribaldry.

A contemporary of Chaucer, Julian of Norwich, wrote about the same time about her visions of divine love. They were written after her own recovery from a desperate illness, and in the context of catastrophic events like the Black Death, peasant revolts and subsequent repression, endemic poverty, and growing religious persecution. Her life was stationary, but her "pilgrimage" was spiritual. Living in seclusion, she nevertheless became a mentor to others.

In its original conception, pilgrimage was seen as a rejection of urban values (materialism, competition, etc.), a kind of "self-exile" from worldly entanglements, to seek forgiveness, acceptance, hope. This is one reason why pilgrimage was marked by generosity to those in need and service to society. Pilgrimage was a mystical experience in which one sought to enter the mind of Christ by sharing the sufferings of Christ. It was a kind of unfolding experience of incarnation or a quest to feel the immanence of

God. Pilgrimage was considered a dangerous undertaking, which is why pilgrims traveled together for protection and mutual support, and why churches became hostels to equip and refresh pilgrims on their way and abbeys became opportunities to receive advice and mentoring.

When I visited Canterbury, I was most impressed by the stone steps leading into the church and up to the altar. The stones have been worn down by the footsteps of countless pilgrims over centuries of travel. One cannot help but be in awe at the persistence and piety, commitment, and endurance of thousands of ordinary people looking for hope in troubled times. You can see the same worn steps in every center of pilgrimage from Jerusalem to Rome to Santiago.

The more I traveled in my career, the more it felt like a pilgrimage. The industrial carpets in airports were worn threadbare at the electronic security gates by the passage of countless travelers. One could not help but wonder what expectations motivated them to endure the lines, and what hopes they had for their final destinations. We live in a time of extreme mobility, physically and digitally. Lifestyle groups are migrating along major transportation corridors in search of affordable housing, employment, and education. They are making, losing, and rediscovering friendships along the way. Many people (younger and older) are trying to simplify and de-clutter their lives. They are not *self-consciously* religious, but they are *intentionally* looking for authentic experiences of the Holy and a sense of the immanence of God.

Ironically, I visited Canterbury in the winter during a snowstorm. It was night. I had neglected to book a room in advance, so I found myself plodding in the snow past the cathedral, looking in windows at the warm glow from nearby homes, yearning for hospitality that was not there. On that dark and snowy night there were no welcoming abbeys or hostels. Today there is a very fine line between being a pilgrim and becoming a refugee. The need for spiritual companionship is greater than ever before.

Journey

I planted, Apollos watered, but God gave the growth. So, neither the one who plants nor the one who waters is anything, but only God who gives the growth. —Saint Paul[1]

---

1. 1 Cor 3:6–7 NRSV.

Me? Mentor? Maybe?

ALL MY LIFE I have been fascinated by the phenomenon of hope. How does it come into being? How is it sustained against all odds? How is it lost, and how is it regained? I have had the opportunities through years and careers and cultures to try to observe this phenomenon. At times I have tried to articulate my observations with colleagues and fellow travelers along the way. Two things have become very clear.

First, hope has little to do with happiness. Hope is neither the result of happiness nor does it necessarily create happiness. It is the result of our discernment of meaning and purpose in our lives. It may make us coincidentally happy, but it will certainly help us be strong in adversity.

Second, hope is not the result of solitary reflection or mindfulness of nature. It emerges in the context of interpersonal relationships that are significant and not just superficial. I see them as influential encounters. They are not easy to track or even define. Some are recognized and some not. Some are long term, and some are not even noticed or remembered, yet in a brief second pack significance for a lifetime.

There is a vast, complex, often invisible network of influential encounters occurring all around us. But the more we become aware of these, the more we realize that, like it or not, we are a part of it. We are participants in a larger quest for meaning and purpose, giving and receiving, sharing and learning, in every influential encounter. The question is whether we have the courage to make our participation intentional.

The very idea of participating in a mentoring relationship is intimidating for modern people. It seems anachronistic and unnecessary, especially as the liberal arts tradition declines in public education and universities. Music, art, literature, philosophy, comparative religion, and cross-disciplinary studies have been replaced by specializations in science, engineering, business, economics, computer programming, and data processing. Mentoring has been relegated to pop culture. It is associated with entertainment superstars, media personalities, popular athletes, pseudo-psychologists, and parachurch cults. Charlatans and narcissists seem to have filled the void. The small group, as "pilgrim band," is associated with elitist sects and brainwashed cults.

Nevertheless, if you look deeper into neighborhood gatherings, local school extracurricular activities, amateur sports teams, musical groups, non-profit organizations, social service volunteers, health care and wellness clinics, fitness clubs and diet regimens, you discover that the practice of mentoring continues to thrive. Indeed, if you linger at the water cooler at the corporate office . . . or hang out in pubs, wine bars, and coffee shops where over-worked employees go at the end of the day . . . or eavesdrop on the conversations at preschools, playgrounds, local sports arenas . . . you will often see the process of mentoring in action. It's just off the record, behind the scenes, and in between appointments.

Mentoring is rarely associated with the organized religions. It has been largely replaced by institutionalism: expository preaching, standardized liturgies, Sunday school curricula, fundraising, and countless committees. Pastoral care focuses on counseling and conflict resolution, and much of that is now being referred to outside secular professionals. Lay visitors are exceptionally kind, but usually tongue-tied about faith. Members are friendly but stay close to their inner circle. Nevertheless, if you listen to serious conversations in the hospitality center and the parking lot, you will see mentoring happen. Indeed, some clergy stay away from the office meeting with members and spend their time in the coffee shop talking with seekers.

"Mentoring" and "membership" are opposite concepts. "Spiritual pilgrimage" and "faith community" mean different things. This is why mentoring is not a priority for both religious and secular organizations.

Religious institutions are more interested in membership programs and stewardship campaigns. The priority is to *assimilate* people who will go on to implement programs, serve committees, and pay for the costs of congregational and denominational overhead. Churches have been steadily declining, and their need for members to sustain institutional survival has been steadily growing. There really is no institutional advantage to mentoring, and indeed, it may be strongly discouraged. Those few professional clergy who trade the office for the coffee shop are more likely to be criticized for failing to pay attention to members.

Similarly, secular organizations are more interested in scalability and profits. Their priority is to sustain an efficient workforce that is not distracted away from organizational purposes. There is no money in mentoring. It is not a fast track in career development, and there is no retirement plan. Some corporations will do limited philanthropy. But this will mainly be in the form of grants and financial donations that represent a tiny fraction of corporate earnings. Employees will be encouraged to work overtime rather than donate time.

Therefore, mentoring happens on the perimeters of religious and secular organizations. Pilgrimage is how we behave on vacation or in secret. It is what you do in your spare time or something for which you volunteer energy on the weekends. Clergy passionate about mentoring tend to do it as a second career or after retirement. One minister I knew volunteered as chaplain to the fire department and retired early so that he could focus on what mattered most. A CEO spent free time and vacations training volunteers for a social service and retired early to prioritize personal fulfillment over corporate success.

Listen and observe. There is a growing dissatisfaction with institutions. Clergy and laity, management and labor are all feeling more and more restless with their chosen careers. The growing demand for limited hours and more frequent holidays is not really about freeing time for more fun, but about freeing time to have a more meaningful life pursuing a higher purpose. And the reason we demand more time to discern meaning and purpose is that we need an urgent reason to hope.

Our need for hope, and our refusal to surrender to hopelessness, is the most visible sign of Spirit at work in the world. The Spirit will just not leave us alone. Perhaps you are restless to do something for someone. Perhaps you have an intuition of a "higher calling."

- If you are part of a church institution, perhaps you have become convinced that there is more to Christian life than going to church and percentage giving. Perhaps you have the audacity to take baptismal vows seriously. The more you ponder your experience of incarnation, the more restless you become. What is the point of hope unless you pass it on?

- If you are part of a secular organization, perhaps you have become frustrated with bureaucracy and sensitive to burnout among your colleagues. Perhaps you have the audacity to want to be fully human full time. The more serious you become about spirituality, the more restless you become. What is the point of personal fulfillment if you don't help others pursue it as well?

It is as if God is inviting you into a different way of life. First thing in the morning, after the last sticky note reminder for tomorrow, in your unconscious sleep and your daydreams at your desk, God (whoever or whatever that is) is beckoning you to do something else.

Hope is generated through inter-personal relationships that are influential encounters. We are all a part of this vast and complex social network but often not aware how much we receive or contribute. Our intentional participation in it is often gradual. Initially it is unconscious and occasional. Then it becomes a behavioral habit of which we are unconscious, but which others see in us and prompts them to confide, ask questions, seek guidance, or receive acceptance. Mentoring is something into which you are precipitated by the Spirit whether you like it or not. If you ask mentors how they started mentoring, they are likely to say that they simply found themselves mentoring others. There was no actual point when they started. They just realized that was what they were doing. Similarly, the thirst for mentoring is often unrecognized or substituted for some other lust or desire. If you ask mentees why they enter covenanted relationships, they are likely to say they just fell into it. There was no specific point when such trusted intimacy started. Conscious participation progressed from unexpected coincidences.

These six indicators are used to confirm what you already find yourself doing or reveal what you have always secretly been seeking in any religious organization or career path.[1]

Humility Before Mystery

In his classic study of monastic culture, Jean LeClercq reminds us that humility is the ability to listen "with the ear of the heart." This is best described in poetic images like hearing an "inner song," or a "silent word," or

---

1. I first attempted to describe these in my self-published book *Christian Mentoring*, 10–26, that I offered via my website www.ThrivingChurch.com.

a "slight murmuring" in the background or at the periphery of daily living that pervades all of life.² Humility is not a hidden *knowledge* but rather an emotional reaction. Early medieval monastics described it as a kind of "stupefaction" (*stupor*) or "admiration" (*admiratio*) before the presence of God. Incarnational experience results in a kind of "astonishment" at the grace of God.³

Humility is not about self-deprecation, as modern people assume, but rather about self-forgetfulness as one is caught up in a greater mystery. Therefore, mentoring is not really a choice prompted by self-glorification. Rather, mentoring is a kind of compulsion or compunction that is irresistible. Indeed, even if one would *rather not* do it, one finds oneself inevitably doing it.

Although mentors can talk about their own experiences of victory over universal anxieties, they never let that go to their heads. The mentor/mentee dynamic reinforces genuine humility.

- They are always ready to learn new things. They demonstrate an uncommon openness to go beyond their comfort zones, associate with strange people, immerse themselves in different cultures, and understand different religions. Yes, they can encourage others to overcome emptiness and meaninglessness, but mentors are constantly learning new perspectives and ideas.

- They are always aware of their personal limitations. They know that every personality, including their own, has both strengths and weaknesses. They wrestle with, and accept, their own shortcomings. They frankly admire the good and greatness in others. Yes, they can empower others to overcome fears of fate and death but frankly admit they are still only human.

- They are always compelled to confess. They own their mistakes and are aware of their essential imperfections. They acknowledge that they are worse human beings than they even realize. They come to God confessing (in the words of the old campfire song), "it's me, it's me, it's me, O Lord; standing in the need of prayer."

Humility is really the ability to accept different roles in life without losing personal identity. A mentor can be visible or invisible. He or she can

---

2. LeClercq, *Love of Learning*, 39, 340.
3. LeClercq, *Love of Learning*, 282–83.

accept praise or criticism without arrogance or offence. A mentor can do great things or menial chores, host a banquet or wash the dishes, and manage popularity and unpopularity with equal calm. Their ability to laugh at themselves is one of the first things people notice about them.

If you are considering mentoring, then answer for yourself these questions. Are you curious? Are you habitually learning new things, befriending new people, mingling with different cultures, and being respectful of other races? Are you self-aware? Can you accept praise calmly? Are you able to accept criticism? Do you genuinely admire people other than yourself? Do you recognize your own shortcomings? Can you laugh at yourself? Do you admit the need for grace? And the ultimate question is: *Can you not do it?*

Desire for God

Humility precipitates a profound desire for God. Those who participate in mentoring relationships are eager to be close to God, part of God's purpose to bless the world, and part of God's global network of faithful servants. They do not love God only in the sense of sacrificial love (agape), but in the sense of passionate love (eros). They often use metaphors for intimacy to describe their experience of God. The more mystical traditions of Judaism and Christianity have both considered the erotic "Song of Songs" in the Old Testament as a metaphor for the soul's yearning and reunion with God. The early monastics spoke of their awareness of the "sweetness" of God that generated a longing for God akin to homesickness.[4]

Similarly, those who participate in mentoring relationships are eager to help others go deeper and further with God. Their concern is not just philanthropic. Indeed, they are not that interested in humanity as a group, but in humans as distinct personalities. This is why mentors and mentees are attracted to a small group rather than a large audience. Mentors are the antithesis of a motivational speaker. They generate profound intimacy among a few radically committed people based on deep trust and high respect. They communicate constantly, in person or online, remaining connected even in a world of speed, flux, and blur.

This element of "desire" is important because mentoring takes time, and progress is difficult to measure. "Success" is often hidden and emerges slowly, and in unexpected ways. Mentoring requires considerable patience and persistence. Unless the mentor truly *desires* a more spiritual life, he or

---

4. LeClercq, *Love of Learning*, 39. Note the reference to St. Gregory.

she will not have the stamina to keep going. The intimate sharing of the personal mentoring relationship may plateau, or later that of the *pilgrim band* is apt to disintegrate.

The desire for God takes great emotional energy. In mutual mentoring, participants share their life struggles and spiritual quests. Mentors are often introverts by nature. The mentoring process can leave participants feeling drained and emptied. Just as doubt is a prerequisite of faith, so also the "dark night of the soul" is a painful step in spiritual growth. Personal and shared spiritual practices help renew the individual, but one benefit of the *pilgrim band* is the additional mutual support. Individually we are tempted to despair. Together we can become what I often describe as *optimystic*: hopeful in ambiguity.

Memories of the Holy

Participants in mentoring relationships always have memories of the awesome presence of God. Some of these experiences are beyond words. Participants may tell stories, draw pictures, or create music as the only means to communicate them. They may also simply be struck dumb and remain silent. Some of these experiences, however, can be set to words. We try to discover or recover experiences of the Holy. We share them, help interpret them, and communicate them to any who have "ears to hear and eyes to see."[5]

Think back on your own life. Have you experienced mystical moments when you felt God close to you? Many modern people have difficulty recovering these experiences, because the contemporary culture of rationalization has led them to "explain them away" in a spirit of skepticism. Interpreting certain experiences as "God moments" seems childish, immature, and even crazy. However, you may be one of an increasing number of modern people who are beginning to be skeptical of the skepticism. You may wonder if there *really wasn't something more* in the experience . . . some intersection with the supernatural . . . some connection with a Higher Power.

As you examine your personal "history with the Holy," it is important that you separate the "sentimental" from the "profound." Here are some guidelines that you can use to test your memories of the Holy.

---

5. I share case studies and experiences of the Holy in my book *Talisman*.

- *A sense of awe*

    Authentic experiences of the Holy impress you with a deep respect for the power of God. It is not a sense of dread or doom, but of wonder, amazement, and reverence. In response, you experience profound humility. You are compelled to surrender to a higher purpose that is beyond yourself and your immediate relationships.

- *A feeling of gratitude*

    Authentic experiences of the Holy generate a feeling of acceptance. That raises your self-esteem, but not in the sense of arrogance or pride. It is more like feeling welcomed into communion and community. Gratitude awakens compassion for others and a desire to share the acceptance you feel with others.

- *A sense of urgency*

    Authentic experiences of the Holy heighten your awareness of time. You become more sensitive to the *passage* of time and anxious about *wasting* time. You are more alert to the *timing* of grace and opportunities for transformation. You become impatient to act, share hope, do things that benefit others.

- *A readiness to risk*

    Authentic experiences of the Holy make you more daring. You are more willing to "throw caution to the wind" and go beyond your comfort zones. You are prepared to look foolish and make mistakes, confident that your heart is in the right place and that you can learn from failure.

These are not fond memories that make you smile. These are times when we are thunderstruck, absorbed, motivated, and daring all at once. Infinity is right there amid our reality. Experiences of the Holy are intimations of incarnation. They reveal how God is uniquely present in each of our lives, addressing the hidden fears and chronic anxieties that shape our lifestyles.

Courage in Anxiety

Participants in mentoring relationships share personal victories amid universally experienced anxieties. In other words, they not only empathize with the anxiety or suffering of others, but they can speak from their own experiences of survival, endurance, and hope. Mentors have "been there, done that" and found a way to move forward in personal growth. They identify with people in need but have little patience with people who are chronically "needy." They are confident that others can be empowered to overcome difficulties, because they themselves have been able to do so. They speak from personal experience.

Of course, this does not suggest that one will never be anxious again. Even mentors will suffer again, worry again, be afraid again, fail again, feel guilty again, and be anxious again. There may even be a time when a mentor no longer has the confidence to be a mentor . . . and must instead seek mentoring. Mentors make no claim to perfection and are not falsely confident that they will always be "okay." At this point, and at this time, with this person, they are able to both empathize and advise. They are givers of hope. This hope is not abstract or theoretical. It is hope that is born from personal experiences of life struggles and victories.

The fundamental anxieties that beset all human beings were defined well by my own influencer, Paul Tillich.[6] I introduced them in an earlier chapter. I apply them to Christian mentoring in my own work.[7] No one escapes these universal anxieties, but mentors can describe their methods of coping and their occasional breakthroughs. Lying behind and hidden within all conversations are existential anxieties that can be raised to consciousness in the *pilgrim band*.

Facing Our Anxieties of Emptiness and Meaninglessness

Everyone is anxious that life might be purposeless and without meaning. Everything that happens is statistically random. We are but cogs in a mechanism or pawns on a chessboard. We are tempted to curl up in a fetal position, withdraw from society, or surrender to mere selfishness. Mentors can share their courage to participate in relationships and life. They model for others how to surrender ego to a higher purpose. They may not explain everything, but they can underline the meaning of some experiences and events. They give people a good reason not to give up.

In Christian perspective, mentors recognize in Jesus the Christ a perfect model for humanity and a spiritual guide through ambiguity. Their

6. Tillich, *Courage to Be*.
7. Bandy, *Spiritual Leadership*.

belief in the immanence of God helps them encourage others to overcome doubt and live with confidence.

Perhaps you doubt that you could ever witness or encourage others through your personal victories over emptiness and meaninglessness. You are naturally self-effacing. But examine your life more carefully. Certainly, there have been times of doubt, and there will be more times of doubt tomorrow. Yet you live. Did you find new meaning in marriage and family life? Did you find renewed purpose in social service? Did you also experience moments of abundant life and joy in critical life transitions?

Facing Our Anxieties of Fate and Death

Everyone is anxious that they may be doomed by genetics, economics, culture, or demonic control. And we are anxious that the hidden network of manipulation in which we fear to live leads only to death and nothing more. We are tempted to abandon hope, get drunk, and despair. Mentors can share their courage to take risks, affirm their identity, rise above chaos, and take control of their lives. They may not always succeed, but they can bear witness to the possibility of changing your direction in life, confronting self-destructive habits, and wrestling victory from defeat. They can share their conviction that death is not the end . . . and that there is some kind of life after death.

In Christian perspective, mentors recognize in the experience of Jesus the Christ a "Higher Power" that gives us a fresh start, and a "Promise Keeper" that reassures us about the future. Their belief in the immanence of God helps them reassure and liberate others to become the best that they can be.

Perhaps you doubt that you could ever exhort or empower others through your personal victories over fate and death. You are naturally modest. But if you examine your life carefully, you may rediscover a greater freedom from despair and hope for tomorrow than you realize. Has a "Higher Power" ever liberated you from self-destructive behavior patterns that you chronically denied (i.e., addictions)? Have you ever overcome the death of a loved one, and rebuilt a life with joy and purpose? Have you struggled to overcome disease? Have you labored to overcome racial violence or cultural prejudice?

Facing Our Anxieties of Guilt and Shame

Everyone is anxious that their failures and mistakes will catch up with them. At the same time, many suffer abuse and are made to feel guilty when they are innocent. Guilt is often associated with mental anguish and physical pain. Shame robs us of self-esteem. We hurt others and are hurt in return. Mentors can share their courage to accept acceptance. No matter how bad their past deeds are, they cling to the belief that forgiveness is possible. They share the courage to stand up to abuse and refuse to be demeaned.

In Christian perspective, mentors recognize in the experience of Jesus the Christ a healer and vindicator. Christ brings wholeness to mind and body and a renewed sense of self-worth. Their belief in the immanence of God helps them comfort and rehabilitate even the worst offenders. They help people "forgive others, even as they themselves have been forgiven."[8]

Perhaps you doubt that you could ever comfort or rehabilitate others. You may be forgetful of your own experiences of renewal. Have you ever behaved badly and sworn never to repeat the same mistake? Have you ever hurt another person and experienced their forgiveness? Have you ever confessed your guilt and felt an overwhelming sense of acceptance? Have you said, "Once I was like this . . . but now I am different?"

Facing Our Anxieties of Displacement and Estrangement

Everyone is anxious that their power and influence will diminish, or that the world will pass them by, or that they will be left behind and forgotten by family, friends, and associates. We feel like strangers in a strange land. We are all alone in a crowd, foreigners in our own backyard, and irrelevant to what is going on around us. We sense that others view us with skepticism or even fear; and we cannot help but view others with suspicion and doubt. Mentors can share their courage to trust and be trusted. They can renew forgotten relationships and risk new companionships. They can demonstrate self-control and selfless generosity. They can adapt to new environments and hold themselves to a higher standard of behavior.

In Christian perspective, mentors recognize in the experience of Christ a rescuer and gatherer. The metaphor they often use is of Christ the Shepherd. They can rescue the lost and accept the rescue that is offered to them as well. They can gather the lonely, and risk gathering with others.

---

8. Matt 6:14 NRSV.

Perhaps you doubt that you could ever restore a relationship or return to community. Perhaps your cynicism isolates you from church or family. But have you ever been surprised by inclusivity? Have you ever been generous and rewarded with a smile? Have you been lost . . . and found? Feared a bad reception, and received a warm welcome?

Mentoring relationships generate hope. Participants demonstrate courage that overcomes anxieties and creates opportunities for grace. Yet a one to one mentoring relationship is often not enough to sustain hope long term. This is why the mutual mentoring experienced in the *pilgrim band* is so important. When anxieties overcome one companion, the others can come to their rescue.

Experience as a Mentee

Mentors have themselves experienced mentoring. Look back on the course of your life—especially on times of transition. You may not have consciously thought about it before, but certain individuals stand out as influential, even crucial, to your progress. These relationships may have been deliberately formed, occur coincidentally in the midst of doing something else, or be entirely unplanned and unexpected. Yet they deepened, redirected, or transformed your life.

Consider first your family relationships. Often individuals who did *not* have direct responsibility for your financial support (i.e., parents) have the most impact in shaping your life: brothers, sisters, grandparents, aunts or uncles, cousins, etc. Such people take a deliberate and self-sacrificial interest in your lifestyle, career, life goals, and overall success as a human being.

Second, consider your personal growth relationships. In the long list of teachers, professors, doctors, pastors, and social workers that have passed through your life, certain individuals stand out. You can still see their faces, recall the timbre of their voices, quote important comments, or remember sharing certain activities. Such people went beyond imparting information and impersonal advice to "take you under their wing" and give you special attention. They saw some hidden potential in you and tried to help you give birth to a new perspective.

Next, consider your business associates and career networks. We all remember how difficult it can be to adjust to a new job, a new office, a new shift, or a new crew. In the midst of all the competitive and suspicious behavior, however, certain individuals sometimes stood out. They had the confidence to befriend you. They "showed you the ropes," gave you tips, and shared sandwiches from their own lunch boxes. In the more "white collar" world, they adopted you as a protégé and guided you through the complexities of work and the stresses of management.

Next, consider your friends. You have probably moved in and out of peer groups all your life, but certain friends have kept up with you wherever you went. They are there for you in times of sorrow and joy. They are ready with personal support, and they are constant cheerleaders in your life. They advised you in the major transition points of your life . . . changing jobs, falling in and out of love, overcoming disease, or relocating to another city. If you lose touch with these friends, and then unexpectedly reconnect, you are instantly bonded again.

Don't forget strangers. Mentors may have emerged in your life in unlikely places. The mentoring that lasted only a few moments at the airport, waiting in a long queue, or on a park bench may have had an extraordinary impact on the direction of your life. It is like "entertaining angels in disguise." You might strain to remember the name of the person, but the experience is forever.

Are you conscious of having received mentoring? Ponder what these mentors said and how they behaved. What did they reveal in word and deed? How did they help elicit hidden potential from within you . . . and how did they help challenge you to confront sidetracks, addictions, and obstacles? How were you different because of this? Your attitudes, behavior patterns, plans, and life goals were reshaped or redirected. In the *pilgrim band*, every participant is simultaneously mentor and mentee. As you have received, so also can you give.

Systems of Mutual Accountability

Those who participate in mentoring relationships always have some experience with serious systems of accountability. They are unafraid of being held accountable. They are assertive in holding others accountable. These experiences of accountability often come from our occupational lives, and sometimes from our lives as volunteers. Most businesses hold managers, support staff, and all employees accountable to specific job descriptions and define anticipated measurable results that are used in annual evaluations. Public schools and hospitals, for example, publicly post "core values" in various visible locations in the building so that the public can hold teachers and health care workers accountable for their behavior.

Experience in non-profit systems of accountability can be especially beneficial if you think you are called to be a mentor. These organizations understand that accountability extends to unpaid volunteers as well as paid employees. Moreover, their systems of accountability go beyond simple skills development and statistically measurable results.

Have you had experience in a *comprehensive* system of accountability? Such accountability includes not only competency and skills development but also accountability for attitude, integrity, and teamwork.[9]

- *Attitude* refers to the underlying commitment you have to the higher purpose or ultimate concern of the organization with which you work. Employees who share a mission attitude don't watch the clock, and they work hard without constant supervision. Volunteers who share a mission attitude sacrifice more time, energy, and money, and evaluate mission results. Your attitude is revealed in your readiness to learn and go beyond your comfort zones. This is a higher accountability.

- *Integrity* refers to the alignment of both your skilled labor and your lifestyle with the values and beliefs of the organization with which you work. Doctors do not abuse drugs; teachers do not behave disrespectfully to minorities; trusted managers do not gamble away their incomes in casinos. Your integrity is revealed in the unrehearsed words and spontaneous deeds that fill your time at work and at play. This is a higher accountability.

- *Teamwork* refers to your ability to be patient, cooperative, and supportive with others. Team players sacrifice ego for the sake of team success. They listen carefully, interact respectfully, treat each other sensitively, and collaborate effectively. Organizations are learning from sports, music, and other high-performance experiences to maximize results. Your teamwork is revealed through your ability to overcome personality and cultural differences. This is a higher accountability.

This more comprehensive experience with accountability is particularly helpful in mentoring. The foundation of all healthy accountability is trust. Trust is not created by lists of rules or regulations. It is generated through

---

9. I talk about this system of accountability extensively in my book *Spirited Leadership: Empowering People to Do What Matters*.

shared attitudes, reliable lifestyle habits, honesty in doubt, and generosity in conviction, shared service, and spiritual practice.

A genuine system of accountability is not revealed through rehearsed words (statements or pronouncements, or sermons or essays). Nor is it revealed through planned or choreographed actions (strategies or structures, or Sunday morning piety or denominational polities). Authentic accountability is revealed through the unrehearsed words (exclamations and conversations, or questions and silences) of daily living. It is revealed through the spontaneous actions (unthinking habits and reactions, daring and unexpected deeds) that shape our lifestyles.

The more you reflect on what you seem to do intuitively and how people spontaneously relate to you, the more surprised you become. The more you realize your own thirst for help to explore the meaning and purpose of life, the more open you become. At first you were skeptical. Who am I that I might be a mentor? What am I that makes me a seeker?

- Yes, I am humbled before the awesome power and love of God and do not pretend to know everything.
- Yes, I urgently desire to be with God and shape my lifestyle around God's purposes.
- Yes, I do remember experiences of the Holy when God profoundly impacted my life.
- Yes, weak as I am, I do have personal experiences of victory that I can describe.
- Yes, mentoring has shaped my life . . . sometimes from unexpected sources in amazing ways.
- Yes, I do have experience with systems of accountability and am not afraid of being held accountable.

This self-awareness sharpens dissatisfaction with classroom education and academic degrees, and with service clubs and church institutions, and with the mere fellowship of sports teams, hobby groups, and drinking buddies. Mentoring is not necessarily linked to any personality type, but many mentors are in fact introverts rather than extroverts. They are often reluctant to begin, energized by the activity, and drained at the end.

You suddenly realize that *you are already treated as a mentor by others*. Family members look to you for advice. Coworkers share confidences with you. Friends and neighbors seek you out amid the struggles and uncertainties of life. Complete strangers speak to you in airports and during soccer games. You may even run from it, but mentoring moments keep finding you. You may decline to talk with people, but they keep coming to you. You may be fearful of the risks of being wrong, but you are compelled to help people do what is right.

And you suddenly realize that *you really do thirst for more meaning and deeper purpose in life.* You can't seem to escape it or excuse yourself from it. Even though you have memories of emptiness, fears of death, and problems with guilt, and even though you also have experiences of defeat, and even though selfishness continues to lead you astray just like everyone else, and even though you have serious doubts about the existence of God . . . *in spite of all that* you still feel the urgency to help others overcome anxieties, feel the touch of the Holy, and discover fresh meaning and purpose.

The dawning realization that, despite all your inadequacies, God is already using you as a mentor comes as both confirmation and shock. It's no use running from it. Now is the time to work backward to prayerfully reconsider the previous six "indicators" that you really are called to mentor. You will seek out mentors for yourself or intensify your training with a current mentor. Your mentor can help you learn from your own past, remember experiences of the Holy, participate in systems of accountability, celebrate spiritual victories, humble yourself before incarnation, and sharpen your desire to be part of God's purpose. What you learn from your mentor, you pass on to those whom you mentor.

The readiness to mentor or receive mentoring implies openness to what I have come to identify as the *pilgrim band*. This is a small, mobile, committed group of spiritual travelers that often gathers around a single mentor but evolves into an experience of mutual mentoring. You do not mentor others *on your own*. You mentor in the context of a group of travelers sharing a journey for purpose and meaning. In the *pilgrim band* you are a mentor . . . and a mentee . . . at the same time.

A Personal Reflection

Let's be frank. Even a saint would not live up to all the criteria I ascribe to a mentor. The best anyone can be is an approximation. And when you think about it, that is as it should be. A mentor is on a journey, too. Journeys can be messy. Sometimes you move forward, and sometimes backward, and what may be sufficient today may be insufficient tomorrow.

You may be more arrogant than you think you are. Your desire for God may run hot and cold. Your memories of the Holy may become indistinct. Your courage will inevitably fail before a crisis, sometimes unexpectedly and sometimes dramatically. Your experience as a mentee may be limited by your upbringing, personality, circumstance, or culture, and what seemed adequate in one situation is woefully inadequate in another. Your history of participation in systems of accountability may be checkered; you may be burdened by regrets and in need of great forgiveness.

Mentors are always and inevitably flawed. They may know it. Sometimes they need a mentor to tell them. You can't possibly be a mentor if you are not ready to be a mentee. This is one reason why a one to one mentoring relationship can and should develop into the mutual mentoring of the *pilgrim band*.

I was raised in a traditional church and trained in traditional seminaries. Last year I recognized the fiftieth anniversary of my ordination. I was equipped then for Christendom, as are most clergy even today. This is because the Christian movement is still mainly institutional, and leaders are supposed to be professionals. Clergy are trained to teach and preach, conduct "good" worship, visit and counsel, facilitate meetings, supervise staff, raise money, preserve harmony, defend policy, and still exercise self-care. Most have limited experience with mentoring, and none have any training to be a mentor.

One of my books is *Spiritual Leadership*, in which I describe eight different kinds of leaders by identity and function.[10] As a consultant I estimate that about 70 percent of clergy are traditional, institutional Christendom leaders. I call them "constant" leaders because they are always very, very busy doing the things they were raised to expect and trained to do. About 20 percent are what I call "organic" leaders because they specialize in seeker sensitive programming and adult faith formation. And about 10 percent are "extreme" leaders. These last function as visionaries, mentors, and pilgrims, but their identities are much more radical. I call them Relentless Futurists, Greek Interpreters, and Determined Travelers. Most of them were not raised in Christendom, trained in seminary, or ordained as clergy. The number of people who gravitate to these last types of leaders has grown from about 20 percent to about 75 percent of the public between 2010 and 2023 (depending on where you are).

---

10. Bandy, *Spiritual Leadership*, 25–36.

It is possible for traditionally raised clergy to become "extreme," but it takes more than extra study or advanced degrees. It requires more than a functional change in what you do or how you do it. It requires a change in *identity*, which is to say, how you are "wired" as a spiritual being. There is a point in ministry beyond which professionalism and ordination cannot take you. It is usually precipitated by a *heartburst* for someone other than yourself and leads to experiences of incarnation beyond the structures of religion.

I think this kind of leadership transformation can be extended to all organizations in all sectors because the postmodern world in general (not just the post-Christendom world in particular) is demanding *more* than professionalism. Education, expertise, and authority are not enough. Wisdom, integrity, and authenticity are the new priorities. "My career" becomes secondary to "our future." This is a traumatic shift for the radical individualism that has dominated the modern era. Personally, I think I have had two near nervous breakdowns along the way . . . and counting.

Heartbursts

ONCE YOU GET OVER the surprise (or shock) of *being* and *becoming* a mentor, new questions become urgent. If you need to seek more intentional mentoring, where do you find it? When should you look for it? How will you recognize it? If you seek to become more intentional mentoring others, where do you find people who might be seeking it? When are you most likely to find individuals open to it? How will you begin?

Yet there is one question that must be answered first. *Who?* With whom, with what kind of person, might I build a mentoring relationship? A mentoring relationship is never forced. It never seems artificial. It is never going to be wholly objective and professional. A mentoring relationship (whether receiving or giving) feels natural. It may seem awkward at first, but it feels right. It is worth the risk. A mentoring relationship is akin to a personal strategy of meditation. Indeed, it is often incorporated into an individual meditation strategy that is already unfolding. While there is objectivity in a mentoring relationship, there is also profound subjectivity in a mentoring relationship. It proceeds more by intuition and empathy than through analysis and program.

The question to ask yourself is this: *Who do I want to be with?* With what kinds of people do I feel the most joy, fulfillment, and relevance? Of course, I do *not* mean that you associate only with people with whom you are *comfortable*. "Comfort" and "joy" are not only different but often completely opposite things. A relationship that brings joy is filled with trust, but it is also filled with adventure. It is a relationship that offers safety and security on the one hand but raises new questions and explores new possibilities on the other hand. Mentoring relationships may extend to people who may think and behave quite differently than people in your past friendship circles, and yet there is a positive attraction and profound respect for their differences.

I call this experience that is at once both immanent and transcendent a *heartburst*. One's heart suddenly opens to someone other than yourself, aware that there is a deeper meaning bigger than both of you. An authentic *heartburst* exhibits three qualities.

1. There is immediate and genuine *acceptance* of the other person, as they are, and not as you imagine them to be or want them to become.
2. There is an initial and growing *respect* for the other person's spontaneity and perspective, regardless of disagreement, prompting conversation rather than confrontation.
3. There is a strong sense of *urgency* for the relationship, awareness of both the timeliness and time limitations of conversation and the need to bypass chatter to talk about matters of significance.

A *heartburst* carries with it a sense of anticipation or expectancy. It is essentially hopeful, not in any emotional sense, but in the existential sense of discerning shared meaning and purpose.

Picture yourself in a crowded room. On the one hand, a *heartburst* may be revealed as you gravitate to someone else. You want to be with this person rather than that person. On the other hand, a *heartburst* may be revealed as another person gravitates to you. They want to connect with you more than others. This gravitational pull may be pleasant or unpleasant. The point is that it is filled with significance. It is an influential encounter.

I think, to a certain extent, it is possible to understand the experience of *heartburst* using the "soft sciences" of demographic and lifestyle research. Once you are aware of *who* you want to be with, then the questions about "where" and "when" answer themselves naturally.

Generational Expectations of Leadership

The Strauss and Howe model of generations tracks leadership expectations for different phases of life. According to this model, generational expectations can be grouped according to age, common beliefs, and values (related to culture, civic engagement, family life, and risk management), and identity with a larger peer group.[1] I use a similar model to describe generational ex-

---

1. The model was introduced in their books *Generations: History of America's Future*

pectations for spiritual leadership.[2] In that book I study spiritual leadership in two ways. *Identity* refers to the way a leader is "wired," the patterns of thinking and acting that predictably shape their leadership. *Function* refers to the tasks, jobs, careers through which their identity is to a greater or lesser degree fulfilled. It is possible for a spiritual leader to *be* one kind of leader, yet routinely *do* things tangential to who they are.

Different generations (in our more complex postmodern world different *lifestyle* mosaics) observe the function of leaders and then intuit the identity of leaders. The wider the gap between *who* a leader is and *what* a leader does, the more likely they will be viewed as inauthentic, and credibility will crumble. And the wider the gap between identity and function, the greater the stress will be for the leader, and self-esteem will lower.

Strauss and Howe Categories			Spiritual Leadership Categories
Generation	**Age**	**Identity and Expectation**	**Identity and Function**
Homeland (Gen Z)	Born 1997–2012	Artist *Image and Music*	Pilgrim—Model *Post-Christendom*
Millennial (Gen Y)	Born 1981–96	Hero *Idol and Role Model*	Visionary—Motivator *Post-Christendom*
Gen X	Born 1965–80	Nomad *Mobile and Pragmatic*	Discipler—Guru *Transitional*
Baby Boomer	Born 1946–64	Prophet *Witness and Futurist*	Preacher—CEO *Christendom*
Silent	Born 1928–45	Artist *Teacher and Wordsmith*	Caregiver—Facilitator *Christendom*

(1991) and *The Fourth Turning* (1997). The Strauss and Howe model is included in the demographic research of www.MissionInsite.com.

2. Bandy, *Spiritual Leadership*, 39–148.

There are two considerations, therefore, before you can make a good start as a mentor. These considerations will become increasingly urgent as mentoring evolves into the mutual mentoring of the *pilgrim band*.

When a leader has a *heartburst* for another, this usually precipitates a re-invention of self. The stress of this change is often revealed whenever there is a staffing change in an institutional church. A staff person is assigned a job description for ministry to a different generation or lifestyle mosaic, and this may coincide with their own wish or *heartburst*. The leader is aware that new skills must be acquired and may seek additional training. What they may not realize is that their *identity* must be reshaped, and this can be very stressful. For example, it is commonplace for clergy (even young clergy) to be assigned to "youth ministry," but the identity that is natural to them, or which has been embedded through traditional seminary education, is that of a facilitator, preacher, or prophet. And they must transform into a new identity as visionary, coach, and pilgrim. The more they succeed in youth ministry, the more maverick to the traditional church that their former peers barely know them.

Second, when a leader has a *heartburst* for another, he or she must set aside all previous assumptions and stereotypes they may have about different generations or lifestyle mosaics. This includes any and all assumptions regarding any demographic marker like age, race and ethnicity, economic or social status, educational background, and so on. When one's heartbursts for another—when one feels compelled to compassion—then one must learn all over again the life struggles and spiritual yearnings of the object of their joy. Mentoring is relevant for each generation, but the choice of mentoring relationship tends to vary for each generation.

Silents and Boomers

Silent and Boomer generations often have formal or informal experiences in religious institutions. They gravitate more easily to a religious professional who has had diverse cultural experiences and is an excellent communicator. These generations are more likely to assume a mentor must be a saint (or recognized as "holy"). Since few people seem to fit the category of "holiness," these generations may be timid about a one to one relationship and prefer to read, learn, or teach in more formal groups or classes.

The Strauss and Howe model suggests that they gravitate to a mentor who is one who teaches about theology or philosophy, shares personal experiences with the Holy, or prophetically critiques the present and discerns the future of society. In my model, these generations often expect a mentor to be gentle and non-aggressive, a wordsmith in preaching or poetry, and alert to cultural nuances. However, they are frustrated with bureaucracy and often on the fringe of institutional life. They avoid meetings but are faithful in relationships.

The Silent and Boomer generations often have anxieties related to loneliness or meaninglessness, and in retirement (or near-retirement) they have questions related to aging and death, or regrets about choices and consequences especially related to careers that may have sidetracked them from personal passions.

Boomers and Gen X

Some Baby Boomers and most Gen X are leading the transition from institutional religion to personal religion, although they may remain periodic adherents (not members) of organizations. They gravitate more easily to a non-professional, spiritually disciplined person who may be on the fringe of institutional religion but volunteer in faith-based non-profits or parachurches. Since they are very mobile in relationships and careers, they seek a mentor who can be equally mobile and adaptable to changing circumstances. Anyone who aspires to be a "mentor" must be available through the week and not just Sunday mornings and offer sound, practical advice for day-to-day living. They are more likely to be in careers related to business, applied science, or health care rather than liberal arts careers in education, social service, or religion.

The Strauss and Howe model suggests that they gravitate to a mentor who is a "nomad." This is a person who tends to be cross-disciplinary and cross-cultural. The potential mentor sees life as a journey but tends to be uncomfortable with ambiguity. Their journey is guided by fixed points of reference, fundamental principles, or reliable certainties. In my model, they tend to be keen on adult faith-formation (if they are related to institutions) or gurus who can share hidden meaning and discern individual purpose.

The Gen X generation often have anxieties about purpose and destiny and may sustain feelings of anger over the economic and career limitations imposed or left behind by the Boomer generation. If the Boomer generation is more concerned about freedom and power, Gen X is often more concerned with limitation and meaning.

Gen X and Gen Y

Some Gen X and most Gen Y are thoroughly postmodern and among the most alienated from, or hostile to, institutional religion. They gravitate more easily to a mentor who shares their skepticism of sacred places, traditions, and processes, and their distrust of authorities claiming to know the truth. Truth is more a verb ("trueing") than a noun ("truth"). It is unfolding and contextual. Therefore, they admire courage more than certainty.

The Strauss and Howe model suggests they gravitate to mentors who are "heroes." Mentors are often extreme risk-takers for an important cause and an example of personal sacrifice. In contrast to other generational expectations, mentors do not have to be moral saints, materially successful, or famous, but they do model total commitment to a personal mission that is personally and socially transformative. In my model, mentors tend to be visionaries and motivators who point to a promising future and inspire hope.

Gen Y share anxieties with Gen X about purpose and destiny, but their feelings of anger tend to be less economic and more environmental. They often seek personal fulfillment over financial success and are more concerned about healthy, holistic relationships than careers.

Gen Y and Gen Z

Some Gen Y and most Gen Z are more indifferent to religion than angry about religion. They gravitate toward mentors with strong cross-cultural experiences, bi-racial and multi-lingual relationships, and open minds regarding gender roles and interpersonal relationships. The boundaries between real and digital worlds are blurred, and so also the boundaries between spirituality and entertainment. Mentors move easily between in-person and online presence.

The Strauss and Howe model suggests they tend to connect with mentors who are "artists" (especially related to music, drama, imaging, and video) and therefore have strong media recognition and influence. In my model, relevant mentors tend to be "pilgrims" who are highly mobile, traveling toward a holy destination that remains ill-defined but highly motivating. Their compassion is often expressed in short, intense bursts of time and energy as they help people along the way, but they may not stick around for long-term social impact. Their moral compass comes from influencers beyond themselves, and they seek companions on their pilgrimage through time and space.

Gen Z often reflects anxieties over emptiness and estrangement that once dominated the Boomer generation in their youth. They often worry about potential post-apocalyptic existence and yearn for promise keepers who can point toward a new reality.

Of course, society is much more complicated than this and there are severe limitations on generalizations based on generations alone. These typologies are based on probabilities rather than scientific research and certainties.

The potential for mentoring relationships surprisingly crosses generational boundaries. Gen X may connect with successful Baby Boomers. Gen Z (sometimes called "Net Gen" for their digitally driven lifestyles) may connect with elders of the Silent generation who are remarkably low-tech in lifestyle, but who have survived historic upheavals and remained optimistic about life. On the other hand, Gen X may struggle to empathize with Gen Y, just as Silents struggle to empathize with Baby Boomers. Among all generations, demographic factors related to age, gender, race, income, occupation, marriage, and family status are less and less important as time goes by. What matters most is lifestyle: the conscious priorities and unconscious behavioral habits that create compatibilities between different groups of people. This is why lifestyle awareness is more helpful than demographic research to determine the potential for mentoring relationships.

Lifestyle Expectations for Mentoring

Today in the digital world there are companies that track the digital footprints of individuals and households. Experian, for example, creates a "family tree" that positions groups in proximate relationship to each other based on demographic information about age, relative poverty or wealth, and single/family status, but then defines seventy-one lifestyle experiences clustered in nineteen lifestyle groups.[3] Together these form a kind of "mosaic" of culture, like individual tiles of diverse shapes, colors, and textures that form a larger picture of cultural diversity. Moreover, companies can design algorithms to group people together who share similar attitudes, priorities, and behaviors to describe compatibilities among people. Just as a portrait painted by a master artist reveals the hidden depths of a human being, so also the behavioral

3. Experian, *Mosaic USA E-Handbook*.

description of a shared lifestyle can reveal the motivations and needs, fears, and hopes of a group of people.

Lifestyle research can be used to intrude on the privacy of individuals for manipulative marketing. And lifestyle research can prejudice assumptions about individual choices. There can be no substitute for eye contact, listening, conversation, and immersion in the sensory experiences and interrelationships of diverse lifestyles. For example, it is difficult to empathize with a group of people without learning their language, tasting their food, participating in their recreations, interacting with their friends, understanding their career choices, living in their neighborhoods, and so on. The fact that corporate lifestyle research is primarily used to shape the strategic planning, fundraising, and marketing of businesses reveals both the advantages and disadvantages of lifestyle research.

One reason that mentoring is misunderstood and ignored in modern society is due to the contradiction between the two forces that shape our society: democracy and capitalism. Democracy only works when you fulfill the moral imperative and treat others as subjects rather than objects. Capitalism inevitably leads us to treat others as objects rather than subjects. Capitalism de-personalizes society and encourages us to use, manipulate, and compete, rather than serve, appreciate, and collaborate. I think there is a correlation in Western societies between the original humanism that gave birth to democracy, and the mentoring that was an essential part of our educational systems, and conflicts with the growing capitalism or materialism of Western societies that reduces people to statistics and profits.

Computer dating services are another way modern people try to find healthy, intimate relationships. The process is similar, although simpler, to corporate lifestyle research. Data about one's attitudes and habits, likes and dislikes, career trajectories and income aspirations, sexual preferences, parenting styles, religious activity and more can be gathered, sorted, and compared to generate potential mating matches. The search for a mate, however, is not the same as the search for a mentoring relationship.

A second reason mentoring is misunderstood and ignored in modern society is due to the identification of ego satisfaction with self-fulfillment. The goal of the first is happiness, while the goal of the second is wisdom. The two quests may use similar vocabulary to describe success: commitment and trust, accountability and forgiveness, peace and contentment, hope and joy. But the meaning and import of these words are very different. The search for mentoring is often rooted in the discovery that happiness is not enough. The process of mentoring can undermine the apparent success of computer dating.

Nevertheless, in our increasingly mobile and diverse world, lifestyle is a more significant factor in shaping relationships than mere demographics. Relationships today are constantly crossing the boundaries of demographic categories. Data management can never replace personal immersion in the lives of others and all the risks, surprises, and opportunities that entails. My point is that you can use lifestyle research to anticipate those with whom you may feel the greatest empathy . . . and discover how you personally need to evolve to be empathic with relative strangers. God can elicit a mentoring relationship with those with whom you feel *comfortable*, and with those with whom you may feel *uncomfortable*. The humility of the mentor allows one to function in different ways without losing identity.

Despite the risks, demographic and lifestyle research can expand our compassion, anticipate human needs, and focus our message of hope. I think it is helpful for the spiritual traveler to filter their relationships (casual or intentional, short or long term, in any and every context) using four filters.

Lifestyle as Personal Choice

Modern people commonly consider lifestyle as a choice. The choice may be conscious or unconscious, but it is still a decision to think, behave, and relate in one way or another. Our choices may be good or bad. We follow and emulate the right people or the wrong people, but we are always in the position of changing our minds. Lifestyle is often reflected in career choices. One chooses the lifestyle of an academic, engineer, farmer, scientist, soldier, etc. It may be reflected in our choices of the hobbies we enjoy, the clubs and churches we join, the music we prefer, or the environments in which we choose to live. Indeed, globalization and internet communication have expanded our personal choices exponentially. As you seek mentoring relationships, you can ponder and prioritize your personal choices and look for mentoring among the people who share your interests. The digital tools I described above may help you do that.

However, we should be aware that, despite the glorification of individualism inherent in modern society, our power to choose and control our lifestyles is much overrated. For one thing, forces beyond our control are constantly blocking, diverting, or subverting our desires. Moreover, what we think we have "freely" chosen has often been prompted by hidden conditions. Depth psychology explores the compulsions and motivations that lie deep in our unconscious minds which influence, if not actually determine, our "free" choices. Indeed, scientific behaviorists argue that "free will" is an illusion. What is clear in global and personal history is that we constantly make decisions to do things that, even at the time, we know to be against our best interests.

Lifestyle as Natural Predisposition

Lifestyle can also be explored because of our natural disposition, temperament, or genetic history. We are content if we follow our natural disposition and discontented when we do not. The best relationships are ones that "fit" with our individual natures. And if we can better understand our natures, then we can select the relationships that would be most harmonious, collaborative, and helpful.

Mentoring opportunities may be enhanced or limited by inherited physical or mental circumstances, debilitating accidents, chronic disease, etc. The best "fit" with our natures may require special empathy with such circumstances. We may seek mentors within personal support, medical, and therapeutic networks. However, we should not limit ourselves to such networks because our humanity need not be defined by these limitations.

Self-understanding is the key to better relationships. As you seek mentoring relationships, it may help to know your personality typology, and there are many tools available. Some personality types get along better, or worse, with other types. However, we should be aware that personality type is not static. It can change and evolve as age, experience, and stress change our personalities. What was "natural" yesterday may not be so "natural" in the future. The teams that function so productively in the workplace may not work well outside the office. Moreover, the more we explore our personality type, the more confused we can become. We seem to have different "personalities" in different contexts. We identify less with a type, and feel we are between types.

Lifestyle as Cultural Influence

Perhaps the greatest impact on lifestyle comes from cultural influences. Cultural habits are passed on through the generations via language, tradition, and family structure. There are behavior patterns shaped by race and country of origin which may be exacerbated by either prejudice or entitlement. As lifestyle diversity increases, peer group pressure (overt and hidden) strongly influences our habits and attitudes. To some extent lifestyle research tools can track these changing and evolving "tribes," but such research can also be used to stereotype and segregate, artificially limiting the opportunities for mentoring.

Mentoring relationships may be found within peer groups, but they may also be found (and perhaps become more significant) beyond our peer groups. Lifestyle diversity may seem an obstacle to finding mutual mentoring relationships, but in fact it is an opportunity to widen our search and expectations for mentoring relationships. Organizational memberships (e.g., churches, clubs, etc.) that are too homogeneous limit opportunities for mentoring, and memberships that are more heterogeneous expand them.

Two things are necessary when seeking mentoring relationships in cultural diversity. First, one must be increasingly self-aware, not of personality traits, but of positive and negative habits revealed in our intentional and unintentional behavior. Pay attention to your *spontaneous* actions and your *unrehearsed* words. These are more indicative of attitudes and assumptions that limit relationships. Addictions as self-destructive behavior patterns that we chronically deny come in many forms and blind us to opportunities for mentoring relationships. Second, one must intentionally practice *humility* before cultural diversity. Suspend judgment and pay attention. Avoid confrontation and embrace conversation . . . even if it is uncomfortable. This opens new possibilities for empathy and understanding.

Lifestyle as Spiritual Formation

The rationalism and materialism of modern life tends to depreciate the relevance of spiritual presence. I do not just mean the influence of religious traditions and institutions. The movement of Spirit in our lives is deeper and wider than any tradition or institution. Spirit can be revealed through organized religion, and it can shatter organized religion. It is often invisible. It is often misunderstood as some other form of psychological or historical influence on our lives. Yet the more one explores life, the more one intuits that there is something more happening in us and in the world than can be rationalized or materialized.

The more one becomes self-aware of the attitudes and habits shaped by nature, personality, or peer pressure, the more one realizes that the meaning of life is neither confined to, nor explained by, such influences. And the more one practices humility amid cultural diversity, the more one senses that the purpose of life lies beyond the self, and indeed, beyond even the collective of individual selves. It is not just that human spirit is more than mind and material, but that human spirit is shaped by God through mind and materiality. Sometimes the movement of Spirit is obvious, but more often it is subtle. Yet it can be decisive for us to discover what it means to be human. And it can lead us to others who share our quest for meaning and purpose. No encounter with another human being is merely accidental.

There are two things that are helpful to discern how Spirit is shaping lifestyle.

First, one must become sensitive to the symbolic power of cultural forms. Any cultural form can become an expression or focus of Spirit. In other words, there is no real distinction between the sacred and profane. The most ordinary, or even the ugliest, or even the most painful experience can become a vehicle for God's meaning and purpose, not just the extraordinary, beautiful, or happiest experience. One needs to view culture with the heart of an artist who can see hidden significance, or with the eyes of a biologist or astronomer who can appreciate intricacy. Both can see the mystery of life in the complexity of culture.

Second, one must be disciplined in spiritual practices. I do not mean just traditional personal or corporate piety like prayer and worship, scripture reading and meditation, and the like. Any discipline may serve . . . artistic or literary, scientific, or military, etc. The key is to lead a *disciplined* life rather than an undisciplined life. A disciplined life is one that is lived intentionally, and accountably, for personal growth and social justice and not just for personal happiness and financial success. A disciplined life is a behavior pattern that observes, reflects, and acts in ways that are just, generous, sensitive, and responsible. Spirit shapes and molds an individual to become more than just the sum of one's choices, or the expression of one's personality, or one's place in society.

Mentors become travelers, and travelers become mentors. The best mentors often describe themselves as the most avid travelers. The ones who know the most are often the ones that confess they know the least, and yet the very least that they know is still more than the traveler seeks. The most effective mentors are also being mentored. They are being mentored by others wiser than themselves, or by others more innocent than themselves. This is precisely the situation of most travelers. All are being mentored by the Spirit.

The challenge of mentoring is not to find people to mentor but to place oneself at the disposal of the Spirit. The Spirit shapes your life but also shapes the circumstances in which you live. There is no such thing as "coincidence" for travelers and mentors. There is only "providence." Even the most casual acquaintance is pregnant with spiritual possibilities. You do not find travelers. Travelers find you. You do not find mentors. You bump into them on the road. More accurately, the Spirit creates situations in which travelers and mentors find each other. It just happens. The more one surrenders to the Spirit, the more mentoring conversations just seem to occur. Sometimes they span a few minutes and sometimes they span a lifetime. Always they are beyond our complete control.

A *heartburst* is not mere sentimentality. It is a combination of pique and compassion. The encounter with a stranger is often felt as a kind of imposition, distraction, or nuisance. Initially it may be annoying because you must focus time and energy away from yourself or your familiar circle of friends. Yet as it demands attention, it also stimulates curiosity. Compassion is the sudden and inexplicable discovery that you *care* for this stranger. You care about their present situation, how it occurred, and where it is leading.

Imagine you see a cute baby in a stroller while you are walking in the park. Your heart goes out to the child, but this is mere sentimentality. There is no obligation implied. You smile and walk on. Now imagine you are in economy class on an airplane, and the middle and window seats are occupied by a young mother and a crying baby. The baby won't stop. The mother tries to calm the child in vain. You are irritated. And yet, suddenly and inexplicably you *care* for the child and mother. You offer to help, soothe the baby, encourage the mother, protect them from the hostile glares of fellow passengers. That is a *heartburst*.

Similarly, a *heartburst* is not mere curiosity. It is a mix of magnetism and imagination. An encounter with a stranger is often felt as a kind of compulsion. You don't just look, you observe. Your attention is fixed when they are present, and their memory lingers long after they are absent. The appearance and behavior of another person or group piques your imagination. You wonder about their needs and motivations, hopes and dreams. You set aside what you are doing and invest time and energy into research.

Imagine you see a group of people in the food court lined up to order fast food. You measure the length of the line, notice which people might slow it down, evaluate the efficiency of the staff, and decide what is best for yourself. Now imagine you are in the same food court and observe a Gen-Z group of mixed gender, race, and ethnicity idly hanging out in their own corner for several hours (talking, laughing, and occasionally cautioned by security personnel). Your interest is aroused. You engage them in conversation, buy them snacks, return several times to build friendships. That is a *heartburst*.

Opportunities for mentoring almost always emerge as a surprise . . . not as a result of strategic planning. They suddenly appear in a conversation after a workshop, or in a coffee shop, or in the airport waiting in the bar for a flight departure. Such relationships may be sustained over time, and some may seem fleeting. But every mentor must understand in all humility that you are just a small piece in a wider, invisible, movement of Spirit. What you experience is both a follow-up from a previous mentoring relationship this person brings with them, and what you share is part of the discernment of meaning and purpose that this person takes with them. You do not know who went before you or who comes after you. You trust the Spirit will follow this person's journey.

This is why I stress that mentoring relationships surprise us as a *heartburst*. You may be prepared for them, but they are not predictable in advance. Preparation is not a curriculum that assumes an ego studying a special content of information, but a spiritual discipline of self-forgetfulness and empathy. Demographic and lifestyle research is pointless unless it serves mutual understanding and reconciliation. Approach mentoring more like a monk leading a spiritual life than a doctoral student researching a dissertation. A *heartburst* emerges from prayer, or more broadly, from communion with the Spirit, rather than accumulated information.

A *heartburst* is like an awakening, a sudden awareness that you are encountering a complex human being seeking meaning and purpose. Whether you instinctively "like" or "dislike" a person is irrelevant. The decision to "approach" or to "avoid" a stranger is taken away from you and replaced by a compulsion to care about the destiny of another human being. Mentoring is not a friendship (although it can lead to a friendship). Friendship is not the goal. Encouraging, challenging, and guiding another in their journey to discover meaning and purpose is the point.

Mentoring does not depend on how much time you have to build a relationship, but about how timely your conversation, however brief, is to the journey of another. It is primarily a *heartburst* rather than a therapeutic *process*. The significance of mentoring is often measured in moments rather than sessions. And when the opportunity passes, you may well wonder what value your contribution might have had, or will have, in this person's life. Indeed, you often discover that your contribution lies not in what you said, but what you have left unsaid, or in a meaning to your words of which you were not even aware. God creates a subtext in every mentoring relationship.

A Personal Reflection

One of the "near nervous breakdowns" in the trajectory of my life started in a small hotel conference room at a hotel near the Houston airport. I was introduced to a new demographic search engine that was being developed, and (more importantly), to the emerging "science" of lifestyle clustering in the digital age. I remember being excited, astonished, and overwhelmed. Here was a tool to study the behavior patterns of groups of people and plan alternatives in ministry not by guesswork but by discernment. More than this, behind the behavior patterns of people, one could glimpse the anxieties that motivated their quests for God. Eventually I would write commentaries for every lifestyle segment and group distinguishing different leadership and program preferences and probing their spiritual needs and longings.[4]

To me, and to the many leaders who use it today, this was revolutionary. I had long been dissatisfied with the basic demographic stereotypes based on age, gender, occupation, income, or family status. Finally, here was a tool to build bridges of empathy between different groups of people, interpret cultural diversity, and customize relevant ministries. More than this, here was a method to explore the diversity of spiritualities in America. To me, this was visual evidence of Tillich's assertion that spirit is revealed in culture. "Culture" could now be described in the behavioral portraits of people and not just the abstract data.

But theory changed to reality when I began work in New Orleans following the devastating hurricanes of 2007. There is a reason New Orleans is often called "the northernmost city of the Caribbean." The two places

---

4. The search engine is www.MissionInsite.com, and the lifestyle research is done by Experian.

in North America where I have felt most like being on another planet are Newfoundland and New Orleans. Such is the diversity of cultures and dialects. I had previously worked among bayou churches and Cajun communities, but after the hurricanes I worked with different churches across the city to encourage leaders and support volunteers. One night I took the wrong exit from I-10 and found myself lost in the lower 9th Ward. All around me were devastated neighborhoods and broken homes. No lights, no signs, no services. The moon revealed a landscape of broken pavement and downed trees. A few people gathered around open fires and homemade shelters. It was frightening and heartbreaking. And that was the moment when I truly felt a *heartburst* for people so completely different from myself. I knew them in theory. Now I knew them for real. Eventually my work extended across southern Louisiana for years to come.

First Steps

GOT MILK? AT ONE time this was a popular marketing slogan for the dairy industry. The marketing campaign they used was humorous, quirky, young, hip, and rhythmic. It managed to connect traditional values with contemporary relevance, old folk wisdom with young folk vitality, and cows, corn, and tractors with cultures, good company, and fast cars. Suddenly the barn was a transportation hub and the meeting place of people looking for a good thing.

In ancient times, and even today in many parts of the world beyond Western culture, mentoring was as ubiquitous as milk. It was a staple in the spiritual diet. You didn't have to persuade people to drink milk. They sought it automatically. And you didn't have to persuade people to seek mentoring. They looked for mentors constantly.

The trend in the postmodern world is that people are once again seeking milk. They are turning away from fast foods, soft drinks, and bad eating habits. More and more people (young and old) are turning away from educational shortcuts, comfortable religiosity, and bad spiritual habits.

It appears that nearly everybody is a *seeker* or a *traveler*. There are still groups of ultra-religious and ultra-rational dogmatists fighting with each other, but most people are not paying much attention to their quarrel. They have realized that spirituality is part of life, and to greater and lesser degrees they are open to surprise. They are convinced that there is a greater purpose and deeper meaning to living—and that meaning and purpose can and should make sense—than either religious or rational dogmatists admit.

As I said in the previous chapter, there are different kinds of seekers, and only some of them really value mentoring and look for mentoring relationships.

- Some seekers avoid taking ultimate responsibility for their quest. They tend to look for magical solutions and superheroes. They value relationships with gurus who can tell them what to believe and what to do.
- Other seekers select little bits of different religions that appeal to their current tastes. They tend to look for vague generalizations and satisfying rationalizations. They value relationships with celebrities who can tell them how to be successful and spiritual at the same time.
- Still other seekers are suspicious of any experts and quite confident that they can think for themselves. They use personality inventories, but are timid about commitment, and value relationships with teachers and therapists.

There are some spiritual travelers, however, who are more serious about exploring spirituality because they are more interested in shaping and living a spiritual life.

They are not needy, self-centered, or simply curious. They have left a comfortable life and convenient assumptions behind and started down the road. The beginning of their journey may not have been a conscious decision, but at some point, the fact that they are on a journey has become a conscious, consistent, and sometimes burdensome awareness. They are deliberately investing time and energy to explore the meaning and purpose of life. They are often risking careers, friendships, and success to go deeper and further with Spirit. They are more interested in experiencing, exploring, and walking with God.

Travelers who seek mentoring are in a quandary. Travelers soon discover that Sunday worship rarely leads to mentoring (although it might lead to education). There is no institution where you can sign up, there is no course that you can take, and there is no professional with whom you can make an appointment. Mentoring just doesn't work that way. Unlike the ancient world, the modern world does not intentionally provide opportunities for mentors and mentees to get together. Indeed, the modern world lives in denial that mentoring is a genuine need.

Over the years I have led many workshops for Christian clergy and laity, and I can't count the number of times skeptical church leaders have doubted that *seekers* and *travelers* really exist because they claim never to have met any. This is invariably because these leaders may be well trained in seminary and extremely competent in institutional churches, but their spiritual lives are undisciplined. It is something they do when they have time, or when they go on retreat, or when they have to prepare a sermon next Sunday. Otherwise, they are just average culturally accommodating "church people."

Similarly, I can't count the number of times leaders in social service, health care, and small and corporate business have doubted the presence of *seekers* and *travelers* in their midst. This is invariably because they are so immersed in management, driven by success, and focused on organizational outcomes that they fail to pay attention to the personal lives and relationships of volunteers and employees. "Team building" and "volunteer empowerment" are things they do in monthly meetings, annual retreats, or formal career counseling. They do not regularly and consistently *pay attention* to the life stories of the workers around them.

The fact is that people who live every day as a spiritual life (or "pray constantly" as the Orthodox practice) rarely need to look for travelers. The travelers find them. The people who consistently and compassionately pay attention to life stories rarely need to strain to see travelers in their midst. The travelers approach them. If you are *ready* to see them, they will *readily* appear.

Transition points and boundary situations are the contexts in which most mentoring relationships are born. Figuratively speaking, these are often the "bus stations" where people are transferring from one stage of life to another—or the "borders" between one state of being and another state of being—when people are apt to reveal their "passports" of identity. Transition points and boundary situations precipitate questions about integrity, loyalty, self-confidence, and purpose.[1]

My mentors have taught me that "boundary situations" are times of high anxiety when finding hope is most urgent. Our lives are rarely "at peace." Sometimes we are living life "on the edge." These can be traumatic events. They may feel like life and death experiences. They can be exhilarating or devastating. Mentoring is often about finding the courage to survive, endure, and boldly step into the future. They often precipitate our quest for meaning and purpose.

Most "boundary situations" lie in between life-at-peace and life-on-the-edge. They are experiences of profound ambiguity and uncertainty. In the broadest sense, the transition between generations and the shift from the modern to postmodern world are cultural boundary situations that precipitate anxieties across all generations and institutions. There are certain

---

1. I first described this phenomenon in my book *Talisman*, 19–20, 76–90.

"boundary situations" that you can discern in the lives of others if you are prayerfully paying attention. These are not just times when we might seek therapeutic counseling, for more is at stake than our physical or mental health. We find ourselves in a "crisis" of meaning and purpose. These are turning points when we feel we are at a crossroads. Mentoring is often about seeking wisdom in the present and direction for the future.

All these boundary situations leave us open to influential encounters that shape our lives, invite opportunities for mentoring, and forge relationships into a *pilgrim band*.

The Boundary Between Participation and Separation

There are intervals when we are content with our relationships or content in our autonomy, but most often we are somewhere in between connection and disconnection. We experience tension between intimacy and individuality. This may involve marriage and family relationships, breaking and forming friendships, decisions about education or employment, etc. Is it time to commit to another person, relationship, organization, or tradition? Or is it time to break from another person, sever a relationship, shift to a different organization, or adopt a new tradition?

The Boundary Between Trust and Trustworthiness

There are intervals when we are confident in those we trust and in our own reliability. More often, we find ourselves questioning our relationships and losing self-confidence. We may be re-evaluating commitments, accepting or declining new responsibilities, torn between righteous indignation and forgiveness, filled with regret and yearning for acceptance. Is it time to confront or negotiate? Is it the time to take big risks or exercise caution?

The Boundary Between Pessimism and Optimism

There are intervals when skepticism is reasonable and we doubt empty promises and false prophets, and there are times when optimism is reasonable, and we believe in the improbable and cling to promise keepers. More often, we are struggling with aging, worried about disease, and afraid of death. We are in despair about the world and building walls to keep life out, or we discern light at the end of a dark tunnel and open doors to bring life in. Is this a time to retreat or advance? Hide from reality or dare new things?

The Boundary Between Faith and Doubt

There are intervals when we are certain about life after death, God, human potential and progress, and other times when we are certain that death is the end, God doesn't exist, and human beings are destined for extinction. More often, we are struggling with ambiguity. We are struggling to make sense of gratuitous evil or struggling to believe in miraculous good. Does God care about one little human being or not? Does a human being really have a spark of decency in his or her soul or not? Is there some kind of life after death or not? Is progress inevitable or not?

All these boundary situations are opportunities for mentoring. These are times when travelers look for mentors and mentors find themselves in surprising conversations with travelers. This is because something deeper is going on here than worries about intimate relationships, financial security, personal health, and retirement planning. These are the times when people question the meaning and purpose of their lives.

All these changes suggest that people who seek mentoring are no longer driven by a desire *to belong*. They are driven by the reality of being *on the boundary*. They have consciously or unconsciously concluded that the best they can do is *partially belong*, and that they will in fact "belong" to multiple groups, relationships, occupations, habits, and obligations. They no longer insist or expect that their lives will be consistent. Contradiction and ambiguity are inevitable. If they cannot reconcile everything, at least they can cope with anything.

In a previous chapter, I shared how mentoring addresses the deeper existential anxieties that drive our quest for meaning and purpose. But I want to stress once again that the role of the mentor is not to answer all questions or solve all problems, but to use their experience to help people think through questions, experiment with new solutions, and persevere through the struggles of life. The *courage* and *fortitude* of a mentor are often more important than their knowledge and ideas. The mentor himself or herself is not a success story but a work in progress. You know you are a mentor when you recognize you are a mentee.

The signs of interest in mentoring represent a kind of hierarchy of awareness. The more unconscious intuitions become conscious insights, the more restless postmodern people become, and the more urgent they become in their search for mentors.

- Awareness often begins with accelerated interest in sacred writings, spiritual personalities, religious perspectives, and the history of ideas. Since the decline of liberal arts education, many are only just discovering history, philosophy, art, and classical literature. This may initially be satisfied by a community college course, a book club, or a study program, but the restlessness persists as people wonder at the existential "stake" revealed in the pursuit of truth, beauty, and virtue.

- Awareness often deepens through engagement with hands-on social service, such as a local, regional, or global mission. Since the decline of the civil rights movements, many are rediscovering the urgency for human rights. This may initially be satisfied with a social service project, a charitable vacation, or by the investment of spare time to care for the "under privileged," but the restlessness persists as people experience gratuitous evil and radical generosity and ask questions they have never asked before.

- Awareness deepens yet again as people question their own career paths, corporate loyalties, and life priorities. As secure, meaningful work disappears, people are trying to merge careers with balanced lifestyles. This may initially be satisfied by a change of occupation or early retirement, but the restlessness persists as people discover that these changes precipitate more anxieties than they resolve. Ambiguity is inescapable in the best corporations and altruistic retirement plans.

- Awareness becomes urgent as people add stress to their intimate relationships. As intimacy and sexuality become more diverse and fragile, people reexamine all relationships. This may initially be satisfied by psychotherapy and marital counseling, or by reshaping circles of intimacy or divorce, but the restlessness persists precisely because true love would rather adapt than give up. The mentoring relationship expands awareness of how to love and of how to participate in the spiritual journey of the beloved.

Awareness peaks with the realization that we live "in between" or "on the boundary" of many distinct and equally valuable cultures. People travel more, mingle with new immigrant cultures, and value multicultural friendships.

Individuals either establish an identity and purpose with reference to absolutes beyond the diversity of cultures, or they lose themselves in the clash of cultures.

Influential encounters occur in times of change. That is why travelers and mentors go searching on the edges of education or on the peripheries of institutions. They hang about the church, but don't join, because their goal is to connect with a mentor rather than to serve on a committee. They take a course from the community college so that they can legitimately lurk in the common room and cafeteria where they might fall into interesting conversations. Since mentoring is most likely to feel urgent in times of transition or boundary testing, travelers and mentors tend to circle around places of transition, such as:

- Transportation and communication hubs
- Sports arenas, fitness centers, and meditation centers
- Coffee shops, wine bars, and restaurants
- Theaters, art exhibits, and cinemas

Wherever people gather to expand relationships, try on new attitudes, explore different perspectives, connect with different cultures, and generally expand their horizons, there you will probably find travelers and mentors looking for one another. When you think about it, much of our time is spent enjoying or protecting our comfort zones. Mentoring connections, however, lie just outside of our comfort zones. With one foot in safe territory, the other foot probing unexplored country, travelers and mentors live a tentative, intuitive, risky kind of lifestyle. It may take a lot of courage for a traveler and a lot of patience for a mentor.

When mentors and mentees do get together, it is helpful to understand how each interprets the event differently. Travelers usually describe the event as "coincidence." Mentors almost always see the event as "providence." If the opportunity is missed, travelers will always walk away thinking "I wish I had asked for directions." Mentors will always walk away thinking "I wish I had said something helpful." Mentors may be surprised by the opportunity, but they are prepared to make the best of it. The traveler should learn something of value to take away, even if he or she doesn't know it at the time. The mentor should have something to give away, even though he or she may not know what will come of it at the time.

Therefore, mentors develop the habit of having intentional, open-ended conversations. These are non-judgmental and gentle conversations that build trust, elicit deeper sharing, and encourage others to speak honestly. Conversations may be short, long, or intermittent, but they always invite profound questions without falling back on easy answers. These are *conversations*. They are not *confrontations*. The mentoring moment is not a debate or an argument. The mentor is not a "prophet," and the mentee is not being asked to repent, convert, or even change. The mentor is not a "professor," and the mentee is not a "student." They are equals in life, but at different places in the journey of life.

Credibility attracts conversation. The hunger for mentoring leads people to make assumptions about credibility based on the smallest clues. Complete strangers will share remarkably personal things at an airport, bus terminal, or transportation center, or at a sports arena, pub, or coffee shop, or anywhere anonymous where people simultaneously lose their inhibitions and feel lost in their identity. Their only clues may be their mannerisms, dress, or overheard comments from people who give the appearance of integrity. Such a thin layer of confidence rarely leads to profound mentoring, but how others observe your spontaneous behavior often opens the door to respectful conversation. So, while on the one hand you must seek out travelers through intentional conversations, on the other hand you must allow travelers to seek you out. These are *influential encounters* that can lead to *influential relationships*.

Seekers and spiritual travelers have hidden antennae that detect authenticity. This has nothing to do with personality. Mentors are often introverts who exude no specific personality. Rather, they are a neutral presence in the situation. They seem "safe" in their initial anonymity. Yet strangers are spontaneously honest with them. And the mentor is honest in return. There is no dissembling or trickery or false humility. It is important that you match vulnerability with vulnerability. In other words, you never invite others to reveal themselves unless you are ready to reveal yourself *to the same degree of stress*. Perhaps that moment of shared vulnerability will go no further.

There is, however, a "mentoring alternative" in every conversation. At the point where most people are deciding whether there is a potential friendship there or not, mentors and travelers see another possibility. It is a variation in the relationship that may, or may not, involve "friendship" but has a unique potential beyond or alongside "friendship." I have observed a pattern behind every influential encounter.[2] For example:

Two people both participate in a service club or church committee. They are different ages, with different professions and incomes, and probably have different family experiences and personal histories. Each one, consciously or unconsciously, thirsts for a mentoring relationship. Their conversations grow incrementally in stages. Conversations may continue physically or digitally (in person and online). The transition from one stage to another may be short or long. Indeed, the conversation can be interrupted and later renewed after days or even years.

- *Affirmation*: Each expresses admiration or appreciation for something the other has said or done. Perhaps it was a daring idea, or perhaps it was a spontaneous behavior pattern, but each respects the integrity or expertise of the other. Remember, this is genuine. If there is nothing to affirm, don't make it up. Don't exaggerate it. Just be honest.

- *Empathy*: Each shares life experiences. They may be positive or negative, but they are *significant* and not mundane. This is no longer a chat. It is an exchange of both information and emotion, the hopes and fears each experience in daily living. The more honest we become, the more vulnerable we feel. Each manages stress in their own way, but each respects the stress another may be feeling. Empathy is not evaluation.

- *Question*: Conversation can last for some time, and wander in many directions, but eventually someone asks a question. It is always an open-ended question, which is to say that there are genuinely different ways to answer it. "What does it mean that . . . ?" "What do you think might happen if . . . ?" "How does this fit with what my father taught, or what my preacher preached, or what some book advocated . . . ?" These are genuine questions for which there is no presumed answer. Conversation becomes shared exploration.

- *Ambiguity*: Every question seeks an answer. Every answer opens new questions. There may be certainties and absolutes, but they cannot be fully contained by either person's mind or completely explained by either person's experience. Each can "get at the truth," but neither

2. Bandy, *Christian Mentoring*, 30–32.

person can "own the truth." Knowledge is always partial. There is always a greater mystery to explore, which means that there will always be anxiety to endure.

- *Variation*: There are many ways to respond to any question. One might repeat some dogmatism or aphorism; offer hesitant speculation; declare indifference. One may offer polite excuses and walk away. But if they stay in conversation, they can explore alternative answers. Each one is free to respond, or not respond, without judgment. The vulnerability of one matches the vulnerability of the other, but both are ready to go deeper.

- *Invitation*: Each person senses an opportunity to share with, and learn from, the other. The invitation to mentoring may be initiated by one or the other, and often it implies that one is mentor and the other mentee. However, in time the distinction between mentor and mentee will be increasingly blurred as each person explores the meaning and purpose of their lives. In the greater mystery of life, it is in fact Spirit that has invited them both into a multi-layered relationship.

There is a larger context in which these kinds of conversations emerge. In part, it is a community context. Each person has been influenced by any number of circumstances, and through any number of casual and formal relationships, to appreciate this opportunity for mentoring. However, there is also a spiritual context. Each person has been influenced by symbols and signs, historical events, and lifestyle patterns, that have created this opportunity for mentoring. This kind of conversation does not occur in a vacuum. This conversation is part of a larger network of conversations, a larger convergence of circumstances, and the larger reality of Spirit moving and shaping culture.

Mentoring that started from a simple conversation, and which may have been pursued sporadically over time, becomes ever more serious and urgent. Mentoring opportunities are intuitional. You do not seek them out. They seek you out. You do not create them. They capture you. Mentoring opportunities emerge as you pursue a spiritual life. The more you discipline your life and pay attention to others, the more you will find yourself in mentoring situations. I invite you to think of mentoring as a lifestyle, rather than a profession. It is a process, not a program. Its primary focus is not on being something, but on becoming something.

A Personal Reflection

The idea of living "on the boundary" has, I think, wide appeal. This reflects what I call the "in-between-ness" of living in the speed, flux, and blur of the world. Change is rapid, constant, and often out of control. When I do demographic and lifestyle research for denominational organizations, I am always struck by the migrations of lifestyle groups along major transportation corridors.

Urbanization goes both ways. People are leaving the city to find affordable housing, quieter surroundings, safer neighborhoods, etc., but they carry with them urban and urbane habits and expectations. People are also commuting long distances to work and shop, sustaining roots and friendships, etc. The digital world has made all of this more intense because people can *move* without physical movement. It's transforming society for the better and worse. When I discover that children in Newfoundland and Labrador are watching television originating in New York and Atlanta, I know that even people in formerly stable or insulated small towns are as much "on the boundaries" as everyone else.

Mentoring occurs in the "in-between-ness" of life. That is where mentoring opportunities seek you out. Paul Tillich noted this in his autobiography.[3] What was true in his life experience before and after world wars speaks to emerging generations today who are especially living in the boundaries between:

- Two temperaments
- City and country
- Social classes
- Reality and imagination
- Religion and culture
- Native and alien land

I have always felt on the boundary between philosophy and theology, reason and miracle, practice and theory. I moved so many times, and lived in so many places, and worked among so many cultures, that I began to feel more at home in an airport than a library. And some of the richest conversations I have ever had have been in pubs and coffee houses rather than churches and classrooms.

3. Tillich, *On the Boundary*, 13–29, 68–73, 91–96.

There are times when mentoring is less likely to happen. There are times when we are living on the creative edge, so busy and focused that we are consumed with activity and have little time to talk. And there are times when we are living at peace with ourselves and the world. It may take a crisis to shatter that serenity. For we only recognize our *need* for hope when we are on the brink of *losing* hope. Most of the time, however, we live "in between": wishing and waiting, making ends meet, in and out of relationships, hoping and worrying, and dreading and dreaming, all at the same time. This is where mentoring opportunities arise. Ready or not, Spirit will invite you in.

Walk with Me

Mentoring may only be a moment of significant conversation between strangers. Two people part and may never see each other, trade email with each other, and never find each other again on social media. No matter. Spirit continues to infuse each life and will connect them with other significant conversations. But some mentoring moments become mentoring relationships.

When two people have a significant conversation, it is common to step away from the crowd. You invite the other to join you. *Walk with me.* The basic process unfolds in three stages.

Share, Listen, Digest

One person shares an observation, idea, or feeling as calmly and clearly as they can. They can use prose or poetry. Their sharing can be punctuated by periods, exclamation points, or question marks . . . or not at all. Sharing can include images, songs, and metaphors. Other people listen. They focus on the sharer. They pay attention not only to what is said or shown, but also to how it is shared, and (if possible) observations of facial expressions and body language. This is followed by a period of silence, which can be a split second or an eternity, but during which what has been shared is digested by the listener. It is pondered, interpreted, evaluated, critiqued, but always with respect and a desire to know the truth.

Respond, Listen, Learn

Another person shares the results of what they have digested. All the possibilities and conditions for the sharer are also incumbent on the respondent. Others are expected to listen in the same way. The emotional tone of the conversation can go up and down. They can discuss calmly or debate vehemently, but always respectfully. There may be laughter but no sarcasm. There are no personal attacks. There are no evasions. In the end, the exchange has helped everyone learn something. They have all contributed to an insight bigger than any one person's mind. They are, perhaps, just an inch or possibly a mile further to understanding.

Know, Doubt, Repeat

Conversation goes beyond understanding. Knowing is not just a meeting of minds but of hearts. The ultimate goal of knowledge is unity of the knower with the known, and the ultimate goal of conversation is the amity of contributors with each other. Conversation has a dual purpose: insight and relationships. The relationship itself can imply many things (forgiveness, reconciliation, friendship, and more). Nevertheless, both knowledge and relationships are limited by the conditions of finitude. It is part of the journey. Now we know in part, later we shall know fully. Therefore, the next step in genuine conversation is doubt. New questions arise, creative ideas emerge, and the conversation never ends.

For conversations to bear significance, they cannot be sabotaged by dishonesty. Conversation is always risky, which is why it is often avoided and replaced by chatter. Participants in a conversation are truly vulnerable to each other. Conversation is an exercise in transparency and, therefore, an act of courage.

Perhaps you have already discovered that the people who boast the most about "listening" are the people who are least able to do it. This is particularly true of religious institutions. Their strategies for listening always involve some form of meeting (focus group, committee, task force, etc.) or some form of survey that is designed or interpreted by a meeting (team of experts, official board, etc.). *Listening* should be personal, non-directive, accepting. Therefore, it is more difficult than it seems.

Listening is really a matter of attitude rather than technique. At the same time one must empathize with the feelings of the other, one must also disassociate from the opinions of the other. It is a paradoxical combination of subjectivity and objectivity that requires great self-awareness on the one hand and exceptional humility on the other. If you really listen to the other, you will inevitably hear something that offends your sensibilities, challenges your assumptions, or just plain makes you mad. And you must be able to set all that aside. You must focus on the humanity of the other and try to sense the deeper anxieties that shape the other's point of view. More than this, you must admit that you yourself have habits and ideas that will inevitably offend the sensibilities of another person, challenge their ideas, and just plain make them mad.

In other words, *listening* is based solely on the understanding that we are both human beings, and no one is just an object to the other. The moment the other person becomes an object, thing, demographic datum, lifestyle category, political opponent, or ideological opposite, listening stops. It is hard to maintain that attitude, and I confess that I have never been completely and consistently able to do it. Jesus did it. And perhaps there are some saints who did it, although all the saints I know (past or present) all seem to be the first to admit that they don't do it well either.

They do, however, offer good advice. The more you listen to the Spirit, the better you can listen to others. Listening skills are enhanced when they emerge from a vital spiritual life. And a spiritual life is a kind of synergy of radical humility, before divine immanence, that results in compassion for humanity . . . which in turn feeds radical humility, and so on, and on. Just as meetings don't precipitate genuine listening so, also, professional training and institutional authority don't generate a spiritual life. Listening to God helps you listen to others . . . and at the same time listening to others helps you listen to God.

Walk with me. Mentoring is really a journey through both time and culture. Mentoring conversations unfold in a variety of different social and cultural contexts, and each different situation shapes and informs the mentoring conversation in new and often unexpected ways. For the Spirit moves through culture and not just through conversation. Mentor and mentee are interacting with everything that is going on around them, and not just with each other. If Spirit is the substance of culture, then culture is the form of the Spirit.[1] Cultural forms, which is to say the sights, sounds, smells, touch, and

---

1. See Tillich, *Theology of Culture*, 42; and *Shaking of the Foundations*, 181; and many

taste of people and things moving around and alongside the conversation, are all vehicles for the Spirit to reveal meaning and purpose. Mentors not only pay close attention to the other person but are emotionally, mentally, and physically sensitive to the contexts of conversations.

This is why spiritual travelers might also be described as "pilgrims" who journey together on a quest. They may travel together for a short or long distance, or all the way to wherever they end up, but along the way they carry on significant conversations about life and living, origins and destinies. And they also stop along the way to eat, drink, serve, and encourage strangers they encounter on the way. This "pilgrimage" is a metaphor common to all religions. We can picture Moses leading Israel to the promised land, or Jesus or Buddha walking with their disciples, *pilgrim bands* on their hajj to Mecca, pious Hindus mingling with mystics bathing in the Ganges, or Daoist sages guiding their followers.

Such images of pilgrimage suggest an inequality between mentor and mentee that modern people may find uncomfortable. The inequality, however, is not a contrast between people who know everything and people who know nothing, or between elites and novices, but simply a contrast between people who are more experienced in the quest for meaning and purpose and those who are less experienced. In mentoring relationships, authentic dialogue is always "unequal." The traveler cannot do anything more than speak from a context of greater separation from God; the mentor cannot do anything else than speak from a context of greater experience with God.

To do otherwise is pretense and an attempt to escape responsibility for our actions or responsibility for the well-being of others. Modern people assume that equality means that everyone's opinion is just as good as everyone else's opinion. This gives the would-be traveler an excuse to avoid taking responsibility for learning, and it gives the would-be mentor an excuse to avoid taking responsibility for teaching. If the recovering mentor is really no different than the alcoholic traveler, then the traveler has no real incentive to stop drinking. If the alcoholic traveler is really no different than the recovering mentor, then neither will sustain sobriety.

What follows is a description of mentoring steps that makes a messy process sound tidy. It assumes that the same mentor is involved in each link of the chain of events. In theory, this conversation is intentionally shaped in a covenant between mentor and mentee. They agree to talk following a

---

other of his works.

pattern of time and space, in person and online, that is reasonably predictable and to which each can hold the other accountable for their commitment. Of course, this may not be the case. But I hope that describing the mentoring chain of events in this way will help you discern when, where, how, and to what purpose you might participate as one link in the chain.

Mentoring *may* be structured in very practical ways. Traveler and mentor may promise to participate in a companionship that may be informally or formally expressed in a covenant. For example, they may agree to a timeline of conversation of three to six months, always with an option to extend their "travels." During that time, they may intentionally connect with each other. For example:

- Meet weekly, at a convenient time and location, for face-to-face conversation.
- Exchange emails frequently to share questions, reflections, and insights.
- Text daily with words of encouragement.
- Customize and share spiritual practices by reading the same sources or following the same prayer cycle.
- Worship together and de-brief afterward.
- Evaluate the mentoring relationship to improve communication or avoid sidetracks.

But mentoring relationships are rarely that tidy or easily controlled. They may start, stop, and start up again—sometimes after considerable time. Mentoring relationships will vary in intensity. There are periods of great emotion, and other periods of calm, and these are not always predictable. Individuals vary in their pace of discernment. Sometimes there are periods of great insights and breakthrough moments, and sometimes there are dry periods when it feels like nothing is happening. The traveler may doubt, but the mentor is convinced that the Spirit pervades the entire conversational journey and encourages persistence and patience.

Imagine watching two people walking together in earnest conversation. Perhaps they are in a city park across the street, and you have the advantage of observation from a hotel window several stories up. It is noon when you first observe them, and they are still talking an hour later. Clearly, they are using their lunch hour for this conversation. It must be pretty important. Around and around the park they go, sometimes sitting on a bench, then moving again. Occasionally their conversation is animated with arms and hands gesturing. One speaks, then the other speaks. Sometimes they stop abruptly, unmoving, listening intently. In our day of cellular communication, it is hard to imagine that one or the other's cell phone hasn't rung several times, but they ignore it.

There are moments when the busy activity of the city intrudes on their conversation. Occasionally they step aside for another pedestrian, assist a child across the street, give a coin to a person in need, or even point to some object of interest, but they always return instantly to their conversation. Such concentration! Perched as you are in the window of your room, you may well wonder just how long this conversation has been going on. Perhaps they meet regularly like this every week. Perhaps the park is an exception, and they normally talk over lunch in some café. Perhaps they carry on the conversation through email and text messages when they are apart.

Mostly you wonder what on earth they are talking about. It could be about any acute crisis, or common interest, but *perhaps* you are really witnessing a mentoring conversation. If one of the people was a priest, you might deduce from his or her clothes that a *Christian* mentoring conversation was taking place, but in the absence of such telltale signs you might still speculate that something spiritual was unfolding. Spirituality is in the air of postmodern living, and even the secularity of modern times has been infused and transformed because of it. More people are wondering about God, seeking the touch of the Holy, and trying to figure out how to connect their desperate lives with God's higher purpose than ever before. Indeed, they are more likely *not* to have mentoring conversations with the priest because the representatives of religious institutions are regarded as having mixed motivations at best. An authentic lay person or spiritually alive, ordinary pilgrim like you will be sufficient.

Return to those two people you observed walking around the park over the lunch hour. You know what it *looks like* from the relative safety of your hotel window, but what does it *feel like* for the two people below?

If the people walking below are actually in the midst of a mentoring relationship, it probably doesn't *feel like* a walk in the park. It feels like whitewater rafting down the Colorado River in early spring. If you could monitor their blood pressure, heart rate, and the dilation of their eyes, even their physiological reactions would not really be appropriate for what we would normally expect of a walk in the park. Both the traveler and the mentor feel the exhilaration and panic of a barely controllable ride down the river.

Sometimes they feel in control of the situation: traveler paddling, mentor steering, making sense of the scenery, and making progress as they journey down the river. They intentionally glide by this rock, struggle over that sandbar, and catch their breath in some quiet pool. Sometimes they feel quite out of control: paddles lost, steering gone, scenery a blur, and under water as much as on top of it. They are swept away by the Spirit, crashing into rocks, carried away by rapids, and spinning in whirlpools.

This is why before they even begin the walk, or start the journey, the mentor always warns the traveler that this *will not be a walk in the park*! It may look like a walk in the park. Outside observers might even envy the conversations if they happen to watch from the safety of their office cubicle or suburban home, but it will not feel like a walk in the park. It will feel quite different. If you want to embark on a mentoring relationship, then be prepared for an unpredictable process of change. Don't count on ending up in the same career, or with the same pattern of intimate friends, or with the same lifestyle habits, or with the same income and stability and accoutrements of living as when you started. It *may* be with you at the end, or it *may* be lost overboard along the way. We just don't know.

Mentoring is a chain of events. Each link might be separated by weeks or months or even years. You might be involved in every event in the chain or in some events of the chain. Indeed, you might be just one link in the chain. Others might provide other links in the sequence of events that eventually leads someone to discover meaning and purpose in their lives. Mentors are really just a part of a larger spiritual presence. The more each mentor is cognizant of participating in a greater movement of Spirit, and the more each mentor strives to live in the Spirit, the more readily they seize the opportunities to mentor someone along the way.

Every mentoring relationship is different. Each person grows at their own pace, and in their own order, largely dependent on their personal sense of urgency, the attention of the mentor, and the work of the Spirit. Mentors tend to be opportunists, rather than planners. They are driven by flashes of insight, rather than agendas. Spiritual growth tends to be marked by consecutive breakthrough experiences. I have observed these in distinct ways.[2]

---

2. Bandy, *Christian Mentoring*, 60–61.

Meetings

Meetings maintain several degrees of separation. One person talks to another person, but they remain distinct personalities and with separate histories. This is why meetings often feel like negotiations and require formal facilitations. There is a process of "getting to know" the other and thereby building trust with another. Trust is cumulative and insight evolves. Mentoring conversations may not be planned in advance, but there is usually a beginning and an ending, and between the two the mentor "goes with the flow." Participants in a meeting wend their way toward meaning and purpose guided by clues shared intentionally or unintentionally by each. Meetings are explorations.

There is a distinct decision on the part of each participant to meet again. Unlike normal meetings for business or planning, however, each subsequent meeting does not necessarily start where the previous meeting left off. Mentoring meetings demonstrate lateral rather than linear thinking. A simple image, phrase, idea that may have seemed minor in one conversation is the starting point for the next. In the Christian gospels this is how conversations between Jesus and his disciples occurred. Meetings were related to each other but shaped by context and guided by intuition. They were more inductive than deductive.

Experiences of the Holy might be characterized in the same way. When asked about spiritual experiences, people often recount mountain views and ocean vistas, natural beauty, childbirth, intimate attachments, homecomings, and other moments when time seems to stand still. Each "meeting" stands alone in significance yet connects in unexpected ways with a subsequent "meeting." The reflections stimulated by each "meeting" with the Holy are not linear and logical, but lateral and emotional. Nevertheless, the individual makes a decision to seek another "meeting" with the Holy on another scenic holiday, life-cycle crisis, intimate reunion, or other occasion when the pace of life slows down and life once again seems to stand still.

The trouble is that it is difficult to distinguish sentimentality from spirituality. Once sentimentality sours, it turns to resentment. People try to recapture a moment and are angered when it is impossible. If the moment is *spiritual*, rather than just sentimental, people try to recover the reality behind the moment rather than the moment itself. Mentoring is not interested in nostalgia. Mentoring uses these experiences as gateways to explore deeper meaning and significance. The conversation between Jesus and the Samaritan woman at the well models this kind of discernment.[3]

Mergers

Mergers reveal several degrees of participation. Mergers go beyond the external relations of meetings between one distinct person and another distinct person, to reveal a deeper unity of experience that binds each participant with another. Beyond the meeting of minds, there is a shared experience of souls. The transformation of a "meeting" into a "merger" is often marked by the silence of companionship. In a meeting, two people sit down and talk together. In a merger, two people sit down and enjoy one another's presence. No words need to be expressed . . . at least not right away.

Mergers are less about explorations of ideas and more about revelations of insights. They start with what happened to each person between meetings and then proceed to unpack the significance of what has happened. Discernment of hidden meanings is instinctive rather than cumulative. The mentor and mentee may share similar experiences, but the mentor, with greater experience, helps interpret what has happened. In a "merger," the next conversation is not so much a decision as a compulsion. There is no real question about seeing each other again. It is an urgent necessity for each.

Experiences of the Holy can be characterized in the same way. These are experiences that are more than formative. They are transformative. When asked about experiences of the Holy, people often use "lost and found," "before and after" metaphors. Such experiences do not just give you pause for reflection, but they decisively reshape, reverse, or restore life. These may involve conversions, remarriages, vocational changes, relocations and migrations, and other situations when time does not stand still but seems to accelerate.

The trouble is that it is difficult to distinguish between self-congratulation, good luck, and God's expectation. Once progress slows down, it turns to cynicism. What they thought to be true, people conclude was a lie. Leaders are hypocrites and they are victims of a conspiracy. Mentoring is not interested in explaining the motives of others or proving the existence of God. Mentoring uses these experiences to reveal the movement of the

---

3. John 4.

Spirit and to explore human existence. The conversation between Jesus and Thomas models this kind of guidance.[4]

Collisions

Sometimes mentoring is precipitated by, or results in, some form of crisis. While it may appear to be an argument between mentor and mentee, it is really an internal argument within the mentee projected onto the mentoring relationship. While it may appear to be frustration with the guidance of the mentor, it is really the mentee's discomfort with ambiguity and their unrealistic desire for certainty. A "collision" feels like a breakdown rather than a breakthrough, but mentors (speaking from their own experience of life struggle and renewal) can help the other see that the one can presage the other.

Mentoring relationships eventually, and inevitably, encourage people to confront the threats to life and well-being that lie deep inside every individual. These threats are often related to chronic depression, inexplicable dread, sudden rage, and profound alienation. Time does not stand still, nor does it accelerate. It just seems to stop. Any awareness of infinity or glimmer of hope is overcome by a desperate awareness of finitude and fog of hopelessness. The mentoring relationship may be temporarily broken, and it is up to the mentor to sustain the same curiosity and compassion for the other that initiated the very beginnings of mentoring.

Experiences of the Holy can be characterized in the same way. The Spirit may be revealed through a whirlwind, a fire, and a storm. It can sweep you away, or scorch you, or overwhelm you. Accidents, disease, divorce, unemployment, homelessness, and death are occasions when meaning and purpose are difficult to discern, yet within these experiences one can hear a voice, see a vision, or feel a presence.

The trouble is that it is difficult to distinguish between personal responsibility, bad luck, and mysterious purpose. Once stability is lost, people turn to recrimination. People blame themselves or just curse their fate. Mentoring is not interested in placing blame or perpetuating self-pity. Mentoring uses these experiences to access God's mystery and discover new hope. "You do well to pay attention to these things, as to a lamp burning in a dark place, until the day dawns and the morning star rises in your heart."[5]

4. John 11:16, 14:5, and 20:24–29.
5. 2 Pet 1:19 NRSV.

A Personal Reflection

In the religious and education sectors, the concept of "small group" has become increasingly accepted as the basic unit of maturation. In business and military sectors, the "team" is like a small group. Positively, this recognizes the importance of interpersonal relationships, conversation, and collaboration in the process of personal growth, learning, and efficiency.

However, it also perpetuates the illusion of continuity. The small group is organized, supervised, and monitored on a manageable timetable. Unfortunately, in our world of change, mobility, and ambiguity we have less and less control over time. Circumstances are shifting, people are moving, life is unpredictable. It is hard to plan strategically more than a few months ahead.

We once thought that social media might rectify this. Participants in a small group or team could sustain their involvement online. Yet there are serious limitations. The internet is saturated with competing conversations. Watching a video is not the same as interacting in real time. And mentoring, in particular, still depends on at least occasional personal presence.

Although I use the metaphor "walk with me," I am uncomfortable with it. One might equally say, *catch up with me*, or *let me catch up with you*. *Jog with me. Dance with me*. We might say *leave me alone* just as we might say *hold me tight*. Mentoring does not depend on the continuity of time. It depends on seizing the moment. We seldom predict whether an influential encounter will be a "meeting," a "merger," or a "collision." We often must decide what is "right" for the "time."

My personal experience is that mentoring is a constant ambiguity. It is difficult to measure "progress" or "success." The number of times I feel like I have missed an opportunity is about equal to the number of times I feel like I made the most of the moment. Indeed, even then I am not sure. For I do not really know the full history or the unknown future of my companion who is walking with me at the time.

The "small group" and the "team" depend on the communication and management systems of larger institutions. The *pilgrim band* depends on the depth of spirituality of the participants. The effectiveness of mentoring is linked to spiritual growth in the relationship. And the effectiveness of the mentor is dependent on his or her flickering sense of the immanence of God. I say "flickering," because Spirit is ultimately a mystery. It can dance around the periphery of our consciousness, one moment with blinding clarity and another moment with obscure nuance. Our best efforts might prove to be least helpful. On the other hand, our worst mistakes might be used by the Spirit for surprising benefits.

Talk with Me

TWO ACQUAINTANCES OR PERHAPS complete strangers share a moment of conversation together. It is honest. It is significant. They are both vulnerable. They step away to carry on their conversation . . . sometimes literally by taking a walk in the park, and sometimes digitally by reconnecting on social media. Eventually, all walks in the park come to an intersection. There is a decision to be made. Does one go forward, turn right, or left? Or does one turn around and walk away?

A synonym for "intersection" is the word "crossroad." All mentoring conversations come to a crossroad, and not just once, but many times. The life stories of mentor and mentee intersect, but also both stories intersect with incarnational experience. Intimacy and immanence emerge simultaneously. But the flow of personal growth and spiritual insight is by nature unpredictable. In a sense, it doesn't really matter which direction the conversation goes. The only thing that matters is that no one turns around and leaves. When that happens, the role of the mentor changes. He or she becomes a "provocateur" and "evocateur."[1]

The mentor helps the traveler continue the walk with an attitude of expectancy. This is not like strategic planning, when organizers define anticipated measurable results. The "outcomes" of maturity and purpose are not that definite. The journey begins with both mentor and traveler opening themselves to unpredictable change and uncontrollable experiences of the Holy. Well, perhaps they can be *partially* predicted by establishing specific goals, and perhaps they can be *barely* controlled as we manage changes and interpret mysteries. But in the end, nothing is certain except that both mentor and traveler will be different.

---

1. Schuster, *Answering Your Call*, 55–107.

Whenever we immerse ourselves in the Spirit, everything changes. Education can be controlled, with each stage marked by a graduation ceremony. Mentoring cannot be fully controlled, and there will be advances, reverses, sidetracks, and the occasional retracing of our own steps. I have observed that there is a strategy to keep the flow of significant conversation going.[2]

Leading Questions

Mentoring conversations are evocative. They are guided by *leading questions*. A leading *question* is open ended, which is to say that it is open to more than one reply. At the same time, it is a *leading* question in that it deliberately launches a particular direction of thought. Lawyers are not allowed to "lead the witness," but mentors must "lead the conversation."

What do you think about this? How do you feel about that? Why do you choose one thing rather than another? Who will you influence, and who will influence you? How will you go about it? When will you start, finish, pause, re-evaluate, give up, or change plans? Where will this course of action end up? All these questions shape the mentoring conversation and guide it in specific directions.

Of course, the mentor wishes to ask the *right* questions. These would be questions that are revealing and fruitful and that open new avenues of inquiry. Unfortunately, it is not always easy to know what questions to ask. Questions elicit unexpected responses. They tease out hidden truths, recover lost memories, explore repressed emotions, awaken new ideas, and birth creative plans. Questions force travelers to think for themselves and take responsibility for their own conclusions.

The "Socratic Method" is most often associated with probing questions that are continuously raised until the traveler arrives at insight. Each question elicits a response, which shapes the next question, until something is fully understood. Aristotle used this principle to guide understanding from the general to the particular. The underlying assumption in both "Socratic Method" and in Jesus' own teaching is that the truth is already *inside you*, hidden in shadow, imperfectly formed, perhaps only a mustard seed that will eventually bear much fruit.

Deep inside, you already know what is good, beautiful, and true, and by asking questions, and wrestling for answers, you will "know" in

---

2. Bandy, *Christian Mentoring*, 46–51.

the pre-modern sense of that word. You will not only comprehend intellectually, but you will align existentially with both *a* truth and *the* Truth. Christian tradition recalls a dialogue between Jesus and his disciples. "Who do people say that I am?" Jesus asks. "Who do you say that I am?" he asks further. And when the traveler replies, like Peter, saying, "You are the Christ," he articulates both a fact and a commitment. Jesus responds, "Blessed are you . . . for flesh and blood have not revealed this to you. God has revealed it to you."[3] Questions assume that in the end you do not know the truth, but the truth knows you.

Challenging Assertions

Mentoring conversations are punctuated by challenging assertions. These may be observations that are deliberately provocative or uncomfortable, but they emerge from carefully listening to the questions and responses that are ongoing in the mentoring relationship. Observations are always offered with reference to the larger context of the traveler's life and environment. They challenge hidden assumptions or biases, illuminate matters of significance for spiritual growth, interpret events with historical or theological principles, and invite discussion or debate.

By asking questions, you imply that the truth is within you. By making assertions, you imply that the truth is out there. Consider this . . . consider that. Look at it this way . . . look at it that way. Understand these perspectives. Experiment with these choices. Uncover the hidden meaning. Interpret the obvious. Discover the roots and discern the purpose. Discussions may often be animated, and sometimes pedantic, but all to the point of maturity.

There really is no place for playing "devil's advocate" in a mentoring relationship. There must be no pretense or subterfuge, lest it undermine trust or leave a traveler guessing about the true intentions of the mentor. If role play is helpful to understanding alternative perspectives, it is clearly identified as just that. The conversation must be entirely honest and perhaps uncomfortably honest.

Christian tradition tells us that Jesus often spoke in parables and metaphors to challenge the disciples to discern truths for themselves. In the parable of the sower, Jesus says, "He who has ears to hear, let him

---

3. Matt 16:13–17 NRSV.

hear."[4] Even when he speaks to them "plainly," his challenging assertions always encourage further and deeper insight . . . and challenge the disciples to take responsibility for their faith. After speaking of the significance of his death, the disciples exclaim, "Now you are speaking plainly!" But Jesus challenges their faith, anticipating that their future actions will belie their claims to understand.[5]

The goal of the mentoring conversation is not to reach intellectual agreement, but to help travelers think for themselves and take responsibility for their own convictions. Certainly, the mentor's ideas and faith will be influential, but mentoring is not about conversion or persuading others to assent to dogmas. We are exploring a larger mystery of truth, which in Christian mentoring is a larger mystery of divine immanence. The maturity that is sought involves understanding of facts, awareness of self, discernment of truth, and the courage of one's own conviction.

Decisive Interventions

Mentoring relationships are delicate things. There are many ways in which they might break apart in dislike or enmity or break down into merely friendly conversations or predictable routines. The task of the mentor is to quickly discern the threat and to take decisive action to confront it. Whenever the relationship seems to have become angry, hostile, or merely emotional, or shallow, unproductive, and boring, there is always some hidden issue that needs to be addressed. There are three kinds of issues that threaten mentoring conversations and sabotage spiritual growth.

Deadweights

The term "deadweight" was originally a nautical term used to describe the tonnage of a ship (including ballast, crew, and stores) that was *unavailable* for productive use in transporting goods. More recently, the term has been used to describe the stage of a rocket when all the propellant is used up. Ballast is what holds you back; deadweight is what drags you down. You must either lighten the ship or jettison the deadweight of the rocket, or the journey will come to a tragic end.

4. Mark 4:9 NRSV.
5. John 16:22–33 NRSV.

The "deadweight" that every person carries will eventually be revealed in the mentoring relationship. Perhaps it is a relationship, personal habit, personality trait, unfulfilling career, unproductive use of time, useless sentiment, unresolved anger, or some other issue in personal, family, business, or recreational life that holds us back from growth. Or perhaps it is a strategy, technique, or behavior pattern that once worked well to further your relationships, career, or stability, but which is no longer effective and is dragging you down.

In the mentoring relationship with the "rich young ruler," Jesus challenges him to let go of the "deadweight" of wealth, and to follow him, commenting that "it is easier for a camel to go through the eye of the needle than for a rich man to enter the kingdom of heaven."[6] Later Christian experience, particularly in the early monastic tradition, revealed that it may be difficult but not impossible. Ancient mentoring often emphasized the need to free oneself from the "deadweights" of the world (prestige, wealth, power, etc.).

Mentors take decisive action. They identify the deadweight, challenge the traveler, and help the traveler do whatever is necessary to break free. Only then will the journey continue or will a stable orbit be achieved.

Roadblocks

A roadblock is a barrier that prohibits further progress. The barrier may be natural, like a landslide or a washed-out bridge, or the barrier may be strategically placed, like a police blockade or a convoy checkpoint. In any case, one either crosses the barrier or turns back.

Roadblocks inevitably emerge in every mentoring relationship. Perhaps it is a personal tragedy, family crisis, loss of income, religious dogma, deep-seated fear, or unexpected situation that stops spiritual growth. Perhaps it is the ultimatum of a spouse, child, parent, or friend, or the threat of a religious institution, government agenda, or corporation that warns you to turn away from spiritual growth.

The Christian tradition can be instructive. Jesus' long-term mentoring relationship with Peter faced constant roadblocks. Even after Jesus' resurrection and "Great Commission," Peter still returned to the obligations of family and the lure of his old occupation. Jesus appears on the seashore to

---

6. Matt 19:16–26 NRSV.

challenge Peter three times: "Simon, do you love me more than these?" He then warns him of the threat of martyrdom for the cause.[7]

Mentors take decisive action. They analyze the barrier, look for alternative ways around it, and help the traveler take courage to continue the journey and pay the price of spiritual growth.

Sidetracks

A sidetrack is a diversion from the main road that ultimately takes you in the wrong direction. Sometimes travelers miss a turn, sometimes they choose the wrong turn, and sometimes they think they chose the right turn and later discover it was not.

It is not always easy to discern whether a fork in the road is a shortcut or a sidetrack, but mentors must be quick to discern the truth. Perhaps this diversion is another stream of thought, or a different kind of question, or a particular enthusiasm, or an unexpected passion. Perhaps this diversion is another media or method of dialogue. Perhaps the diversion is an excuse to avoid talking about what really matters.

Christian tradition once again provides a helpful illustration. Jesus reserved some of his most uncomfortable remarks to address sidetracks to faithfulness. Even seemingly worthwhile tasks can become sidetracks for spiritual growth. "Let the dead bury their own dead," Jesus says. "No one who puts their hand to the plow and looks back is fit for the kingdom of God."[8]

Mentors must be quick to identify sidetracks that are taking the conversation—and the traveler—in the wrong direction. They must explain the mistake, retrace steps to the main road, and reestablish the goals of the mentoring relationship.

All these deadweights, roadblocks, and sidetracks emerge in every mentoring relationship because inevitably mentoring leads to the stress of change. Schuster's reference to "sabotage" is particularly revealing, because very little of this is mere coincidence.[9] The source of the sabotage is often the traveler himself or herself, revealing unconscious psychological attitudes or addictive behavior patterns that halt spiritual growth. The source of sabotage may also be outside forces from marital and family

---

7. John 21:15 NRSV.
8. Luke 9:62 NRSV.
9. Schuster, *Answering Your Call*, 57–75.

situations, or from corporate and career pressure, or even from religious institutions. Occasionally, the source of sabotage may be the mentor personally, for we are all imperfect.

Interventions may be rare in the mentoring relationship, but they will inevitably be required. No matter how evocative the questions might be, or how provocative the assertions might be, there will be moments when the mentoring relationship itself is in peril by internal or external forces. Mentors act to free the traveler, encourage the traveler, and focus the traveler. They will confront any obstacles that keep the traveler from spiritual growth, even if the obstacles are occasionally the mentors themselves.

Pregnant Silences

In the mentoring relationship, what is unsaid can be just as important as what is said. The gaps can be as profound as verbal conversations. Mentors are often tempted to "micro-manage" the spiritual growth of travelers but need to allow space in their relationship. That space, however, is not a matter of indifference. What fills that space is the activity of the Spirit. One might quickly assume that means silent prayer (mentor for traveler, traveler for illumination, etc.). However, I think such intentional piety is less significant than we suppose.

Silence is never absence. In silence we become attuned to the sounds, smells, scenes, and movements around us. Even the smallest thing can unconsciously trigger a memory, stimulate an idea, create brief eye contact with a stranger. What we often dismiss as "distractions" are often God's mysterious designs. The more I experience mentoring relationships, the less I believe in mere accidents. What we call prayer (intentional, directional, pious thinking) is often just an extension of ego. It is another way mentors try to control the Spirit. Their egos remain at the center of the action.

The Spirit is revealed in and through culture in macro and micro ways. We may see glimpses of Spirit in great architecture, but Spirit may equally reveal itself through a coffee pot. In treating trauma, therapists are aware that there are hidden, invisible "triggers" that suddenly transport a trauma victim back to the emotions of a traumatic experience without their even realizing what is happening. But on the other hand, when seeking meaning and purpose, mentors are aware that there are hidden, invisible "triggers" that suddenly transport the spiritual traveler forward to fresh insight without their even realizing what has inspired them.

True, mentoring relationships allow spaces for meditation and reflection. But the absence of conversation can sometimes be even more fruitful. Too many words get in the way. Too much time together clouds discernment. The relationship itself gets in the way of personal growth. This is why I prefer to have mentoring conversations in a setting with potential distractions—in a restaurant, at the airport, or in a sports arena. Rather than walk together in the woods, I prefer to walk together along a city street.

These spaces of silence may last a few moments or a few weeks or months, and in some mentoring relationships the spaces may last years before the relationship is renewed. However, when the relationship is renewed and conversation begins again, both mentor and traveler realize that something new and deeper has emerged. The conversation does not just carry on from where it ended, but it seems to have taken a leap forward in maturity and understanding.

I hope that by now I have made my point that mentoring is *purposefully messy*. There is a purpose to it. Mentor and traveler yearn to experience the Holy, live in companionship with Spirit, and find their place in God's movement through the world. The journey to get there, however, is very messy. The style of the mentor in asking leading questions, making challenging assertions, intervening in decisive ways, and welcoming pregnant silences is that of an innovative musician or dancer rather than a methodical researcher or lecturer. Mentoring is messy. Move forward, backward, and to the side; twists, turns, leaps, and pirouettes . . . the mentor seems to be moving to music that the traveler can't quite hear yet. Even the mentor is not quite sure what the next move will look like. Life is messy, figuring life out is messy, and the Spirit shaping life is messy.

It is also true that mentoring is *messily purposeful*. There is a discernible pattern to mentoring. However messy the journey might be, once you look back and examine it, there is a sensible flow to the process. It may be misleading to describe this flow in *stages* of mentoring, because that might imply some linear curriculum from "introductory" to "advanced" mentoring that would resemble a program rather than a relationship. One does not complete an oral exam for "Purposeful Living 101" and then register for "Deeper Meaning 201." It might be better to say that mentoring proceeds from crisis to crisis, or from breakthrough to breakthrough. Each "stage" is marked by stress and stress release, consternation and discovery, or discomfort and serenity. A breakthrough in spiritual growth might move the traveler into brand new territory, or unexpectedly return the traveler to revisit previous territory, but overall, there is a discernible progress to be made. The goal, after all, is to discern meaning and purpose, and until that becomes clear we remain restless for more.

In Christian tradition, one of the classic mentoring relationships is that between Jesus and the young Pharisee Nicodemus.[10] According to tradition, they meet more often than once, and Nicodemus is even present at the death and burial of Jesus. Their mentoring relationship includes meetings and mergers, but in the lengthy conversation recorded in the Gospel of John their encounter is more like a collision. The mentee is astonished by Jesus' claim that "you must be born anew." How is it possible? Jesus answers: "The wind blows where it chooses, and you hear the sound of it, but you do not know where it comes from or where it goes. So it is with everyone who is born of the Spirit."[11]

Talk with me. That simple invitation leads to a more complex journey. The timeline may be short, long, or intermittent. The challenges are sometimes predictable, and often surprising. The growth may accumulate slowly or come in spurts of maturity. Mentoring may well use the language of pilgrimage, temptation, and discipline. But the accumulating effect is personal confidence, deeper serenity, and clearer purpose. The result is an acute sensitivity to the immanence of God and renewed courage for living.

A Personal Reflection

The virtual world has dangerously undermined our ability to have significant conversations. We communicate in short, ungrammatical bursts, which leads to constant misunderstandings. Our vocabulary includes more acronyms and jargon but fewer words that qualify nouns and verbs. Increasingly we see the world as anime, not as reality, which makes it much harder for us to cope with personal and historical events. Indeed, communication used to reference historical events, great ideas, and influencers who shaped culture for centuries. Now we do not even remember historical events, do not know how ideas have evolved, and only pay attention to influencers who shaped culture last week. In a society filled with chatter, we long for influential encounters and significant conversations.

There are three elements to communication. The *form* of communication refers to the structure, method, or media of a message. Obsession

---

10. John 3:1–21.
11. John 3:8 NRSV.

with *form* leads to "political correctness" in vocabulary. The *content* of communication refers to the data, detail, or information in the message. Obsession with *content* leads to pedantry and argument. The *import* of communication, however, refers to the significance of a message. It is the consequence, magnitude, or momentousness of the message. Influential encounters, and conversation within the *pilgrim band*, focus on import rather than form or content. It explores the substance ("weight," "meat") and the thrust ("point," "heart") of the message.

In a world in which *words* are unhelpful, images and sounds become more potent to convey import. Conversations are precipitated by a picture or a movie, a lyric or a rhythm, an object, or even by a perfume or aroma. Why are tattoos so popular today (as in ancient times)? The answer is that images etched into the skin reveal what is *import*ant in our lives. They not only are a declaration of identity but reveal what is momentous in your life. The very sight of them precipitates conversation.

Jewelry, clothing, architecture, and even technology hardware, can become symbols of significance. I call these objects, images, tastes, and sounds "talismans." They are the expression of meaning that is beyond words. In a culture of limited vocabulary, talismans are the means to communicate both your roots and your hopes. These need not be expensive or complicated. They may be new or old. Without a word being spoken, bonds of understanding and empathy build. Such symbols become a focus for meditation and convey the nuances of spirituality. They evoke feelings and provoke conversations because they not only *remind* travelers of meaning, but they also serve as portals through which meaning is *revealed* by Spirit.

Personally, I often wear a pocket watch and carry a Greek "trisagion" (Byzantine prayer beads) in my pocket for meditation. The pocket watch is a reminder of childhood trauma and redemption. The trisagion includes a prayer of my own devising that summarizes what, for me, is the struggle for meaning and purpose. Many a curious question about these talismans has led to an influential encounter.[12]

---

12. I elaborate on the significance of prayer beads in the first, older edition of my book *Talisman* (2006), 98–102.

Walk Together

Mentoring relationships often start with two acquaintances, or perhaps complete strangers, walking and talking together. They may cross many physical intersections and travel unexpected digital paths, but as long as they keep going, they will almost inevitably connect with someone else. These may come as accidental encounters or intentional invitations. Often, they come at just the "right time" to energize or redirect a developing mentoring relationship. The conversation, intimacy, trust, and discernment expand and soon they are something more than friends.

We may talk seriously with each other, or humorously with each other, but never frivolously with each other. We strive to talk *significantly* with each other, and if we don't have anything significant to say we tend to remain silent and wait for it. Often the waiting is rewarded with the addition of new companions. Truth can only be uncovered when others who are on a similar quest provide the objectivity that helps us do it. Therefore, spiritual travelers travel best when they are not alone but accompanied by other travelers. I have come to think of this as a *pilgrim band*.

The *pilgrim band* is a fluid experience, and participants may come and go. They may walk together for a time, pause and later catch up, alternate between periphery and intimacy, or seemingly vanish and later reappear. At any given time, however, I have found that the most influential *pilgrim bands* consist of five, seven, eleven, or perhaps thirteen participants in close physical and/or virtual contact. The odd numbers help the *pilgrim band* avoid polarizations. Fewer participants often encourage groups to plateau in spiritual discernment and relational intimacy. More participants often encourage exclusivity. Perhaps the paradigmatic *pilgrim band* numbered thirteen (including Jesus), but even then, we see the development of an "inner circle" that seems to dominate the others.

I have said several times that mentoring relationships demand vulnerability and honesty, and that they involve both personal discovery and spiritual discernment. However, in group dynamics these do not occur instantaneously. They evolve. As new participants join the *pilgrim band*, or as past participants leave and rejoin the *pilgrim band*, it takes time and intentionality for the group as a whole to sustain vulnerability and honesty and deepen relationships and spiritual discernment.

Pilgrim Band Group Dynamics

All participants in the *pilgrim band* should be cognizant of the basic dynamics of deepening relationships and spiritual discernment. In mutual mentoring, it is not just up to a single "mentor" to monitor the process. Each participant helps the other. The processes described here may seem straightforward and tidy, but (once again) the reality is messier. This is partly because each participant has a different personality. More significantly, participants belong to different lifestyle mosaics shaped by culture, personal history, and demographic markers (age, race, language, education, etc.). It takes time for empathy to deepen and for vulnerability and honesty to mature.

Moreover, the transitions from each stage in the deepening of relationships and discernment are often precipitated by a kind of crisis. This can vary in intensity for each individual, and each individual makes the transition in their own way and their own time. Such crises may appear as "roadblocks," "deadweights," or "sidetracks," and the companions of the *pilgrim band* help one another address them as they appear.

Deepening Relationships

The flow of deepening relationships in the *pilgrim band* is more intense than in a typical small group that forms around shared affinities (e.g. hobby, sport, book study, program, and the like). This is because the affinity of the group is already clear and is already acknowledged to be a risky and passionate journey toward meaning and purpose in life.

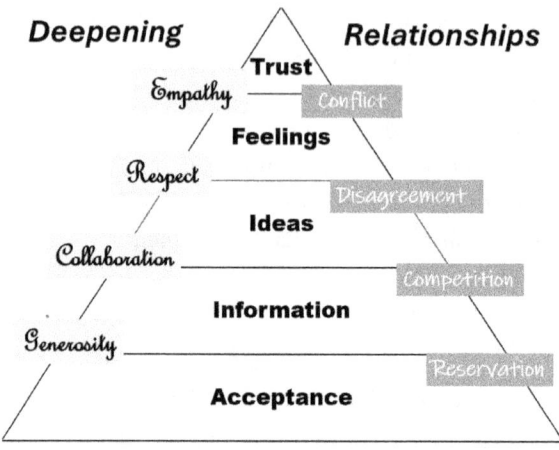

Acceptance into the *pilgrim band* is based on recognition of certain shared characteristics. These include an intention to generate a lifestyle that blends humility, inquiry, and compassion; a willingness to be transparent and honest; and passion to explore the meaning and purpose of one's life. It is also based on expanded openness to different demographics or lifestyles. While there may be a sense of "covenant" to interact together within a set of core values, and to honor together certain bedrock beliefs, there is no "contract" that suggests obligations of membership. We recognize from the very beginning we are no more than fellow spiritual travelers, and our routes may (and probably will) diverge along the road.

Theoretically, "acceptance" is wholehearted. But the reality of living under the conditions of existence is that acceptance is always "halfhearted." There are always reservations, because we cannot ignore past rejection or present bias. Therefore, participants in the *pilgrim band* go out of their way to practice generosity (patience, benevolence, kindness, and more).

Information is often the next step. Participants share more about themselves and their personal histories. Included in this "information" will be individual experiences of incarnation (unsettling or affirming), past experiences with systems of accountability (positive and negative), and recognized existential anxieties that they believe drive their quest for God. Clearly, this information is more internal than external. It goes beyond "name, address, and serial number" to identity, trepidation, and aspiration. There is a readiness to share one's soul however bruised or beautiful it might be.

Inevitably, shared information leads to comparisons with others in the *pilgrim band*, and a kind of competition to "outdo" one another in either pathos or success. We try to earn greater respect, enhance our image, or exaggerate our importance. The remedy is for the *pilgrim band* to emphasize equality and strive for collaboration. Our past is only useful if it is pooled together and used to shape the present and contribute to the journey.

Ideas include rational insights and non-rational intuitions with which we reflect on meaning and purpose. Most participants in a *pilgrim band* bring with them an enormous body of experience, thoughts, and perceptions that can be shared and compared. Participants especially focus on *consistencies* and *inconsistencies*. The former encourages further exploration. The latter challenges hidden assumptions and biases. It is often this earnest discussion that is most visible to outside observers.

Sharing ideas can, and should, lead to disagreements. These energize our desire for truth, but they can also get out of control and cause divisions. The *pilgrim band*, however, recognizes the difference between "truth" and "trueing" and can agree to disagree. This is not resignation, but an attitude of expectancy for a future, perhaps unexpected, insight. It is this mutual expectancy, and regard for the perspective of another, that generates respect.

Feelings often follow ideas because disagreements reveal passions that we know and emotions that have unconsciously lingered from our past. Ideas, and the words, concepts, and gestures revealed intentionally and unintentionally in disagreement, can be "triggers" that reveal deeper emotions. Spiritual travelers may be able to tame their egos, or practice calm, but underneath they are very passionate about the expressions of meaning and purpose in love, power, and justice.

Conflict, however, can be a catalyst for empathy. These piques of passion can be understood by a deeper respect for the life experiences, existential anxieties, and creative intuitions of one's companions. When these can be expressed within the shared values of participants, and the spiritual identity of the group, the result is a deeper bond of trust that outlasts disagreement. It is this trust that endures as spiritual travelers converge and diverge and regroup on the journey.

Trust, not fellowship, is the ultimate goal of relational development. Trust is based on consistent, positive, behavioral expectations (like love, joy, peace, patience, kindness, gentleness, generosity, humility, and self-control). However intense the relationships become, the bonds of mutual support continue.

I think it is important to understand that the goal in deepening relationships in the *pilgrim band* is not primarily *friendship*. That may often be a by-product that is valued, but the companionship of the *pilgrim band* is very fluid. Participants may "like" or "dislike" each other, at different times or in various contexts. But they will continue to trust each other regardless of whatever competitiveness they might feel in other aspects of their lifestyles or careers.

Deepening Discernment

The flow of deepening spiritual discernment is more intense than in a classroom or educational program. This is because the companions in the *pilgrim band* have a more existential stake in the journey that goes beyond career expertise or rational satisfaction.

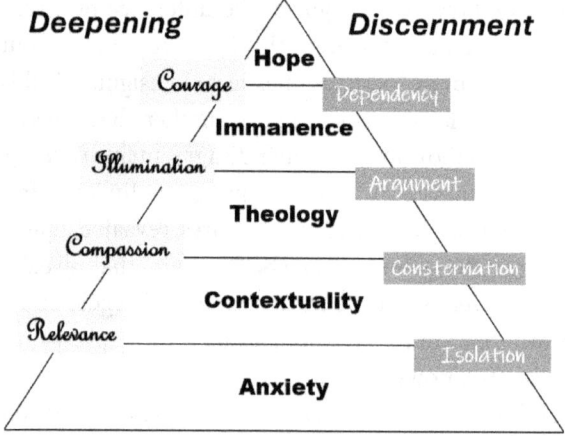

Anxiety precipitates deepening discernment in the *pilgrim band*, just as anxiety initiates all mentoring relationships. We do not join a *pilgrim band* out of curiosity, or even a desire to learn, but because we are driven by existential anxieties that interrupt and unsettle our lives, and we desire to find courage for living. The first step in discernment is to become aware of the specific anxieties that are paramount in one's life and find ways to honestly share them with one's companions on the journey.

The risk in doing so is that one might feel more, rather than less, isolated. It is difficult to find words to express our sense of being empty, lost, lonely, estranged, trapped, dying, broken, or victimized. Initially, we may need to resort to images or songs or symbols to express ourselves. Yet the struggle to communicate often makes us feel helpless. The companions of the *pilgrim band* help us reveal ourselves, because they can identify with our helplessness. They help us see the relevance of our motivations to the life situations of others.

Contextuality is usually the next step in discernment. The companions help each other explore personal histories, cultural connections, traumatic experiences, or critical transitions in the "boundary situations" of life. "Contextualizing" life is mainly done through storytelling and discovering the intersections between one person's story and another's story. But it also involves sharing the first glimpses of God's immanence and opening awareness of the movement of Spirit in one's life.

These explorations can be simultaneously illuminating and frightening. Individuals usually feel increasing discomfort revealing their life situations and growing consternation over the vulnerability that they are feeling. The *pilgrim band* helps each other overcome consternation by showing ever greater compassion. This may be kindness and inclusiveness, but it can also involve forgiveness and reconciliation.

Theology follows the awareness of anxiety and the exploration of contextuality. This is a more rational stage of discussion that might involve sacred texts, religious perspectives, creeds and liturgies, philosophical systems and cultural critiques. It may be broadly "systematic" or related to specific issues. It may be moral or metaphysical. Participants seek to understand, insofar as they are able, the movement of Spirit in personal and social history.

Inevitably, theology leads to argument. There is a risk that this could break relationships and dissolve the *pilgrim band*, but this can also be a catalyst for illumination. This is a more intuitive sense of unity in diversity. It is the realization that truth cannot be contained by any expression or articulation of truth. "Import" will always exceed "content" and shatter any cultural "form." Argument gives way to awe.

Immanence is an ecstatic leap beyond rational theology. It is, perhaps, the most singular step that separates the *pilgrim band* from the therapy session or educational classroom. It is the evocative and provocative experience of incarnation or "God-among-Us." Now the process of spiritual discernment (pursued "from below") becomes a portal of experience through which Spirit reveals itself (received "from above"). These experiences are "theonomous" in the sense that life and culture come together in a unity of love, power, and justice.

The danger, of course, is that we can become dependent or "addicted" to the adrenaline rush of God's immanence. For after all, under the conditions of existence it is fleeting. We can waste time and digress from the pilgrimage, trying to recreate or preserve or protect these Kairos moments. Instead, experiences of incarnation are incorporated into the courage of the *pilgrim band* as they continue to face the ambiguities of living.

Hope, not consensus, is the ultimate goal of the *pilgrim band*. They do not strive to think alike, but rather to help one another persevere, endure, and stay positive about life. I think it is important to understand that the goal of deepening discernment in the *pilgrim band* is not agreement. Shared commitments to an institution, tradition, or cause may be a valued by-product, but companionship is based on constant personal and spiritual growth. The participants will always honor the courage of conviction of each other.

The "group dynamics" of the *pilgrim band* always includes an unseen companion, namely, Spirit. Spirit is the ground of trust and the power of hope. It is what elevates the *pilgrim band* beyond the fellowship or consensus of institutions like the church. The *pilgrim band* has an eschatological sense of identity. It embodies the unity of Spirit and culture that can be temporarily realized but is yet to be universally fulfilled.

Pilgrim Band Spiritual Practices

Participants in the *pilgrim band* have usually personalized their spiritual practices. However, they also share spiritual practices that are incorporated into daily, weekly, and annual disciplines. These practices may change or evolve as group dynamics deepen and the spiritual journey continues. After all, no *form* of spiritual practice is in itself sacred. As the Spirit leads, the forms change.

The annual group practice tries to bring the pilgrim band together physically in one place, at one time. It does not necessarily take the form of a retreat or a cloister. Indeed, given the blur of secular and sacred in the postmodern world, they might well meet in an urban setting and include music, theater, visual arts, and other shared events that can be provocative and evocative of Spirit.

The weekly practice of the group may involve both physical and virtual participation and occur at any agreed time. Again, the time may vary because any time can be sacred time. Older generations with experience in traditional religious organizations may commit to Sunday worship, especially if it involves Eucharist. Younger generations, however, are more likely to connect weekly with a non-profit involved in a specific social service. The "hands-on" aspect of service is especially important as an exercise in humility.

The daily shared discipline of the *pilgrim band* is what sets them further apart from any traditional "small group." The enthusiasm and rigor surpass that of institutionally managed fellowship groups. There can be enormous creativity in this daily discipline that is shared by *pilgrim band* participants wherever they might be at any given time. In the animation of the postmodern world, and the fluidity of religious movements, individuals have increasingly borrowed practices from a variety of traditions and adapted them to their personal lifestyles.

First, *mobility* and *miniaturization* are essential. Traditional practices assumed a passive or stationary lifestyle. Monks retreated to a monastery, hermits lived in a cave, clergy stayed in the study. Members attended church once a week, and church buildings were built in neighborhoods assuming most people would walk to get there. They tended to rely on hard copy books, annotated Bibles, sacred properties, and cumbersome objects. Even now, when Baby Boomers travel, they still tend to check luggage.

Today mobility, not passivity, is the context of spiritual practice. Everything you need should be readily accessible on a cell phone. Devotional objects are worn around your neck, carried in a pocket, or tattooed on your flesh. Images and sound bites are often more useful than words. The traveler needs to exercise their spiritual practices flying economy class, sitting in the middle seat, at the rear of the plane. Carry a backpack or acquire what you need when you get there.

Spiritual practices may be employed, created, and shared online. However, a discipline is not a discipline if it cannot be done regularly and predictably, or instantly and surprisingly. The true spiritual traveler cannot count on internet access or convenient cell phone towers at every place and time. So, spiritual practices must be available and doable in both hi-tech and low-tech ways.

Second, *sensory experience* is essential. Spiritual practices should not be exclusively cognitive and focused on words. The shared practice of the *pilgrim band* may involve sights, sounds, tastes, and aromas. The younger the participant in the *pilgrim band*, the more evocative and provocative multisensory experience becomes. As I said before, I think of such objects and images as "talismans." Music can be in any genre. Objects can range from similar jewelry, to tattoos, to apparel like prayer shawls, or T-shirts. "Talismans" are symbols that remind us of significant ideas, but they are also portals through which Spirit reaches into our hearts.

Sensory experiences are aids in meditation. They help focus and open our minds but also exercise and direct our feelings. Sensory experiences are less "controllable" and "manageable" than verbal prayers or liturgies. When the mind strays from words, it may be less about sloth and more about revelation. Daily spiritual practices feed our passions and energize our journeys. They cause us to laugh or weep together. We celebrate in joy and lament in sorrow. Such creativity can inform and animate future conversations within the *pilgrim band*.

Third, *memory* and *repetition* are essential. Internet access and artificial intelligence create the illusion that we do not need to remember anything. Map directions, formulas, statistics, definitions, and concepts are readily available. Crises in life occur, however, precisely at the times when we have "lost connection" because the internet is unavailable, or we are too upset, too overwhelmed, or too much in a hurry to be digitally dependent. When you have been in an accident and are being wheeled into the emergency room for surgery, you can't find hope on the internet or even ask your friend.

The *pilgrim band* imitates *ancient* practices of memorization. They must remember and repeat words when their hands are full, or when they are doing manual labor or serving in the community. They must be able to visualize images or sing a song instantly, during a crisis, when there is neither time nor opportunity to look anything up on the web or search a table of contents. Tech assisted memory can be helpful, but it is not reliable, and it is not instantaneous. In the time it takes to turn on a cell phone or click a button, temptation has already carried you away and crisis has already overwhelmed your life.

The urgency for immanence is what motivated early Byzantine monastics to develop what became known as the "Jesus Prayer" based on the story of the blind beggar beseeching Jesus, "Son of David, have mercy on me."[1] This is used as a response to the biblical admonitions to pray con-

---

1. Luke 18:38 RSV.

tinuously, pray in the Spirit on every possible occasion and situation.[2] The automatic repetition of the prayer that becomes a constant background for daily activities is described in the anonymous account of a nineteenth-century Russian peasant in *The Way of a Pilgrim*.[3] It reminds me of the constant dependence of Millennials on social media and cell phones.

"Muscle memory" is perhaps an even better comparison. "Muscle memory" is what athletes refer to, and rely on, when they have been unable to practice a sport for a long period of time. They get back into shape because their muscles soon move in the right way, at the right time, to get them back into the rhythm of the sport. It is the same with spiritual practices. You do not need to remember an entire verse . . . all you need is a key word. You do not need to remember the whole song . . . all you need is the refrain. You do not need to visualize a detailed image . . . all you need is a color or a symbol. Participants in the *pilgrim band* rely on "triggers" to stimulate their memories. That is why small devotional objects or talismans were often used in ancient times past and are now used in trouble times in the future.

A "spiritual practice" is any activity that relies on some cultural form to connect a person with something of ultimate significance. In the inertia of the Christian institution, spiritual practices included the seven sacraments and the use of bread, wine, water, and vestments to bring people into the presence of God. These also included liturgies, lectionaries, and objects like buildings and Bibles, windows and icons, etc. These incorporated different languages and aesthetic styles, dress and body movements, or calendar dates, ceremonies, etc.

The contrast between "faith" and "faithfulness" is very clear when it comes to spiritual practice. Church members find spiritual practices boring. The *pilgrim band* finds spiritual practices exciting. The institutional church encourages spiritual practices out of a sense of duty and as a way of reinforcing institutional authority. This is why spiritual practices become standardized as practitioners say or do the same things, in the same formulas and rites, at the same times and in the same places.

The *pilgrim band* embraces spiritual practices out of a sense of anticipation. They are driven by a thirst for God and a desire to live life with profound meaning and significant purpose. Therefore, spiritual practices are not standardized but customized. To be sure, there is much to learn

---

2. 1 Thess 5:14–18; Eph 6:18; 1 Tim 2:8 RSV.

3. Anonymous, *Way of a Pilgrim*, and *Pilgrim Continues on His Way*.

and imitate from other spiritual travelers (past and present). But there is nothing sacred about any specific spiritual practice. These, too, are just cultural forms that Spirit employs to be useful and shatters once they become useless.

Spiritual practices fit the individual's lifestyle like skin on the human body. You do not need to think about it, command it, or control it. Your skin flexibly moves as you need it to move. You may need to protect it from chafing and sunburn, but under normal conditions you just assume it works. A traveler's spiritual practice should match the rhythm of their walk in their spiritual journey.

Many people imagine a spiritual discipline to be cumbersome . . . like wearing a suit of armor. In fact, medieval craftsman customized a suit of armor to fit precisely over the unique physiology of the wearer. Knights wore suits with armorlike skin. It never limited the spontaneous movements of their bodies. It never threw them out of balance or inhibited their activities. When St. Paul encouraged the Ephesians to "put on the whole armor of God," he was not asking them to make an uncomfortable fashion statement. The "belt of truth," "breastplate of righteousness," "shoes of peace," "shield of faith," "sword of Spirit," and "helmet of salvation" enable the spiritual traveler to "stand their ground" in evil times and walk with confidence into the unknown.[4]

Pilgrim Band Intentionality

The journey of the *pilgrim band* is messy because changes in group participation always influence group dynamics. Deepening relationships and deepening discernment ebb and flow up or down, or leap from one stage to another. On the one hand, Spirit is impacting our lives and shaping our journey. On the other hand, old habits, hidden assumptions, and subtle egotism can hold us back. Therefore, participants in the *pilgrim band* incorporate three daring and diligent practices throughout the journey.

Tough Love

Each member of the *pilgrim band* is radically honest with the others and expects radical honesty in return. There may be affirmation or criticism.

---

4. Eph 6:10–17 NRSV.

The affirmation may be surprising and occasionally embarrassing, carrying with it a heightened sense of responsibility. The criticism may be unexpected and hurtful, carrying with it a demand for repentance and change. All of it is guided, however, by the unwavering desire to bless the other and to help the other grow.

Tough love is as difficult to administer as it is to receive. Since members of the *pilgrim band* really do care for one another, they may be hesitant to speak the truth, waiting for a "right time" that never comes. We may be fearful of hidden manipulations in ourselves, using affirmation or criticism as a means of advancing our own authority. The more honest we are, the more we risk honest responses. Even if we risk anger, or endanger the relationship itself, it is all for the purpose of the mutual growth of companions in the *pilgrim band*.

Steady Concentration

Members of the *pilgrim band* prioritize time and energy to think for themselves. They do not simply mouth slogans and creeds, or waste time in idle chatter. They ponder the relevance of the core values and beliefs that they hold precious to the business of daily living. They consider the sources of faith through sacred literature, biography, and prayer. It is a *steady* concentration that permeates lifestyle and is not limited to an hour of study or a burst of attention.

Steady concentration is perhaps more difficult today than ever before, given the distractions of the highly mobile and multimedia world. Helping one another multitask and still focus is part of the mutual accountability of the group. Group members share insights with one another, ask questions, and engage in dialogue, and when the thread wanders each member refines the point. Steady concentration is not really about reading and meditation, but about lively conversation and shared insight.

Expanding Compassion

Each member of the *pilgrim band* connects the internal dialogue of the group with external interaction with culture. The *pilgrim band* is not a fan club for specific kinds of tastes and opinions; it is not a society for the preservation of any particular culture. It is just the opposite. It is eclectic. It is attentive to the diversity of cultures and the diversity of needs surrounding them. A true *pilgrim band* is always learning a new language, appreciating a new cultural form, and exploring creativity more than conformity.

If one person becomes more sensitive to the needs and life struggles of people around them, how much more sensitive will the combined observation of the group be? Each member calls the attention of the others to the experiences of life going on around them. Individually and as a group they reach out to bless others in practical ways, encourage others by sharing the insights of a pondered faith, and pray for others as they follow their own paths.

These three practices correspond to the monastic ideal of spiritual life. The spiritual life rotated around a circle of *humilitas*, *conversatio*, and *humanitas* (humility, meditation and study, and service). The center of this circle was the immanence of God, either experienced as reality or expectation.[5]

Today institutional religion and the *pilgrim band* are on increasingly divergent courses. This is very true outside America but emerging rapidly within America. People are choosing not to participate in a church or dropping out of participation in a religious institution. Even though many people continue membership in a church, the fact is that their spirituality is increasingly customized or personalized in ways that diverge from standardized faith and practice. Churches often describe themselves as communities *of faith*. The *pilgrim band* is best described as a community *of hope*. Hope breaks the dogmatic boundaries of faith.

Mentors build on their one to one relationship and help spiritual travelers find like-minded, or like-hearted, companions. Today, like in ancient times, *pilgrim bands* are highly mobile small groups of highly committed seekers, who intentionally practice spiritual disciplines, shape everything around a spiritual life, and support one another on the road. They don't tend to "settle down" for long in any given church or institution. They are too restless and too driven and feel too much urgency to go deeper and further into life in the Spirit than to participate in bureaucracies or preserve old buildings.

Imagine, then, what a contemporary *pilgrim band* might look like. The small group of spiritual travelers may include men and women, young and

---

5. In 2005 a denominational agency asked me to write a position paper on the waning credibility of clergy. The result was my book *Why Should I Believe You?* I argued that the Christian movement divided into an institutional (diocesan) version and a monastic version, and today the latter is becoming more resurgent. See Bandy, *Why Should I Believe*, 26–36 and 96–108.

old, and people of diverse cultures and interests. Each person takes seriously their shared identity of core values and beliefs, and each commits to the spiritual growth of the others. Members may meet weekly, physically or virtually, over a meal, trade messages that affirm and critique, communicate insights and raise questions, and alert participants to the emerging needs of others. Even as they are physically far apart, traveling to different countries, they continue to be in virtual conversation.

They constantly pause in their journey together to help others. They do whatever they can to heal the broken, befriend the lonely, guide the lost, bring justice to victims, give hope to the anxious, and offer the entrapped a fresh start. Every act of compassion is inspiration for the deeper reflection that they share with one another. If one member of the group is caught in a cycle of anger, alienation, obsession, doubt, guilt, arrogance, or accommodation, the others rescue him or her through tough love. If one member is in need, anywhere in the world, the others fly to his or her aid. All of this is done as part of a *journey*. After all, they are pilgrims traveling to a holy destination. Nothing stops or sidetracks them for long.

A Personal Reflection

June 2023 was the fiftieth anniversary of my ordination. At that time, candidates for ordination were required to write a summary of their understanding of ministry. I happened to find it buried in my files. In about five thousand words I said that . . .

> The minister pursues the spiritual life. This is the source of their dynamism, and the ground for their authenticity—and thus the spiritual life is the very meaning of their being-in-the-world and the implicit purpose of their being-for-the-world.

All papers were critiqued by anonymous authorities. I'm not sure whether the comments on my paper were written by a member of the bishop's cabinet or a seminary professor. It was evidently acceptable, but the final comment at the end was interesting. "So, what really counts for you is a general ministry of being human, religious, and a Christian person in that order, but not a special ordained ministry. Just think about it. Where does that come in?"

Having thought about it for fifty years, all I can do is recognize the uncomfortable sense of (yet again) being on the boundary. It is the boundary between religion and spirituality. The more I listen and observe, the more I realize I am not alone.

On the one hand, there are many who are restless with the limitations of religion. Authorities that people see as less than credible are demanding loyalty to traditions that are less and less meaningful, agreement with ideologies that are increasingly judgmental, obedience to doctrines that are frankly unintelligible, and participation in rituals that are culturally irrelevant. Spirit bursts all limitations. We celebrate our freedom.

On the other hand, there are many who are restless with the freedom of personal spiritualities. There are no criteria to separate the profound from the trivial. There are no checks on personal opinionating. There is no refuge to escape the cacophony of competing demands, and there is no benchmark with which to approximate truth. Spirit challenges our self-centeredness. We crave limitations.

Arbitrary limitation exacerbates our anxieties about fate, death, abuse, and we long for the freedom to think for ourselves and live our lives as we wish. But absolute freedom exacerbates our anxieties over loneliness, emptiness, and meaninglessness, and we search for relationships to cherish and a purpose for our lives. The paradox of life today is that Spirit breaks all forms that would contain it, and yet Spirit requires some form to reveal itself. I observe that there are new forms emerging, but they are not the old forms with which we were familiar.

Talk Together

It takes determination to be a traveler rather than a tourist. A tourist wanders, starts and stops, on a whim. Travelers are far more sacrificial and purposeful. In essence, mentors help mentees in the same way that roadside assistants help travelers or that pilgrims serve others along their way.

- Remember what started you on the journey.
- Focus on where you are headed.
- Don't wander, don't misbehave, and don't hinder the journeys of others.
- Pause only to aid others who need it.
- Seek help when you are in some kind of trouble.
- Discern God within, beyond, and beside you on the way.

Follow the road that is a straight line that links your soul with Spirit via compassion for all the people you encounter on the way. However, while we may walk together, the path is not easy. We must *work at it*.

It is more natural for a human being to have meaning and purpose in their lives than not. Meaning and purpose perpetuate one another. The more our lives have meaning, the more they have purpose. The more we fulfill our purpose, the more our lives have meaning. True, there are traumatic situations that interrupt this perpetual motion. But meaning and purpose generate courage, and courage usually helps us regain the momentum of meaning and purpose. This is what my past mentors might describe as the *power of being*.

We tend to assume, in comparison, that meaninglessness and purposelessness are simply an *absence* of meaning and purpose. It is "nothing," whereas meaning and purpose is "something." That is not true. There is a potency, a momentum, to meaninglessness and purposelessness as well. This is the *power of non-being*. The power of non-being undermines courage. In some cases, courage is replaced by resignation or resentment. In other cases, it is replaced by despair. But this is not an empty void in our souls. It is a power unto itself and self-perpetuating unless the power is broken. It is the immanence of God, or the "incarnation" of the Holy in our lives, that breaks the cycle and renews our courage to be. The *power of being* overcomes *the power of non-being*.

The metaphor of addiction may be useful here. An addiction is a self-destructive behavior pattern that we chronically deny and which we cannot overcome by our own efforts. The substance an addict abuses is a *thing*, but the habit that compels an addict to use it is a *power*. This is why addiction intervention is not just a therapy or learned skill. Addicts can value the therapy and learn a skill, and *still* be addicted. What is needed is the intervention of a "Higher Power." What does this "Higher Power" accomplish? It does not take away the addiction. It restores our courage to face and overcome it one day at a time.

Mentoring is like that. Deepening self-awareness, encouraging self-discipline, and mutual support are all important. But there is more work to be done. The mentoring relationship is a means to break the *power* of meaninglessness and purposelessness that has us in its grip. Like an addict, many modern people are in denial that such a power exists, or that this power is in control of their lives. They have come to believe that anxiety about meaning and purpose are "natural" to life and that a sense of meaninglessness and purposelessness is in some way normative to living. Paradoxically, while they may be alive, they are nevertheless caught up in non-being.

Mentors understand this situation consciously or intuitively, but the point of mentoring is not metaphysical speculation or philosophical reflection. The power of meaninglessness and purposelessness is more concretely revealed in several "vicious cycles" of attitude and behavior. At different times in our lives, among different generations and lifestyle groups, and in different social contexts, some "vicious cycles" may be more dominant or controlling of our lives than others. Each "vicious cycle," in its own way, perpetuates the power of non-being. The hardest work of mentoring is to identify these vicious cycles and help the mentee break them.

Temptation is more complex and subtle than most people realize. The power of meaninglessness and purposefulness (the power of *non-being*) is experienced as a kind of self-perpetuating victimization. The psychological impact of victimization often results in victims eventually becoming victimizers themselves. And victimizers become victims all over again. Manipulation is an *external* force that generates an *internal* struggle. Temptation is an *internal* struggle resulting in *external* manipulation.

Historically, Christianity (and other religions) have personified temptation and manipulation as the devil's work, even claiming that human existence is a kind of "spiritual warfare." Religions have employed extraordinary tactics ranging from prayers of supplication to aggressive intervention to exorcism. Yet in the context of mentoring relationships, it is all ineffective. It fails to discern the complexity and subtlety of temptation and manipulation. The "tempter" cannot "push our buttons" unless there are already buttons to be pushed in our psyche. We are tempted to do only what our secret desire has pre-programmed us to do. We are manipulated only because, deep inside, we secretly want to be manipulated. The most profound reason we struggle to discern meaning and purpose is that we are already addicted to meaninglessness and purposelessness.

"For I do not do the good that I want, but the evil I do not want is what I do.... Wretched man that I am! Who shall save me from this body of death?"[1] The words of St. Paul continue to haunt us in the mentoring relationship. The earliest apostles, who were the first Christian mentors, had a much more profound understanding of temptation. They understood that temptation is a kind of vicious cycle of defeat, as an internal weakness that invites external manipulation, and as external manipulation that plays upon internal desires. The power of non-being, our self-destructive habits that lead to meaninglessness and purposelessness, cannot be broken simply through assertiveness training and conflict resolution.

> Blessed is anyone who endures temptation. Such a one has stood the test and will receive the crown of life that the Lord has promised to those who love him. No one, when tempted, should say, "I am being tempted by God"; for God cannot be tempted by evil and he himself tempts no one. But one is tempted by one's own desire, being lured and enticed by it; then, when that desire has

---

1. Rom 7:19, 24 NRSV.

> conceived, it gives birth to sin, and that sin, when it is fully grown, gives birth to death.[2]

Jesus promises the apostles that he will send the Holy Spirit as an "advocate." The "advocate" breaks the vicious cycle of temptation.

> And I will ask the Father, and he will give you another Advocate to be with you forever. This is the Spirit of truth, whom the world cannot receive, because it neither sees him nor knows him. You know him; because he abides with you, and he will be in you ... I have said these things to you while I am still with you. But the Advocate, the Holy Spirit, whom the Father will send in my name, will teach you everything, and remind you of all that I have said to you.[3]

For the earliest Christians, the experience of the Holy Spirit was specifically aimed at breaking the vicious cycles of temptation and manipulation that undermine faith and sidetrack the spiritual life.

The *pilgrim band* helps one another resist the temptations of self-defeating habits that break the processes of deepening relationships and deepening discernment. Paul worries that violent oppression may have preyed upon the weaknesses of Christians in Thessalonica and writes:

> For this reason, when I could bear it no longer, I sent to find out about your faith; I was afraid that somehow the tempter had tempted you and that our labor had been in vain. But Timothy has just now come to us from you, and has brought us the good news of your faith and love.... And may the Lord make you increase and abound in love for one another and for all, just as we abound in love for you. And may he so strengthen your hearts in holiness that you may be blameless before our God ... at the coming of our Lord Jesus with all his saints.[4]

It is through the interventions of Paul's *pilgrim band* that these ancient spiritual travelers stayed together, remained faithful, and continued their journey to meaning and purpose.

Spiritual growth can be so *frustrating*. We deepen our self-awareness, develop spiritual habits, and periodically experience the immanence of God or "God-among-Us." Yet again and again we feel alienated from

---

2. Jas 1:12–15 NRSV.
3. John 14:16–26 NRSV.
4. 1 Thess 3:5–13 NRSV.

Spirit, lose the discipline of spiritual habits, and return to the habits of pessimism and despair. Hope is difficult to sustain. Repeatedly, we fall back into hopelessness.

Once again, the metaphor of addiction is useful here. Intervention seeks to replace self-destructive habits chronically denied with life-affirming habits intentionally pursued. But this requires more than the insights of a sponsor or family member. It requires the ongoing support and shared wisdom of a group. Frustration is a chronic reminder of our imperfection. The *pilgrim band* helps one another find the courage to face the manipulations and temptations that frustrate their spiritual lives . . . and overcome them.

Frustration on the spiritual journey always has an external and internal aspect. The frustration can be focused *externally* on the world as the *pilgrim band* interacts with world, and it can be focused *internally* with the interaction of the participants themselves. The one mirrors the other. Often the external frustrations result from internal frustrations projected onto the world. The correction of external stress with the world is not achieved by changing the world, but by changing ourselves.

The Vicious Cycle of Anger

The cycle of anger is usually the first bitter fruit of frustration. The *pilgrim band* is counter-cultural by nature. It is perceived as odd (and perhaps extreme) behavior by family, friends, and strangers. It invites misunderstanding and attracts both mild and extreme criticism. Participants in the *pilgrim band* can become angry. Anger invites retaliation, which generates more anger, leading to estrangement from former relationships.

At the same time, acceptance in the *pilgrim band* is always half-hearted for newcomers and fragile even for veteran companions. Individuals can feel misunderstood, under-appreciated, or rejected. Anger encourages criticism, and emotion escalates hostility. The *pilgrim band* can become polarized by personality conflicts and violent disagreements over ideas.

This is one reason why I favor odd numbers in the makeup of the *pilgrim band*. Resolution comes from mediation through one participant who can empathize with both sides. This is someone compatible with the lifestyles of both parties, who sympathizes with the existential anxieties that drive their quests for God, and who can interpret the deeper motivations of one with the other.

The same kind of mediation works to resolve disputes with the outside world. However, I find that once an internal cycle of anger is broken, an external cycle of anger is also defused. Once the harmony of the *pilgrim band* is restored or affirmed, resentment toward the world is eased even if anger from the world continues. The *pilgrim band* can travel peacefully even through hostile environments.

The Vicious Cycle of Guilt

The vicious cycle of guilt often accompanies or follows the cycle of anger. Anger toward others is often only a projection of anger toward yourself. This is particularly true for participants in the *pilgrim band* whose quest for God stems from experiences of abuse or victimization. They are prone to self-hatred and consequent depression. The joy of the *pilgrim band* is compromised as every participant second-guesses their words and actions.

The world often scapegoats the righteous for their inability to guarantee justice. In the same way, the *pilgrim band* can be blamed or taunted for their limitations, mistakes, and shortcomings as the realities of living fail to reflect the ideals they pursue. Some participants take this guilt upon themselves and feel responsible for all people, all suffering, and all social evil. The same cycle of guilt is visible within the *pilgrim band* itself. Individuals blame themselves for any hurt or misunderstanding. They scapegoat themselves and "whip" themselves mercilessly as if they were inherently evil.

Resolution comes from forgiveness, but it also comes from absolution. This means that guilt is shared across the companionship of the *pilgrim band* (internally) and across the pluralism of culture (externally), so that individual responsibility is limited and realistic. Self-hatred is replaced by self-acceptance. I find that once absolution is experienced within the *pilgrim band*, self-hatred is healed and guilt for the condition of the world becomes manageable.

The Vicious Cycle of Arrogance

The vicious cycle of arrogance is often an extreme reaction to anger and guilt. The inward journey of the soul toward God is replaced by an outward display of piety for religion. Empathy toward strangers is replaced by a need for recognition both in the world and among one's peers. Arrogance invites rebellion, which in turn reinforces an egotistical desire to manage, judge, and ultimately control others.

Outwardly, the *pilgrim band* appears condescending toward the world, and the world feels belittled by the *pilgrim band*. Their standard of behavior is imposed on others. Their very success in leading change in the world, or building credibility as spiritual leaders, encourages them to jealously guard power and influence. Inwardly, the dynamics within the *pilgrim band* become more competitive as each one tries to outdo the other in scrupulous obedience or worldly achievements. The fluidity of spiritual life is replaced by the solidity of corporate identity.

The corrective for arrogance always lies in role reversal and menial service. There is an intentional shift from the "highest rung" of power and prestige to the "lowest rung" of powerlessness and humiliation. The spiritual traveler deliberately chooses to vacate the "C Suite" to scrub floors in the restroom. In the same way, each participant of the *pilgrim band* stoops to "wash the feet" of their companions. I find that once the internal dynamic of the *pilgrim band* changes, the compulsion to compete with the world is reduced.

The Vicious Cycle of Accommodation

Whenever arrogance remains unchecked, the cycle of accommodation is inevitable. Accommodation relaxes standards of behavior and spiritual expectations in a futile attempt to preserve the status of the *pilgrim band* in the world. This may come from the world toward the *pilgrim band* as forces advocate competing visions, or it may come from within the *pilgrim band* as individuals seek to curry favor and support from their companions.

Accommodation always obscures identity. And the more the identity of the *pilgrim band* is blurred, the more we depend on external voices to tell us who or what we are. The purposefulness of the band wavers. We are tempted to "settle" for whatever spiritual insight we have achieved so far, and "settle down" in a more comfortable routine. The equality of *pilgrim band* dynamics tends to become a hierarchy of influence.

The remedy lies in disruptive creativity. In part, this comes from reinforcing the core values that shape the behavior of the *pilgrim band*. And in part, this involves the recovery of the original vision that inspires their quest. The restlessness of existential anxiety is reawakened, and the urgency of hope is sharpened. Externally, this is generated by expanding our sphere of relationships among lifestyle mosaics beyond our comfort zones. Internally, this emerges from a more radical incarnational experience. The one leads to the other.

The Vicious Cycle of Obsession

The cycle of obsession is often a reaction to our attempts to resist accommodation. Disruptive creativity can fixate on a single issue, problem, or belief that dominates our attention and demands all our resources. A single idea or program is given ultimate importance as the pivot on which everything else turns. Obsession, however, encourages oppression and prompts rebellion, which often reinforces obsession.

The vicious cycle of obsession can be very subtle because confrontation is often disguised as "prophetic witness." It feeds off the piety of self-righteousness. Unlike genuine prophetic witness, the "prophet" stands apart from, but does not share in, the suffering of sinners. In the world, they remain "safe in the suburbs." Inside the *pilgrim band*, they claim to be secure in their certainty and above criticism. Seekers become "true believers" in a cult rather than participants in a community. They take themselves *very* seriously.

The remedy lies in laughter. This may seem frivolous, but comedy is an antidote for tragedy. When we take anything too seriously, our sense of irony comes to the rescue. We are able to see the humor in our pride and the irony in our situations. Humor is a great leveler. It may even be sarcastic and mocking. Humor challenges travelers to observe their own foibles and laugh at themselves; humanize their heroes and shatter their idols; and calm their passions and regulate their lifestyles. The *pilgrim band* helps travelers see a bigger picture and align themselves with a higher purpose rather than personal satisfaction.

The Vicious Cycle of Doubt

When the cycle of oppression is broken, spiritual travelers are often drawn into a cycle of doubt. They laugh at themselves and recognize the ambiguities of life . . . but go too far. Principles become mere perspectives. God's purpose is lost in personal preference. Faith becomes a matter of opinion. Morality becomes a matter of taste. Doubt makes us indecisive, and indecision reduces commitment to the spiritual journey.

Externally, doubt is reinforced by perceptions of gratuitous evil (undeserved, unexplainable suffering). Internally, doubt is reinforced by a growing sense of futility in life and irrelevance to the spiritual quest. Doubt is not really a crisis of faith, but of hope. The *pilgrim band* feels a loss of momentum and the holy destination seems remote and inaccessible. Doubt in God's transcendence (power and omnipresence) results from distance from God's immanence (revelation and relevance).

The remedy for doubt is not propositional certainty but intuitive joy. While there is gratuitous evil, there is also unexplainable grace. The *pilgrim band* sharpens its awareness of miracles. These may suggest a supernatural breaking of the laws of nature, but in fact miracles are penetrations of the infinite into the finite. They are experienced in all forms of love, all expressions of beauty, all struggles for goodness, all approximations of truth, and all experiences of renewed life. Once hope is renewed in the *pilgrim band*, courage is renewed in the face of adversity. Doubt is overcome by confidence.

The Vicious Cycle of Alienation

The cycle of alienation often follows the cycle of doubt. Cynicism is perhaps worse than doubt because it is a dogmatism of non-being. While doubt invites dialogue, cynicism cuts off conversation prematurely. It breaks community. It not only distances a participant in the *pilgrim band* from the quest for meaning and purpose, but it separates the pilgrim from his or her companions. Alienation tends to be contagious and unity declines.

Cynicism is especially powerful among the entitled and affluent because their fear of loss is greater. Ironically, the powerless and poor are often more confident in faith and cling more strongly to hope. Within the *pilgrim band*, those who have given up most for the spiritual life are often most vulnerable to cynicism. They may have been the most articulate, the most intellectual, and the best strategic planners.

Therefore, it is up to the more introverted, intuitive, and spontaneous participants of the *pilgrim band* to rekindle hope. The remedy for alienation is the renewed credibility of those closest to the Spirit and their invitation to deepen communion with the Spirit. By "communion," I mean the sense of the immanence of God in the forms of daily living as well as the symbols of spiritual practice. The *pilgrim band* stays together, and travels together, because of their sense of "God-among-Us."

Each of the seven cycles is "vicious" in its own way, and each can be interrupted and resolved by specific actions. However, the seven cycles also represent a single cycle of self-destructive behavior that can sabotage the impact of the *pilgrim band* for the good of society and ultimately lead to the dissolution of the *pilgrim band*.

- Anger leads to retaliation or polarization and generates guilt.
- Guilt encourages depression as self-hatred is repressed by false pride.
- Arrogance leads to condescension and control.
- Control encourages accommodation to culture and becomes obsession.
- Obsession invites criticism and fosters doubt.
- Doubt nurtures cynicism and a sense of futility.
- Alienation undermines unity of purpose and companionship.

On the other hand, the cumulative interventions that break each cycle contribute to deepening the bonds of companionship and the urgency of spiritual discernment.

- Mediation leads to reconciliation.
- Forgiveness leads to self-acceptance.
- Humility increases generosity.
- Creativity sharpens vision.
- Humor gains perspective.
- Confidence increases hope.
- Communion reveals Spirit.

The conversations within the *pilgrim band* often come back to these concerns. It is not just about the internal dynamics of the *pilgrim band*. It is also about the relevance and impact of the *pilgrim band* on the cultures and contexts through which they travel.

The greatest obstacle to discerning meaning and purpose is not any specific problem, mistake, or misunderstanding. It is our *habit*. We fall into habits of thinking and behaving. These habits are automatic, often difficult to see, and always difficult to break. This is the reason why discovering meaning and purpose in life is so hard. This is also why the *pilgrim band* is so helpful, because it often takes the wisdom and intervention of our closest intimates to see a habit, break a habit, and avoid falling back into the habit. My presentation of "vicious cycles" may create the impression that these can be incremental. Breaking one bad habit can lead to forming another, different bad habit. But these need not be sequential. One can start anywhere, but the longer the *pilgrim band* walks together, the more likely each participant will uncover and overcome multiple layers of bad habits.

Conversations within the *pilgrim band* as they travel range widely and can include almost any topic. Conversations may be related to art and literature, history and culture, philosophy and theology, mental and physical health, social conditions and economic situations. They can share ideas related to theoretical and practical science, business, or international affairs. They can explore moral behavior, ethical issues, or war and peace. Participants in a *pilgrim band* come from all walks of life and bring with them education and professional insights, expertise and training, and all manner of diverse experiences.

Conversation is most vital when the *pilgrim band* is limited to five to thirteen people. If there are fewer participants, conversation eventually becomes exhausted or repetitive. If there are more participants, participation becomes unequal and unduly influenced by the interests of a few. Conversations are always energized as new participants join, while others leave to follow different paths, and still others return from different experiences.

Conversation may be loosely structured. This helps groups focus and build continuity in conversations. And it creates different contexts for individuals to express themselves in the ways best suited to their personalities.

- *Study*: The group may choose a book or use some specific media to orient their reflections and focus conversations. These might be nonfiction or fiction, biography or philosophy, devotion or theology, prose or poetry.
- *Service*: Conversation evolves in the course of social service, while volunteering for some project in the surrounding community or through advocacy of some global mission.
- *Spiritual practice*: This may include the study of traditional sacred texts, ancient or contemporary commentaries, or the wisdom of past saints or modern heroes.

- *Labor*: Conversations evolve in the course of hands-on, physical activity necessary for survival and daily tasks related to food, clothing, housing, and health care.
- *Silence*: Silence is a special form of conversation in which participants stop talking and *listen* with the inner ear of the heart to Spirit.

Conversation may be loosely or highly structured, but however it unfolds it should include *all*, and not just *some*, participants of the *pilgrim band*. They study, serve, practice, and labor together. No matter how conversation is structured, the form of conversation never constrains imagination or creativity. No matter what the content of conversation might be, it is always open to surprise and the inbreaking of Spirit. Conversation aims to go beyond the mundane to the significant.

A Personal Reflection

It has always been my custom in mentoring and coaching to keep track of conversations. I tend to keep logs, journals, and notes of conversations that arise from study, service, spiritual practice, labor, and silence. Every day, and in the history of our days, life is filled with conversations. Much of this is chatter. Some of that is significant. But what shocks me is that it is often difficult to discern which is which. What seemed idle conversation can blossom with enormous significance. What seemed so profound can be revealed barren and useless.

I think it is the *momentousness* of conversation that is most precious. The significance of mentoring boils down to mentoring moments. It may be a split second of time. It may be a word, a glance, or a touch. Conversation can be rich, nuanced, multi-layered, and complex, but all of that is forgotten over time. What remains is the import, impact, or momentousness of a conversation as it influences and shapes our lives.

All the *pilgrim bands* in which I have participated (sometimes consciously and intentionally, and sometimes unconsciously and coincidentally) have felt like old-time prospectors panning for gold. The water of life rushes down from the melting snow of the mountains, overflows the "sluice gates" constructed by religion, and slows in the shallower portions of the river where we can wade but not drown. There, prospectors gather to sift through the silted deposits looking for nuggets of beauty, perfection, and truth. They share their wealth with one another.

Yet contemporary pilgrims, like old-time prospectors, never seem to retire and settle down. They continue to pan for gold, looking and searching, in every season and any weather. They are not discouraged if all they glean is gold dust, the smallest specks of value. Nor are they satisfied with the occasional large nugget. They are filled with an eternal optimism and in awe of the limitless wealth of creation both hidden and revealed in the water of Spirit.

Trek Together

Spiritual travelers may walk and talk together in many ways, down many paths, through multiple media, for short or long times. Their conversation unfolds along the way. It is stimulated not only by internal thoughts but by external events and circumstances. The more philosophically rich, topically varied, and culturally diverse their journey becomes, the more creative and profound their conversation becomes. There are ups and downs, struggles and victories, one day at a time, for the long haul. The combination of walk and talk becomes a trek.

I tend to look back to ancient times to understand mentoring methodology. Mine have Western roots. Others may have Eastern roots. There are Egyptian, Greek, and Latin antecedents, many of which were recognized and shaped by the writers of Wisdom Literature in Jewish history, and later by the early desert abbas and amahs of Christian origins. Here is my sense of the scope of conversation covered by the *pilgrim band* on their journeys.

Feeling the Spirit

Experiences of incarnation are central to mentoring conversations. As we know, Spirit can use any cultural form, event, or context as a vehicle of grace. This immanence of God is brief. It is an intimation, a hint, a suggestion of what the fullness of God in the limitations of existence might be like. Spiritual travelers are alert to them as they journey. Some experiences might be quickly apparent and others hidden. Some may be understood immediately, and others only in retrospect. Most often they elicit feelings and provoke discussions now, but also awaken memories and evoke creative ideas later.

Early Christians understood such experiences as "sacraments." Religion tends to limit these to specific institutional rites. But these include any moments in which spiritual power is revealed through material things. It is both a symbol that informs and reminds a person of spiritual meaning, and (however briefly) a portal through which Spirit touches the mind, heart, or soul of an individual. These are "sacred" moments in which "God is among Us."

Birth and Rebirth

Any experience of creation and transformation feeds the conversation of the *pilgrim band*. The birth of a baby, and indeed the birth of any animal or the budding of any plant, is often described as a miraculous event. It is an awesome and mysterious moment. Even if it can be "explained" as a biological phenomenon, the beauty, purity, and potentiality of the event has a spiritual meaning or divine import beyond the event itself.

The same is true for experiences of rebirth. A transformation in life is like being "born again." For example, an addict healed from a habit of self-destruction, a spouse finally divorced from an abusive relationship, a slave obtaining freedom, or a criminal released from prison are all dramatic experiences of a fresh start. The same can be said of recovery from natural disaster or the metamorphosis of an organism. The bare statement of facts cannot express the joy of renewal.

Commitment and Sacrifice

The *pilgrim band* is itself a serious, accountable commitment or covenant, making the companionship itself an experience of incarnation. Spirit is always the invisible, sometimes incognito, party included in the journey. The paradigm for accountable commitment for traditional religions was usually associated with institutional membership, but the ancients had a broader understanding of the seriousness of the relationship (compare the followers of Socrates, disciples of Jesus, companions of Alexander, and more).

Companion is perhaps the best expression of commitment and sacrifice as a symbol of incarnation. It implies agapeic love, readiness to sacrifice one's life out of loyalty to another, selfless generosity toward a beloved partner. It assumes that there is a cause or community "worth dying for," the meaning and depth of which is constantly being tested and explored through the vicissitudes of living.

Repentance and Forgiveness

Accountable community anticipates the inevitability of error and abuse, but incarnational experience implies forgiveness rather than vengeance. We need to expand the idea of agapeic love to its most counter-cultural extreme. If the *pilgrim band* is a kind of mutual bodyguard, then one would naturally expect that harm to one would justify reprisals by the others. The opposite is true, making incarnational experience as forgiveness an irrational act. This is expanded even further because it applies to society itself or the global community. Incarnation is experienced not only in the preference for peace rather than war, but even to the elevation of love over law. The tension between love and law is the incarnational paradox of justice.

Repentance is necessary for forgiveness, but incarnational experience blurs the logic of the process. Does repentance lead to forgiveness? Or does forgiveness lead to repentance? Must guilt be assigned to celebrate love? Or does guilt only emerge when love is celebrated? Thus, the idea of "atonement" is not an essential part of the repentance/forgiveness dynamic. To be an experience of "God-among-Us," forgiveness is always undeserved. Incarnation is astonishing to some, and infuriating to others, because it breaks the cycle of reciprocity.

Oneness and Timelessness

Although we speak of spiritual travelers *on a journey*, experiences of incarnation are often interruptions to that journey. In this sense, incarnation is an ecstatic event. It is an event that lifts you out of chronological time into Kairos time. Process is interrupted by timelessness. One is in communion with Spirit, or, to say it another way, the subject/object mode of existence is transcended by a sense of oneness with Spirit. Ego is left behind, although identity is not lost. There is an immediate participation of the soul with the divine.

Religion has always tried to control the experience of incarnation by encasing it in ritual that is overseen by experts. This is one reason spiritual travelers leave the religious institution to engage in a journey. The journey itself is a renunciation of institutional control. The traveler is deliberately vulnerable to Spirit that is beyond control. Given my own Christian background, I cannot help but recall the story of incognito Christ meeting disciples on the road to Emmaus, and how the risen Christ is revealed at the table. They say: *Did our hearts not burn within us!*

Intimacy and Trust

Although ecstasy is temporary and unpredictable, incarnational experience also emerges in chronological time within consistent personal relationships. The virtue involved may be defined as responsibility or fidelity, but the experience itself is one of profound intimacy that is dependable over time. Institutional religion has tended to associate this with marriage, but the diversity of the twenty-first century has expanded the meaning of intimacy and trust beyond institutional and, indeed, gender expectations.

The significance of incarnation may include, but clearly transcends, sexuality. This is because authentic intimacy again transcends subject/object dualism in what might be described as reckless trust. It is the risk of absolute vulnerability in the hope of ultimate understanding. The miracle is that people are willing to take that risk, compelled to do so out of a quest for self-transcendence.

In the age of social media and constant mobility, "friendship" has been watered down to a list of contacts and likability. As an incarnational experience, "friendship" is a more intense bond of comrades or confidantes. Such relationships today are highly prized but difficult to find and sustain. Relationships of such deep trust are associated with concepts of "honor" and "integrity," which are often lost in a consumer society. Just as there is "risk" in intimacy, honor and integrity are often courageous, counter-cultural acts.

Vocation and Fulfillment

Although incarnational experience is often associated with self-sacrifice or selflessness, it can also be associated with self-affirmation and self-fulfillment. It is the distinct awareness of being "special," not in the context of personality, but in the context of destiny. Unlike a job or career, vocation is not really a choice. It is more like a compulsion and traditionally has been described as a calling. It is not about doing or training, but about being and becoming. And it is not about functioning in a particular way, but about living in a particular way. One can pursue a vocation across any number of careers.

Vocation implies fulfillment. The word that captures the spiritual nature of fulfillment is "joy." One can be happy in a career and joyless in life. Similarly, one can be unhappy doing a job, but joyful in life. The recognition of deep, profound satisfaction or contentment is more closely associated with relationships than activities. It is an alignment of identity and purpose that is only revealed through the lens of Spirit. It reveals the paradox of incarnation, in that a person may even do something they prefer not to do yet find fulfillment in doing it. You participate in, or contribute to, the movement of Spirit in history.

Acceptance and Hope

All experiences of incarnation culminate in, or point toward, unconditional acceptance and hope. We never quite realize the high ideals, understand all the hidden meanings, or live up to all the expectations that are revealed in any experience of incarnation. No matter how hard we try, we inevitably fail. Fear of failure, therefore, is more serious than finding fault. Conversation within the *pilgrim band* is helpful for self-examination only if there is a possibility of perfection.

Failure is rooted in the nature of existence itself. It is the result of our inability to escape finitude. The final failure is death. This fear is not just about ceasing to live, but about the fading of all our accomplishments and our "deletion" from memory. Our existential dilemma is not just that history might, but seemingly must, repeat itself, and whatever gains and contributions we have made for a better world come to nothing. In the age of enlightenment, faith in progress led us to believe that we could achieve our own self-transcendence, but that optimism about human nature is contradicted by the nature of existence.

Hope depends on Spirit, which works in and through history, just as it works in and through ego, yet transcends history and ego. Perfection is only possible, and self-examination is only useful, if it is grounded in the confidence of being acceptable despite our failures. History does not, and ultimately will not, keep repeating itself. Even if our great or small contributions go unrecognized and forgotten, they contribute to the flow of Spirit and benefit the world in ways that we cannot ever imagine.

Serving the Public

Radical generosity is also a topic of conversation as pilgrims walk together in a spiritual journey. Ancient philosophies and religious traditions all emphasize the importance of acts of mercy. Generosity is *radical* in the sense that mercy does not just demonstrate humility but also the willingness to accept humiliation. The spiritual traveler is willing to stoop lower, sacrifice more, and give away everything including their pride for the sake of suffering humanity. Any pious individual can strive to be humble, but only the mutual support of the *pilgrim band* can engender the courage to share suffering, or, more radically still, take the place of the sufferer.

Radical generosity is tied to lifestyle empathy. In an earlier chapter, I defined the experience of *heartburst* as an important aspect in initiating and nurturing mentoring relationships. Empathy can be explained in the demographic categories defined by lifestyle research (as I said in an earlier chapter), but it is clearly not limited to these categories. Suffering forms its own micro-cultures that cross boundaries of age, gender, income, and so on. The immersion of the spiritual traveler in such a micro-culture may be the primary affinity that unites a *pilgrim band*.

Christian tradition identifies incarnational experience with Christ "incognito" among the poor and powerless. Jesus names a list of ways people suffer that is paralleled in other religious traditions. And he concludes with the words: "As you do it for the least of these, you do it for me."[1] Ancient Christians believed: "For just as the body without the spirit is dead, so faith without works is also dead."[2] To wish anyone peace, health, and safety without responding to their physical, mental, emotional, and relational needs was hypocrisy.

- *Feeding the Hungry*

    These are the ways in which we address the physical needs of the world through gifts of food, training for self-reliance, and caring for the environment.

- *Providing Drink for the Thirsty*

    These are the ways in which we help people satisfy their yearning for knowledge, quality relationships, and deep spirituality.

---

1. Matt 25:31–40 NRSV.
2. Jas 2:26 NRSV.

- *Clothing the Naked*

  These are the ways in which we protect the abused, rescue the vulnerable, and restore self-esteem to victims of violence.

- *Visiting the Sick*

  These are the ways in which we care for the physically, mentally, or emotionally ill and support those who are under unusual stress.

- *Housing the Homeless*

  These are the ways in which we provide havens for those who need safety and rest, guard personal privacy, and reunite families.

- *Ransoming Captives*

  These are the ways in which we spend our wealth and risk our lives to rescue those who are trapped by bigotry, poverty, or politics.

- *Honoring the Dead*

  These are the ways in which we help people confront death and dying with dignity and hope and help them remember the best about friends and foes alike.

Acts of generosity may involve providing *solutions* for these social problems. However, generosity is often more about *presence* than *problem solving*. Generosity is bigger than outreach. It is also about immersion in the suffering of others and being a hopeful presence among those who suffer.

Earlier, I described how the mentoring relationship helps the spiritual traveler avoid sidetracks that take them out of alignment with their spiritual purpose. However, the *pilgrim band* together can help a spiritual traveler discern the difference between a sidetrack and an opportunity. A sidetrack is anything along the way that reinforces self-interest or manipulates strangers. An opportunity is anything along the way that contributes to justice or brings people closer to God. Those stops along the way for acts of mercy are not sidetracks, but stepping stones toward their holy destination.

The more content we are to settle for status quo, and the more reluctant we become to risk humiliation, the more our generosity becomes a sidetrack rather than an opportunity. This is most apparent as the generosity of the individual spiritual traveler, or the camaraderie of the *pilgrim band*, becomes institutionalized. Generosity is expressed through financial donations and fund raising, administrative or board leadership for non-profit organizations, or advocacy for government policy. While these are all expressions of *humility*, acts of mercy are increasingly mediated or filtered through bureaucracy. They are not face-to-face. Acts of mercy that are central to the spiritual journey are always personal.

Personal service is the hardest expression of mercy. The most profound acts of mercy are spontaneous and unrehearsed. Organizational strategic planning and policy development do not focus on the hardships of service. Acts of mercy are about personal relationships, sincerity in sharing hope, and active modeling of virtues of love and compassion. Empathy means that hope is revealed from *within* the life struggles of others.

Becoming Authentic

Spiritual travelers may be *pursuing* a life of meaning and purpose, but it is worth noting that they are *leaving behind* a consumer society of self-interest in which the primary preoccupations are to live happily and delay dying as long as possible. Spiritual travelers are preoccupied with *living well* and *accepting death* whenever it comes. In Western culture, from ancient times through the Renaissance, this was the ethical dilemma of human beings living in and enduring the moral ambiguities of life.

The journey of the spiritual traveler is often arduous and confusing, and the traveler wonders if they are making any difference to society or any progress in spiritual maturity. The *meaning* of life becomes tangled with other preoccupations with culture. The *purpose* of life becomes lost amid other expectations. The conversation of the *pilgrim band* helps each traveler gain perspective on their progress.

In traditional religion the regular evaluation of one's life is often called "confession." Catholic and Orthodox churches practice this as a distinct sacrament regularly observed and confidentially shared with a priest. Protestant churches practice this as part of the Sunday liturgy confidentially shared among believers. Absolution or forgiveness guarantees eternal salvation if you happen to die a moment later, or at least a fresh start for the new week. Unfortunately, neither practice works well in a consumer society of self-interest where conscience, confidentiality, and credibility are hard to find in any institution.

Spiritual travelers rely on the *pilgrim band* to practice radical honesty with themselves and with each other. In a sense, travelers "keep each other honest." Individuals can dare to plumb the depths of self-deception, and the group can hold one another accountable to higher ethical standards in a context of high trust. Over the centuries, one can observe a pattern or methodology for honesty. You can trace it from prophets like Amos and Hosea and Aristotle's *Nicomachean Ethics*, through the beatitudes of Jesus, Paul's letter to the Galatians, the monastic teachings of Evagrius and others, Dante's *Divine Comedy*, pilgrim immigrants to America. The most relevant translation of "deadly sins" and "lively virtues" is the contrast between addiction and authenticity.

Addicted	Authentic
Pride	Humility
Envy	Gratitude
Gluttony	Moderation
Greed	Generosity
Lust	Respect
Anger	Patience
Sloth	Diligence
Despair	Hope

Religious institutions have tended to use this method to define a state of being, making these "either/or" choices subject to evaluation by external authorities. Spiritual travelers in the *pilgrim band* know that life is more ambiguous than this. The only honest answer to cross-examination would be "yes and no." Both addiction and virtue are behavior patterns and not itemized lists. At any given time, in any given situation, spiritual travelers are *caught* by one and *committed* to the other. Our companions help us resist one and persist in the other.

The role of the *pilgrim band* is not to pass judgment. It neither accuses nor excuses. That is a matter for conscience and Spirit. Instead, the role of the *pilgrim band* is to mitigate self-hatred and encourage personal growth. They may encourage the individual to treat themselves with gentleness or severity.

Religions (and church institutions in particular), tend to promise purity and certainty, and society tends to expect it. Spiritualities (and *pilgrim band*s) are more realistic. They understand that the limitations of existence force us to live in constant tension between good and evil. Religions can be the source of great good and great evil. Christians (and any religious adherent) can be heroes or villains. The inevitable ambiguity of living means that it is not always easy to tell which is which in either the short or long term. Most outcomes are ambivalent. Spiritual travelers constantly live in these eight moral or existential tensions:

Living in the Tension Between Pride and Humility

The moment we become self-aware of our self-forgetfulness, ego reinserts itself into service. Yet the boundary between self-esteem and self-promotion is often blurred. Righteous behavior blends into self-righteous attitude. Spiritual travelers are often blind to their own arrogance, and the honesty of the *pilgrim band* helps the traveler accept their limitations even as they explore their potential.

Living in the Tension Between Envy and Gratitude

The moment gratitude compares itself to the success of others, life becomes competition. Yet the boundary between thankfulness for what we have and the desire for what others possess is often blurred. The desire for self-improvement leads to comparisons with the accomplishments of others. The honesty of the *pilgrim band* helps the traveler measure personal success by approximating high ideals rather than winning races.

Living in the Tension Between Gluttony and Moderation

The moment moderation is touched by inspiration, the more we become obsessive/compulsive over fulfillment. The boundary between passion and consumption is often blurred. Our joy in beauty, goodness, and truth is expressed in our acquisition of things, growing our reputations, and building our libraries. The honesty of the *pilgrim band* helps the traveler choose wisely and live simply.

Living in the Tension Between Greed and Generosity

The more we give away, the more we strive to gain. Wealth and poverty are tied to power and powerlessness. To aid the powerless, the more we need to become powerful. The wisdom of the *pilgrim band* helps the traveler determine his or her percentage of giving (money and resources, physical and emotional energy, etc.). The greatest challenge for radical discipleship is not tithing (the percentage given in God's service) but rather reverse tithing (the minimum required to sustain personal and spiritual wellness).

Living in the Tension Between Lust and Respect

Deepening intimacy within and beyond the *pilgrim band* can blur the boundary between passion and love. Even the desire for God can blend into a lust for life. The *pilgrim band* helps each traveler wrestle with the boundaries of relationships, checking the temptation to objectify other human beings, undermine their dignity, or take away their autonomy. Together, in any given moment and situation, they help each other discern what it means to honor God and each other.

Living in the Tension Between Anger and Patience

The moment feelings of compassion are expressed in actions for justice, the boundary between patience and anger becomes blurred. The more the quest for justice is resisted, the less compassionate we become. Yet the more compassionate we feel, the less assertive we become. There is holiness in righteous anger, but not in self-righteousness. There is holiness in righteous restraint, but not in ethical complacency. The wisdom of the *pilgrim band* helps the traveler discern the boundary . . . and experience grace in ambiguity.

Living in the Tension Between Sloth and Diligence

The moment we separate "work" and "play" we deny the fullness of life and limit the potential for service. Institutional religion defines "work" with "professionalism" and "play" with "vacation." The former is an exercise in diligence and the latter an excuse for sloth. The relationships of the *pilgrim band* help make work become fun and play become productive.

Contemplation and service infuse all aspects of living. God embraces all aspects of life.

Living in the Tension Between Despair and Hope

Despair and hope are two sides of the same life under the conditions of existence. There can be no hope without despair, and no despair without hope. The power of the *pilgrim band* is not that together we can find answers to the problem of evil, but that together we can endure, persist, and in the fullness of time overcome evil. When one person weeps, (s)he weeps for all. When one person laughs, (s)he laughs for all. The *pilgrim band* is united in the weeping and united in the laughing, and Spirit is moving within that unity.

The "trek" of the *pilgrim band* is a constant movement between three sacramental experiences. The more aware we become of the Spirit moving in our lives, the more we have wisdom and courage to live authentically in the ambiguities of existence. The more authentic we strive to become, the more we are moved to generosity toward the world. And the more we experience, give and receive love, the more we feel the immanence of God.

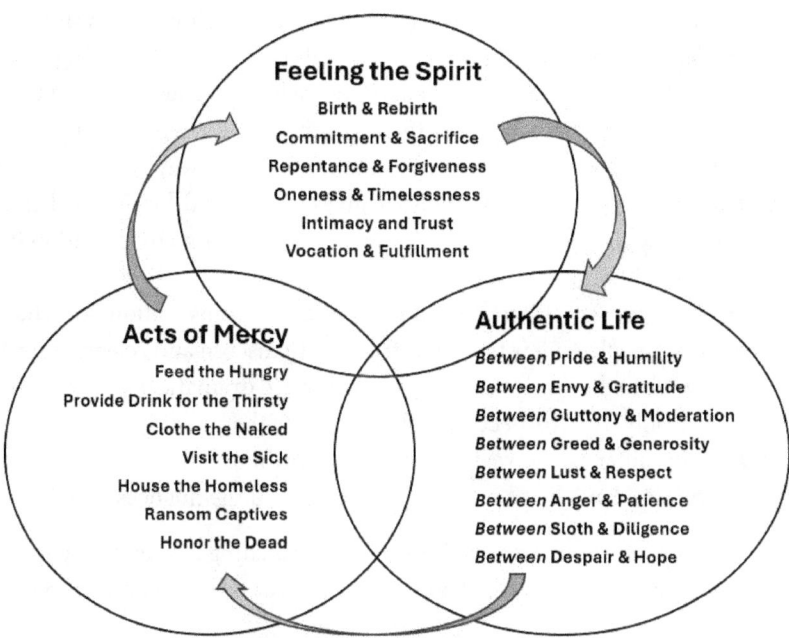

We are prone to talk *at* people, or talk *about* people, or talk *beyond* people, but rarely actually talk *with* people. A careful look at any shopping mall food court reveals the difference between *chatter* conversation and *significant* conversation. Sure, there is a high noise level. Body language reveals the truth. Most people are slouched in their chairs, only half-turned to their neighbors, text messaging, talking on cell phones, laughing, and only partially listening to several conversations at once. Their eyes are not focused on any given speaker, but roving over the food court, looking for something (or nothing), because what they are hearing is titillating or boring, and hardly important.

But wait! Look over there! There, in a quieter corner, out of the way from distractions or eavesdropping, sit half a dozen people in *significant* conversation. Things of importance are being shared. Each squarely faces the other. Cell phones are holstered, eyes are locked, only one person speaks at a time, and the others (astonishingly!) pay attention. Even if the emotion of the moment causes one to stand or move about, he or she circles the table, leans in, and listens. The conversation may get animated, or even emotional, but whenever there is confrontation there is also conciliation, and whenever there is laughter, it is followed by sudden, and even deeper, seriousness.

Can you begin to imagine the conversation along the way? The *pilgrim band* is talking and walking (emailing, texting, "tweeting," and communicating as often as they can, and in whatever media they prefer). Along the way they are pausing to help others and serve the zip codes through which they travel. Each one in his or her own way is both mentor and traveler. One moment a member gives advice and holds another to accountability. The next moment he or she is receiving advice and being held accountable.

So, have you experienced Spirit this week? The conversation flows back and forth as people review their life struggles to discern and celebrate spiritual victories. Some stories are obvious, some are dramatic, and others become clear only in retrospect. Sometimes events that previously seemed so trivial and ordinary are revealed to bear extraordinary meaning and promise. The *pilgrim band* helps one another explore all the nuances of Spirit.

- One felt the immanence of Spirit while watching children play in the park, seeing one child in tears while an older brother comforts her.

- Another glimpsed the power of Spirit while chatting across continents with their companions as they create "Houses of Grace," providing healing environments for people in difficult circumstances.
- Yet another experienced the work of Spirit that transformed the pain of bitter argument into joyous reconciliation with their parent or partner.

It may be that individuals have simply not sensed the Spirit at all this week, no matter how they search through their memories. There is no invention or exaggeration here. Companions are not in competition with each other. They are honest with one another. The conversation sharpens their perceptions and fills them with greater anticipation. Regardless of this week, where will Spirit emerge, and what will Spirit do next week?

It's noon, and one of the group members is on his way out of the office for a take-out sandwich from the deli across the street. He checks his cell phone for text messages. *Helped any strangers lately?* A mere glance around the busy urban center reveals plenty of opportunities. There is the homeless person begging for coins, the elderly couple walking nervously across a high-traffic street, two motorists shouting insults at each other after a fender bender, and another woman honking in road rage behind them. There is the harried retailer, and the stressed-out colleague, and the sorrowful looking elderly woman, and the teenager telling a racist joke, and the guy gliding by in the electric wheelchair, and the weary policeman, and more. Twenty-nine minutes later, the group member is out of time and out of money, returning to the office having decided to fast that day. He texts back: *Yes.*

It's Saturday morning, and a small group is clustered comfortably in the corner of the coffee shop. The members are in earnest conversation: leaning forward, sipping their drinks unconsciously while a range of emotions flash across each face, talking, listening, gesturing, and connecting with one another. One computer is open, and you can see the face of another participant from far away.

Are you making any progress in getting home? They are talking about individual strengths and weaknesses, spontaneous deeds, risky actions, unrehearsed words, and crafted speeches. They are sharing what they planned to do, what they did, and how they feel about the difference. Their honesty is astonishing. People are talking about their sexual temptation, greedy behavior, and uncontrolled anger. They are lamenting and laughing about their laziness and insensitivity. They are confessing their selfishness at sports events, or their jealousy at the office, or their obsession with the stock market.

What is more remarkable is how they challenge each other. *Your faith sounds way too self-satisfied! Don't apologize for being careful, even if you missed an opportunity to serve! Giving two percent of your income to charity isn't much to boast about!* You can see them all reassessing their own situations. Perhaps they are not as good or bad as they thought they were. You can hear the alarm or relief in their voices.

But what is most remarkable is how they encourage one another. *Keep going! Try this! Watch out! There is another way—a second chance! Next time you will be better prepared!* There is acceptance and sympathy in their eye contact, and reassurance and kindness in their dialogue. There is single-mindedness and purpose when they break up and exit through the door. They all drive off in different directions, but all seem to be headed for the same destination.

A Personal Reflection

No doubt you have heard the expression that describes moral character: *Walk the talk.* The *pilgrim band* takes this to an extreme: *Trek the talk.* A "trek" is more arduous and intentionally covers difficult terrain. It takes longer and continues even when there is no end in sight. It is riskier and more dangerous. Many people go for a walk. Fewer people undertake a trek. A trek is not something you "decide" to do for a day. It is a habit that you do automatically when you get up in the morning. When I translate historic spiritual practices into contemporary language, what was once ritual becomes lifestyle.

Another way a "trek" is different from a "walk" is that it forces you to concentrate on the ordinary. A "walk" allows us the luxury to notice extraordinary beauty. A "trek" forces us to watch our step, anticipate hazards, and see extraordinary beauty in ugly things. A "walk" allows us to see the sublime as if it were rare. A "trek" allows us to see the sublime as if it were everywhere.

The contemporary connotation of the word "trek," however, is that it is a noble, uplifting, and even glorious experience. There may be occasions when it feels like that. Most often, I think, a "trek" feels more like a "slog." That is, the journey of the *pilgrim band* often feels like seemingly endless and enervating hard work. It's more like cutting a path through the jungle than following a trail across the mountains. There is less of a breeze. There are more mosquitos and snakes. And you sweat copiously.

Dante's long allegory of redemption is framed as a pilgrimage with mentors (Virgil and Beatrice) who guide him through hell and purgatory to paradise. And perhaps there is no better description of the pilgrimage state of mind (or state of being) than the opening words of the first canto of the *Inferno*:

> When I had journeyed half of our life's way,
> I found myself within a shadowed forest,
> for I had lost the path that does not stray.
>
> Ah, it is hard to speak of what it was,
> That savage forest, dense and difficult,
> Which even in recall renews my fear:
>
> So bitter—death is hardly more severe!
> But to retell the good discovered there,
> I'll also tell the other things I saw.[3]

A pilgrimage is not an easy trek, and often feels like a slog, but the rewards are huge. You can feel the Spirit come alive, become a blessing to everyone around you, and discover your authentic self.

---

3. Dante, *Divine Comedy*, 59.

Transitions

THE MENTORING RELATIONSHIP IS often unpredictable. We move forward, then go back to revisit past steps, and sometimes there are gaps in the conversation. We try to organize the mentoring relationship into covenants that can be renewed and redesigned as we go along, and the overall relationship may last days, weeks, or years. But more often than not, mentoring relationships escape our best efforts to manage and control them and vary in intensity as they unfold. We walk physically and virtually with ever-changing companions: meeting and walking, separating and reuniting, and often just waving to one another encouragingly. Mentoring may be a return to ancient methods of maturity, but we do not live in ancient times. Mentoring today unfolds in the modern world of speed, flux, and blur.

If one to one mentoring is part of a larger movement of Spirit, invisibly handed off from one mentor to another, then *pilgrim band* is also a fluid experience. A group walks together for an unpredictable amount of time, in a certain direction. But individuals may step away into different relationships to travel in a new direction. In ancient times, change often occurred during a layover in an inn, a hospice, or a "waystation" at some intersection. Some travelers go one way, some another, some stay in place for a time, and some continue the journey with the same group.

At some point, and perhaps at several points, spiritual travelers eventually sense that the time has come to part. Each traveler must go their separate ways. The mentor has given about as much as he or she can give. The mentee has received about as much as he or she can receive. Participants in the pilgrim band may be drawn away to other responsibilities, called in different directions, and, sometimes, need to get out of each other's way.

A particular mentoring relationship, like any relationship, can eventually become more of a hindrance to spiritual growth than a help.

It can become a comfortable habit, filled with a great deal of affection. But whenever the preservation or perpetuation of a relationship becomes *more important* than the spiritual growth emerging from it, the relationship needs to end. This does not mean that the *friendship* needs to end, but that the intentional practice of leading questions, challenging assertions, decisive interventions, and pregnant silences are no longer effective. The friendship can remain, but the mentoring relationship must be established with someone else.

This decision to end the mentoring relationship is not easy to make. Travelers have been *positively* dependent on each other for guidance, but the negative risk is that participants in mutual mentoring might become *co-dependent* in their relationship with one another. The mentee requires the affirmation of the mentor to continue in spiritual growth, and the mentor requires the affirmation of the mentee to continue to be confident in guiding spiritual growth. The minute that travelers become consistently comfortable with each other, they are no longer *staking* or *risking* themselves for spiritual growth.

The moment the ambivalence of "yes and no" leaves their relationship, effective mentoring ends. Mentors are always worried about their incompetence: "This may be right . . . but it may be wrong." Travelers are always worried about their inexperience: "This may be constructive . . . but it may be dangerous." When the mentoring relationship becomes so confident and comfortable that mentors are *certain* and travelers are *sure*, the risk goes out of the relationship and effective mentoring ends. I have observed some common issues.[1]

The first thing that blocks closure to the mentoring relationship is the "Traveler Complex." This refers to pilgrims who are convinced that they are "never quite ready" to take responsibility for their own personal growth. The pilgrim perpetuates the mentoring relationship out of fear, not expectation. The reality is that no one is ever ready to take responsibility for their spiritual life. The incarnational experience will always be a mystery and never fully grasped. The meaning and purpose of life will always be vast and never fully completed on this side of existence. The vicious cycles will never be completely broken and rendered powerless. The point is that there will never be a time when we are *completely* competent. The awareness and acceptance of our own incompetence is essential to the process.

---

1. Bandy, *Christian Mentoring*, 127, 128.

The "Traveler Complex" means that the pilgrim clings to the mentor or to the *pilgrim band* the way that a capsized sailor, in fear of drowning, clings to his or her rescuer. Yet they must catch their breath, calm themselves down, focus on the distant shoreline, and eventually swim for themselves. If they don't, both will drown. There is no *guarantee* that the capsized sailor will reach the shore. Who knows? A shark may attack, a hidden reef may intervene, or a cramp may slow them down. But unless they have the courage to swim for themselves, the quest for meaning and purpose will remain unfulfilled.

Pilgrims often begin a mentoring relationship with childish naiveté. They soon learn that the alignment of one's life with God's purpose is more difficult and demanding than expected. Yet even after they have considerably matured, the inner child reemerges on the brink of independence to hold them back. Like teenagers leaving home for the first time, they look back with frightened eyes. The mentor must wave encouragement but close the door.

The second thing that blocks closure to the mentoring relationship is the "Savior Complex." This refers to mentors who are obsessed with the idea that they are ultimately responsible for the quest of the pilgrim. The mentor perpetuates the mentoring relationship out of egocentrism, not spiritual purpose. The reality is that no one can take ultimate responsibility for the pursuit or completion of anyone else's journey. Some pilgrims hit the target. They are satisfied with the meaning of their lives and aligned with what they perceive to be God's purpose. Yet it is only temporary. Spirit will sooner or later stir up discontent and doubt and force them back into the journey. Some will come close. Some may miss the target altogether. Some may do well for a time, and then fall prey to one of the vicious cycles of temptation. The point is that the mentor cannot control the futures of others.

The "Savior Complex" means that the mentor clings to the pilgrim the way that a rescuer clutches a drowning person, even after they are safe. The rescuer must hold tight, whisper encouragement, point out the distant shoreline . . . but then give the other a shove in the right direction. Otherwise, the rescuer will become the drowning person. After all, mentors are not people that finally landed on a beach safely and then turned back to leap into the ocean. They are swimmers themselves. They capsized. Someone else helped them to swim. They are swimming in the right direction. Along the way, they help others who are newly capsized. *But then they must continue swimming.* The journey of the mentor is not done either.

Mentors often begin a mentoring relationship with false confidence. They soon learn that helping others discover meaning and align with purpose is more difficult and demanding than expected. Even as they accept the risks and ambiguities involved in helping guide others, their sense of guilt and potential self-condemnation increases. *What if* my guidance is awry? *What if* this traveler drowns anyway? *What if* my faith is misplaced, or my judgment is skewed, or my advice is poor? These mentors are like parents saying goodbye to their teenager for the first time. They are moved by the frightened eyes. But they must close the door and pay attention to the next child.

The third thing that blocks closure to the mentoring relationship is "Group Think." This refers to the tendency of the pilgrim band to gradually replace *discernment* with *consensus*. Spiritual growth requires work, risk, and, ultimately, courage. The wisdom one gains is just as unsettling as it is satisfying. There is always the temptation to avoid personal responsibility by appealing to group solidarity. Just as a mentee does not require the permission of a mentor to think, speak, or act—and just as a mentor has no authority to tell a mentee how to think, speak, or act—so also the *pilgrim band* as a group can neither be expected to provide, nor are they able to guarantee, whether a course of action is appropriate or not. Only the pilgrim can investigate their own soul and search out their own spiritual path.

Just as doubt is the existential corollary to faith, so also autonomy is the existential corollary of companionship. There is no escape from such ambiguity under the conditions of existence. Faith and doubt, unity and disunity are "natural" to the human condition. Therefore, it is not only entirely possible, but quite inevitable, that a mentor and mentee part company. And it is not only possible, but inevitable, that a *pilgrim band* should dissolve, and participants go different ways. Sooner or later, they get in each other's way. They become more hindrance than help. Only Spirit is absolute.

This does not mean that mentoring relationships and *pilgrim bands* end in anger. Quite the opposite. If the experience of mutual mentoring has been authentic, then the participants part in love. There is grief, but only in the larger context of hope. The participants may continue to be friends (even in disagreement), and they may continue to be in communication. But their spiritual journeys take each traveler down different roads and with new companions.

In a time of transition, it is important for those who have shared mutual mentoring to understand that the journeys they take are not personal *choices* (as if their autonomy determined their destinies). Nor are their different journeys really *obligations* (as if their journeys were controlled by institutions or world authorities). Their transitions are *compulsions* just as the incentive to pilgrimage was a *compunction*. They are moved by the power of Spirit.

The decision to join a *pilgrim band*, or leave a *pilgrim band*, is an act of courage elicited and empowered by Spirit. First, there is the courage to participate and the courage to trust and be trusted. The spiritual traveler joins himself or herself to the companionship of mutual mentoring with all the risks and opportunities that entails. But second, there is the courage to separate and the courage to accept one's authentic self. The spiritual traveler leaves the companionship of mutual mentoring with all the risks and opportunities that entails.

The mentoring relationship, powerful and influential as it may be, is only part of a larger network of spiritual relationships. Some are visible. Other friends, colleagues, neighbors, church members, and strangers will take over responsibility for the next steps in spiritual growth and accountability. Since we often do not yet know who those people will be, we realize that the key spiritual relationship is invisible. In the Christian gospel, Jesus promises to send the Holy Spirit as "counselor" and "guide."[2]

Any single mentoring relationship is only a part of a series of mentoring relationships. The *pilgrim band* is part of a larger movement of pilgrims. Sometimes the mentor and traveler can see it, and the mentor literally hands off the traveler to another who can guide him or her in the next steps of the journey. Sometimes neither mentor nor traveler can see it, and both trust in the Spirit. The Spirit continues the conversation with each pilgrim. The Spirit asks leading questions, poses challenging assertions, makes decisive interventions, and creates pregnant silences.

The idea of bringing closure to a relationship by "commending the traveler to the mercy of God" sounds trite to modern ears. This is not just because Christendom has overused the phrase, but because its repetition in liturgy has made it sound pedantic and otherworldly. It is because there is a profound skepticism in modern times that Spirit is, indeed, *merciful*. Many believe Spirit exists. But most believe that it is, at best, *indifferent*.

---

2. John 14:14–17 NRSV.

That Spirit should actively—or even habitually and strategically—take an interest in *my* living is a surprise.

If the *pilgrim band* believed, deep inside, that Spirit was indifferent to their journey, or haphazard about mercy, then pilgrimage would be unbearable. And if the traveler believed, deep inside, that Spirit was indifferent to his or her quest, or easily distracted by more important people and more desperate situations, so that chronologically speaking they were basically on their own, then mentoring would be a waste of time. Who could endure such self-discipline? Who could help you when you were helpless?

Spirit is what provokes the mentoring relationship, and Spirit is what evokes the *pilgrim band*. It is a small miracle that the mentoring relationship began at all, given the temptations of the world and the selfishness of human beings. It is another small miracle that *pilgrim bands* continue to emerge and thrive, diverge and renew, all the time and in every social context given the very same conditions of existence. *Despite existence,* mercy endures. *Despite failures,* spiritual growth continues. *Despite the limitations of humankind,* there is a destiny for each individual human. The *pilgrim band* can provide the form and content, but significance and fulfillment lie with God.

A Personal Reflection

My motivation for writing this little book is different, I think, than for all my previous books. This book is not intended to be systematic theology, nor pastoral theology, nor even church growth strategy. It is not intended to be an educational curriculum or program in faith formation. It is really an extended reflection on how I have spent my life and why. I am reminded of what one of my earliest mentors quoted as I left high school for college. He was the Spanish teacher who introduced me to the early twentieth-century existentialism of Miguel de Unamuno:

> I hope, reader, that some time while our tragedy is still playing, in some interval between the acts, we shall meet again. And we shall recognize one another. And forgive me if I have troubled you more than was needful and inevitable, more than I intended to do when I took up my pen proposing to distract you for a while from your distractions. And may God deny you peace, but give you glory![3]

---

3. Unamuno, *Tragic Sense of Life,* 330.

God has certainly delivered the first, but the second continues to be an open question. This little book is not intended as a handbook to slavishly imitate, but only as a summary of things to think about and a suggestion of when to think about them.

On the other hand, I am reminded of the advice of a series of mentors who guided me through the life and reflections of Augustine, whose most cherished image was the journey of the soul toward God. In the words of Roger Hazelton, "Augustine's theology is devotionally stimulated and oriented, just as his devotion is theologically sustained and controlled."[4] The same is true for me. Hope and intellect are inextricably bound together. Understanding cannot rest while the journey is incomplete. Spiritual life demands theological reflection.

---

4. Hazelton, "Devotional Life," 400.

Spirit

The "in" of the divine Spirit is an "out" for the human spirit.
—Paul Tillich[1]

---

1. Tillich, *Systematic Theology*, 3:112.

On Being Spiritually Present

Mentoring relationships are formed in the midst of life. They emerge from, and are sustained by, the busyness of living. Mentoring is not something undertaken on vacation, or at leisure, or whenever we can make time for it. Life is a constant existential dialogue. Questions constantly arise. Answers are constantly sought. Every "answer" provokes a new "question." Every question carries an implicit answer. Every situation is pregnant with meaning, no matter how trivial it may seem. When it comes to mentoring, there is no time like the present.

What does it mean to be spiritually present? Clearly it implies accessibility, availability, and the readiness to make time to relate to another human being. Today there is a great deal of talk about living in the *present*, in contrast to living in the past or the future. We speak of being physically present, mentally alert, and emotionally sensitive. Focus, pay attention, avoid distractions, get in touch with your body, your feelings, and your surroundings. See the other as a person to be understood and not an object to be used.

- Many consider living in the present as a state of *mindfulness.* We are aware of our external surroundings and our internal workings. We focus on breathing rather than doing. We step back from the "world" to center the self. Mindfulness is a gentle self-acceptance that inspires peaceful co-existence.

- Others consider living in the present as a *social responsibility.* To "be present" for another implies moral obligation. We are obliged to care for others and not just ourselves. We focus on justice. We prioritize the powerless. We engage the world now, as it is, and work to make the world a better place.

The attitude of living in the present today resonates with the advice of ancient stoics. The path to peace is to be content with yourself, honor the light of reason within, live harmoniously with others and the laws of nature, and be grateful for the universe and your place in it.

Is there anything unique about being *spiritually* present? Even if that includes mindfulness and social responsibility, is there something deeper here? Is there something more to mentoring than behaving as guru or social advocate? How is the mentor distinct from other important roles as counselor or therapist or social worker or priest?

Being spiritually present is different from "mindfulness" because it is never content with awareness. It is perpetually open to the future. The mentor is not so preoccupied with awareness as to be insensitive to transcendence. Gurus tend to be indifferent to change. Mentors value the present moment, but are open to, and expectant of, purposeful change.

Being spiritually present is different from "activism" because it is never confident about the achievement of permanent justice. It is always skeptical of success. The mentor is not so confident about human potential as to forget the necessity of grace. Activists tend to expect perfection. Mentors value social revolution, but are open to and expectant of personal transformation.

Being *spiritually present* is a behavior that is based on a different perception of reality. To *be spiritually present*, one must see reality as charged with spiritual presence. In one sense, this is a choice. Spirituality is an alternative interpretation of meaning that may be unconsciously inculcated by culture or consciously selected as counter-cultural. Yet in another sense, the perception of spiritual presence is not a choice, but an inevitability. The presence of Spirit is, as it were, thrust upon us. We may try to avoid it, and for extended periods of time we may be blind to it, but Spirit constantly and surprisingly interrupts our lives.

The interruptions of the Spirit may be pleasant. The moment we fall in love, marvel at nature, or create a work of art . . . and the moment we learn something new, make an intuitive leap of logic, discern a hidden truth, or transition into a new stage of life . . . we become aware of spiritual presence. The interruptions of the Spirit may be unpleasant. These may be moments of suffering, failure, doubt, powerlessness, and even humiliation. But whenever we realize that we are not in control, at the limits of our understanding, or at a boundary in our existence, we become aware of spiritual presence.

ON BEING SPIRITUALLY PRESENT

Whether by choice or compulsion, being spiritually present elevates intuition over rationalization. A philosophical tradition sometimes described as "Life Philosophy" began with Henri Bergson and influenced future thinkers like Pierre Teilhard de Chardin, Alfred North Whitehead, and Paul Tillich, as well as future environmental theorists. They all reject pure rationalism or technical reason as the only means with which to understand the world. Bergson wrote:

> By intuition is meant the kind of intellectual sympathy by which one places oneself within an object in order to coincide with what is unique in it and consequently inexpressible.[1]

He combined "intuition" (which recognized the internal relationships of all things in space) with a concept of "duration" (which recognized the internal relationships of events across time).

> Inner duration is the continuous life of a memory which prolongs the past into the present, the present either containing within a distinct form of the ceaselessly growing image of the past, or, more probably, showing by its continual change of quality the heavier and still heavier load we drag behind us as we get older. Without this survival of the past into the present there would be no duration, but only instantaneity.[2]

Bergson described the combination of intuition and duration in his concept of the vital force (*Élan vital*) uniting self-transcendence and self-conservation.

Once acknowledged personally, spiritual presence becomes more obvious socially. No matter how hard we try, or what algorithm we devise, we cannot predict (much less control) the future. We can count the cards and calculate probabilities, but the boundary between bad luck and good luck is always ambiguous. The boundary between fate and destiny, chance and providence is blurred by existence. We live on the verge of disaster and the edge of death. Yet at the same time we live on the verge of victory and the edge of life.

To *be spiritually present* implies a rejection of the adequacy of technical reason to interpret reality. By itself, it dehumanizes existence by reducing persons to facts. There must be a depth to reason that is not "irrational" but rather a recognition of something that precedes or transcends reason

---

1. Bergson, *Introduction to Metaphysics*, 7.
2. Bergson, *Introduction to Metaphysics*, 94.

in power and meaning. Therefore, to *be spiritually present* goes beyond mindfulness and social activism (as beneficial as these might be) to be sensitive to the very ground and power of being. It is the simultaneous assumption and expectation of revelation.

Society today is an extreme example of autonomous self-sufficiency. We allow ourselves to be governed by world-ruling techniques of rationalism, materialism, and an increasingly flawed confidence in progress. What is missing is the *hallowing of existence*.[3] This intuition of the Holy is what emerges when the structure of reason conflicts with the depth of reason, and we find ourselves on a quest for greater meaning and purpose. We are not forsaking reason, but we are open to ecstasy that is symbolically expressed through imagination and culture.

"Truth" is not a series of facts however logically constructed. It is not something we can ever possess or control. "Truth" is an unfolding process in time and space. It is an ongoing experience of "trueing" . . . becoming true.[4] But the "truth" constantly lies outside our minds. We know that life happens. We yearn to know what life means. That yearning is the perception of spiritual presence. "Spirit is a dimension of life that unites the power of being with the meaning of being."[5]

To be spiritually present, therefore, is to be aware of deeper meaning behind events and open to Spirit shaping and reshaping both personal experience and social history. This does not to belittle human reason and creativity but rather reinforces and accelerates both. For the very *impulse* to think rationally and the *desire* to act creatively is rooted in spiritual presence. To be spiritually present does not imply the seeming passivity of mindfulness, nor the activism of social justice, but both simultaneously. Being spiritually present is a precarious balance in living because spiritual presence is a paradoxical dimension of life.

Religion always attempts to make clear distinctions between the secular and the sacred, and even sets the one in confrontation with the other. Specific rites, objects, or persons are considered "sacramental," while all else is considered "profane." Spirituality, on the other hand, recognizes the blur between the secular and the sacred. Spirit is revealed through cultural

---

3. Tillich, *Religious Situation*, 47–48.

4. I was introduced to the idea of "trueing" early in my doctoral studies in Toronto in philosophical theology via the dialogue inspired by the theologian and Shakespearian scholar John Meagher, reflected in his later book *The Truing of Christianity*.

5. Tillich, *Systematic Theology*, 3:111.

forms but cannot be contained by cultural forms. Any activity, object, or person can be grasped by the Spirit to become "sacramental," just as even the most cherished rites of religious institutions can be abandoned by the Spirit and become "profane." Cultural forms can point toward Spirit but never become absolutely spiritual. To say this another way, the "secular city" and the "realm of God" overlap in mysterious and unexpected ways. Those who strive to be spiritually present recognize this ambiguity.

There are two elements to being spiritually present, which are not usually included in being physically present, mentally alert, and emotionally sensitive, nor in being morally responsible and socially active. Religion often identifies these characteristics as confessional faith and agapeic love but tends to limit these to particularly dogmatic affirmations or institutional programs. These are interpreted and evaluated by officially designated "sacred" authorities. Spirituality, on the other hand, broadens these characteristics to describe a way of being and becoming, revealed by Spirit, and encouraged through the mutual mentoring of the *pilgrim band*.

Optimystic Attitude

I first used this term twenty years ago in a mentoring relationship for the spiritual rehabilitation of a pastor. He had been professionally disgraced for misconduct but was now in a rigorous process of renewing spiritual credibility and restoring professional credentials. "Rehabilitation" is a good metaphor to describe the situation of many spiritual travelers today. The term is directly associated with recovery from substance abuse, correcting criminal behavior, and returning to "normal" life. But the term "rehabilitation" is also a good metaphor to describe the trajectory of many spiritual travelers who are transitioning from a lifestyle of despair, discouragement, or oppression to a new lifestyle of joy, hope, and empowerment.[6]

Traditional religion doesn't really have a term for "rehabilitation." Instead, the church combines a variety of abstract terms like "conversion," "atonement," and "sanctification" in a rather complex theology of sin and salvation. That has led the church into a confrontational relationship with culture. The church, by its very theological position, always tends to be exclusive. And the route to inclusion is very difficult and sometimes impossible. In the mentoring relationship I mention here, the pastor's career,

---

6. Bandy and Ratzlaff, *Christian Optimystics*.

marriage, and life were virtually destroyed by a "zero tolerance" institutional policy which, in the name of justice, contradicted the gospel of love.

In the broader, more inclusive, context of spirituality rather than religion, the mentor is in a very different position than the traditional priest or clergy. Mentors bring to every relationship an "optimystic attitude." This is the primary reason spiritual travelers in need of "rehabilitation" avoid institutional religious leaders whose attitudes are fundamentally pessimistic and legalistic. The term "optimystic" combines two different ideas.

The word "opti" is the ancient term for *choice* or *intentionality*, in contrast to behavior that is automatic or instinctive. Mentors are hopeful *by choice*, but not necessarily *by nature*. Their overall experience with the world may be negative (which often gives the appearance of depression or pessimism), but their *choice* is to be positive. Hope is not a trait of personality or a remnant of cultural identity. It is a choice that is often made against all odds. It is an indefatigable hope that is renewed even in times of seeming hopelessness.

The term "mystic" is the ancient word that describes someone who apprehends truth beyond appearances. This is someone who sees deeper meaning beyond rational reasoning. Mystics are not illogical. Indeed, mystics may be among the most logical and scientific thinkers. Yet they are not content with reason, because the human mind cannot contain universal truth. It can only grasp partial truth. The mystic experiences reality as open to symbolic signification and creative interpretation.

Yet the term "mystic" implies more than the ability to "read the signs" of significance. The mystic is also one who is likely to be *grasped* by the ultimate meaning that is beyond the control of the human being. My mentors understood the universal significance of symbols as "Ultimate Concern," but that term is too limited, too abstract and rational, to convey the mystical experience. Instead, my mentors understood the ecstatic experience of awareness (the Kairos or "Aha!" moment) as the revelation of the "Power of Being." God reaches *through* symbols to convey truth. The *content* of a symbol is one thing. The *import* of a symbol is quite another. The symbol becomes a portal through which the infinite penetrates the finite and lifts the finite to participate in infinite significance.

Being spiritually present, then, is about having an optimystic attitude. And this attitude is not a "natural" one. It is a choice, and sometimes a radical and foolish choice. It is, therefore, an act of existential courage, or, as my mentor suggests, the "courage to be." Perhaps you might say it is a reasonable decision to be unreasonable. I indicated in a previous chapter how different lifestyle segments are motivated by different anxieties in their quest for God. They initially gravitate to spiritual leaders because they model the kind of courage they themselves require facing life.

The role of the mentor is not that of a guru or a seer. One's consciousness is not just "taken over" by the supernatural, and you do not simplistically become a mere mouthpiece for a ghost from beyond. The mentor chooses to courageously speak insightfully about the present, and positively about the future, by combining a reasonable interpretation of historical events with an intuition of the greater import of those events. This is what the ancients called "wisdom."

Unassuming Amity

The second element to being spiritually present has to do with love, but the term has been applied in so many ways (profound and trivial) that it must be qualified in the context of spirituality. The classical distinctions we learn in public school define love as *eros* (desire or sexuality), *phileos* (friendship or companionship), and *agape* (selflessness or self-sacrifice), and as we grow up, we realize that the boundaries between these experiences are constantly blurred ... perhaps so vague and inconsistent as to be unrecognizable. Institutional religion tends to attribute the first and second to human nature (negatively or positively) and the third to divine nature (achievable by humans in a limited way and only through grace). Yet being spiritually present is not about love expressed in any of these ways, but as a state of being prior to all of these experiences.

The mentoring relationship is based on an unassuming amity between mentor and mentee. And I would argue that it is this unassuming amity which is the real quest for spiritual travelers. They may *mistake* other forms of love for unassuming amity, but soon discover that such forms of love are not as helpful in their quest for meaning and purpose as they think. For some, the quest is *romantic*, and they are constantly searching for the perfect sexual partner. For others, the quest is *philanthropic*, and they are constantly searching for the perfect teammate. And for still others, the quest is *tragic*, and they are constantly searching for a savior. All these prove unsatisfying.

Similarly, there is constant temptation for the mentoring relationship to devolve into one of these sidetracks of love. The intimacy of mentoring *might* lead to a sexual relationship. The helpfulness of mentoring *might* lead to partnership in a social service organization. The idealism of a mentoring relationship *might* lead to an unhealthy co-dependency. But it does not have to be sidetracked if we are clear about what love really means in the context of spirituality.

The Greek word for love that is perhaps closest to my meaning is *pragma*. It is a relationship of trust that is in essence "pragmatic." Practicality is more fundamental than romance, service, or even sacrifice. Partners in the relationship have a sense that they have more to lose traveling separately than together. It is to their individual advantage for personal growth that they continue in conversation.

Love expressed in a mentoring relationship is *unassuming*. That is to say, mentors do not assume that they are attractive, righteous, or even necessary for the journey of the spiritual traveler. They are simply there, they can be helpful, and they care about the quest for meaning and purpose. Meanwhile, mentees do not presume that a mentor will always be there, can always be helpful, and can answer all questions. The mentoring relationship is an urgent, significant conversation between travelers who pass each other, or temporarily accompany each other, down the road.

Being spiritually present is a state of *non-neediness*. Mentor and mentee value each other but do not *need* each other. Pastors and counselors are all too familiar with "needy" parishioners and counselees. They are entirely focused on themselves, constantly demand attention, and are incapable of saying goodbye. The challenge in a mentoring relationship is not quite the same as what psychologists mean by "self-differentiation." This is because "self" is not really part of the equation. There is only "differentiation." Yes, there is usually recognition of lifestyle compatibility and empathy with the life struggles of another person. Nevertheless, there is no personal stake in the outcome of the relationship one way or another. If the relationship is helpful, well and good. If it is not helpful, there is no need for personal regret or recrimination.

The state of non-neediness is as close as we might come to an egoless relationship. Unassuming amity brings no personal expectations to the relationship beyond basic respect. It is based on the premise of accepting people as they are, and not as one wants them to be. It is approached with the assumption that two parties each quest for meaning and purpose in their lives . . . but no assumption that the meaning and purpose of one's life should be the same meaning and purpose for another life.

Personally, I have never been able to fully realize a purely ego-less relationship or fully achieve the state of non-neediness. There is always, for me, an element of pride or self-satisfaction, or a sense of disappointment or regret, in every relationship. I always look back thinking that "I wish I would have said this . . ." or "I'm glad I realized that . . . ." Indeed, I have only met two people in my life who I think did realize this state. One was a patriarch (archbishop) of the Greek Orthodox Church, and the other was a janitor in an industrial warehouse.

Together, optimystic attitude and unassuming amity make those who seek to be spiritually present catalysts for hope. They are on a journey that starts with the awareness of Spirit (immanence) in and through culture. This is a process of intuition rather than analysis. The presence of the Spirit is never *deduced*, but it is always *suspected*. It is experienced as a constant or chronic discontent, the suspicion that there is something of greater significance lying beyond the obvious materialistic finitude of the world.

I remember vividly an "ecstatic" moment fifty years ago walking in a pine forest near Princeton University, as I mentally prepared to begin doctoral research and tutoring responsibilities in Toronto. Perhaps it was akin to Bergson's sensitivity to vital force as "intuition" and "duration." But I suddenly understood the tension between freedom and limitation that requires resolution. I remember how excited I was to tell friends my thoughts about how freedom mediates power and limitation mediates meaning. And I remember their bewilderment about what I meant and why I should be so animated about it.

The journey that begins with awareness of the immanence of Spirit continues in the daily process of living life alongside others who are also living their own lives. The sense of freedom or autonomy empowers us to extend our influence and take control of our destinies. Yet while freedom is exhilarating, the mere exercise of will is aimless and egocentric. The complex network of relationships between people, within culture, bound by the physical world, limits our freedom. These limitations help us understand the relevance and significance of our lives for the world. Yet extreme limitation erodes our freedom and renders us powerless. Both absolute freedom and absolute limitation lead to hopelessness.

The ambiguity of living between power and limitation, or between freedom and meaning, can be interpreted in different ways. It is the tension between controlling your own destiny (autonomy) and your destiny controlled by outside forces (heteronomy). It is the tension between radical subjectivism and radical objectivism, or the tension between ego or outside authority as the final arbiter of truth, or the tension between self or selflessness as ultimate concern. Hope lies in a resolution that my mentors have variously described as "theonomy."

> The permanent struggle between autonomous independence and heteronomous reaction leads to the quest for a new theonomy, both in particular situations and in the depth of the cultural consciousness in general. This quest is answered by the impact of the Spiritual Presence on culture. Wherever this impact is effective, theonomy is created, and wherever there is theonomy, traces of the impact of the Spiritual Presence are visible.[7]

My point, however, is that the hope of theonomy is not only historical and cultural but also relational and personal. It is a potential that emerges in and through the mutual mentoring relationships of the *pilgrim band.*

The journey carries the spiritual traveler beyond the tension of freedom and limitation to reunion with Spirit. Such transcendence can only be expressed metaphorically in song, poetry, or image. Those who are spiritually *present* are those who anticipate the spiritual *future.* The end of the trajectory of hope is the final consummation of peace. This is not just a "passive" serenity of the individual, but also an "active" harmony in society as a whole. It may be experienced as mindfulness at one time, and as social action at another time. Peace is only experienced in fragments (often unexpected and surprising) by those who are spiritually present, but such experiences renew their courage and hope.

What does it mean to be spiritually present? It means more than being conversant on the topic of spiritual presence. It implies a way of life, or at the very least, a fundamental attitude toward living. If you strive to live intentionally spiritually present, you can expect to live in both acute and systemic ambivalence with society.

Acute ambivalence with society means that spiritual pilgrims are likely to be directly criticized or attacked from two different directions.

First, the desire to be spiritually present is attacked by radical secularity. These critics reject both religion and spirituality. The former is dismissed as political manipulation of the world and the latter as psychological delusion in the individual. It emerges, for example, among some scientific and health care circles in which truth simply means facts, and facts must be

---

7. Tillich, *Systematic Theology*, 3:252.

verified by empirical analysis. "Spirit" is an intellectual evasion in the first circle and an unhealthy deception in the latter.

Those who would be spiritually present respond by pointing out the inner contradiction of radical secularity. This is the contradiction between how we think and how we live. It is not just that we consistently live by making decisions based on subjectivity rather than objectivity, but that we *instinctively* do so. We can refuse to do what is "correct" to do what we believe, deep inside, to be *right*. We can choose to see beauty when everyone else sees ugliness. The moment the human being says, "I choose," the human mind transcends itself. We can deny the obvious, imagine the improbable, and risk all for the impossible. Thinking is an expression of the power of being. Descartes is often quoted as saying, "I think, therefore I am." He had it backward. "I am; therefore, I think."

Second, the desire to be spiritually present is attacked by radical supernaturalism. These critics fear the inherent ambiguities in spirituality and retreat into the supposed certainties of religion. Since there is no room for ambiguity, this group falls back on authority. It is not just that the Bible or some other book is interpreted literally, but that only certain people are empowered to interpret it correctly. Religious extremism in any religious tradition is based on the notion that "truth" can be grasped by a properly indoctrinated human being.

The response, of course, is to observe that "truth" grasps the human being. The subsequent ambiguity in every claim to own the truth means that *authority* must be replaced by *community*. That is, the search for truth becomes a joint effort in which the whole of humankind participates. That participation is a constant conversation. "Agreement" is only a temporary rest from perpetual dialogue. And that dialogue is not in the form of arguments between rival claimants of truth, but rather in the form of conversation between equally earnest seekers of truth. The response to those who say, "I know" in relation to what they believe is to say, "I think" in relation to how we live.

Both threats to being spiritually present are forms of dogmatism. The origin of dogmatism is not this or that claim about truth, but rather a fundamental disrespect of another person. The radically secular group can only be angry or condescending. The radically supernatural group can only be critical or combative. Both exercise a form of self-righteousness that contrasts sharply with the unassuming amity of the one who is spiritually present. Both reveal an ultimate pessimism about life that contrasts sharply with the optimystic attitude of the one who is spiritually present.

Lest this sounds too abstract and theoretical, those who are spiritually present can focus the debate to be more realistic and practical. What is at stake is not just our understanding of truth, but our confidence in justice. Both the radically secular and the radically supernatural entrench subject/object dualism to the point of intolerance. People are treated as objects (whether as entities or ideologies to be manipulated), rather than subjects (beings of inherent value). It is not just religious extremism that creates holocausts, but scientific extremism as well. Both groups attempt to deny or avoid the fundamental tension between freedom and limitation that is the nature of finitude and that shapes culture. Radical secularists exaggerate freedom over limitation, rendering the moral imperative a matter of opinion. Radical supernaturalists exaggerate limitation over freedom, rendering the moral imperative a matter of ideological assent.

The act of being *spiritually present* is to curb power with justice, but in tension with love. This is only possible if subject-object dualism is overcome by Spirit. For human beings cannot fully participate in the lives of each other unless each participates in spiritual presence. This is always ambiguous under the conditions of finitude, but it is a fundamental principle for the spiritual traveler.

While criticism can be *acute* from both sources of dogmatism, pilgrims more routinely experience *systemic* ambivalence with society. No matter where they go, what they do, or with whom they associate, the pilgrim is never quite *in sync* with culture. Just as Spirit simultaneously employs and shatters any cultural form as a vehicle for meaning, so also the pilgrim is constantly using and discarding, or at the very least constantly changing and adapting, cultural forms to sustain meaning and purpose. No one form can be unconditional. No one symbol or spiritual practice is indispensable.

This explains the pilgrim's ambivalent relationship with religious structures, liturgies, and organizations. What is helpful now may become unhelpful later. This is not just because one might outgrow a particular religious form or practice, but because the impact of the Holy through any form or practice is reduced with familiarity. At some point, a religious form or practice presumes on our unconscious to be sacred rather than signifying or channeling the sacred. Any form or practice of religion can be unconsciously elevated to Ultimate Concern, and Spirit itself will break the idolatry. Surprise is more important to being spiritually present than continuity.

On the other hand, this explains why the pilgrim is constantly seeking, creating, or experimenting with other cultural forms and religious practices. Even though Spirit cannot be contained by any form or practice, it is only revealed and experienced through some form or practice. We cannot live in a manner that is spiritually present without them. Form reveals import. But import is only experienced indirectly through form. Continuity is more important than surprise.

The ambivalence toward religious structures, liturgies, and organizations is equally felt toward any secular form, career, or organization. Therefore, the pilgrim always has the sense that they are never permanently settled. They are always in transition. They are not defined by any relationship, job, social position, or functional role. They are restless for growth, curious to learn, open to surprise, and thirsty for God.

This *systemic* ambivalence to society is probably more common than any *acute* ambivalence with society because most of our associates in life are not on the radical fringe but among the moderate middle. It is in the relationships of the pilgrim's life, rather than in any given function or status, or any given membership or activity, that we see the greatest continuity that sustains meaning. For pilgrims tend not to gravitate toward people who are dogmatists or dilettantes, but rather toward those who are seriously experimenting with ideas and radically committed to the quest for meaning and purpose.

On Faithfulness

THROUGHOUT THIS JOURNEY I have made distinctions between religious *institutions* and religious *movements*, and specifically between the Christian *church* and Christianity as a *movement*. There are important theological nuances behind these distinctions. Institutionalization implies solidity, continuity, or reliability. We rely on institutions to guarantee certainty and control behavior. Movements imply fluidity, change, and unpredictability. We participate in movements to guide us through ambiguity and encourage imagination. Institutions require hierarchies and governance. Movements require partnerships and mentoring.

Just as institutions tend to fix religion in space (locations, buildings, doctrines, and policies), so also the institutional church tends to anthropomorphize God. We assign metaphoric titles (like *Lord* or *Father*) or use pronouns (like *he* or *she*) to talk about God. We tend to visualize Christ as a historical figure, invisible friend, or supernatural bodyguard. Christianity as *movement*, however, best describes God as *Spirit*. God is everywhere, all the time, with everyone, influencing every event. God may be transcendent and unknowable, but Christ is the experience of God's immanence. Thus, the Christian *movement* is sensitive to incarnational experiences beyond our control or understanding but crucial to hope and well-being.

Divine immanence is existential, not merely emotional. What does that mean? It means that God is in the midst of existence in all of its physical, rational, and emotional aspects. God is in the most microscopic diversity of humanity just as God is in the most macroscopic harmony of the universe. God is in and between spaces and God is in and inside the passage of time, which is to say that God is omnipresent. No matter how different each human being might be, God is there because God is Spirit. The *Power of Being* is the source of life but revealed in the activity of living. People often associate the immanence of God with a particular emotion that is evoked by some natural occurrence. But emotion is only a sign of divine immanence, and not a reliable sign at that. God is just as "immanent" in sadness as in joy, in boredom as in ecstasy, in suffering as in contentment.

Modernity was a period of increasing *inertia*. Postmodernity is a period of *animation*. I deliberately refer you to the discussion of postmodernity available in Wikipedia, rather than any single historian's point of view, because that is where most postmodern people would look for understanding. Wikipedia suggests two phases of postmodernity:[1] the first in the 1940s and 1950s when analog limited media channels; and the second starting in the 1960s and 1970s when cable television and new forms of digital media accelerated and expanded access to information. Not only the internet but mass migrations prompted by war and environmental change have magnified the transition between eras even more dramatically. Institutional religion cannot keep pace much less maintain control.

Inertia describes the way things were, when people sank roots, accepted the limitations of space and time, defined themselves by simple demographic categories, and resisted change. We valued and preserved the solidity of life. *Movement* describes the way things have become, as people uproot, break out of the limitations of space and time, describe themselves in evolving lifestyles, and embrace (courageously or anxiously) inevitable change. We value and celebrate the fluidity of life.

This transition from modernity to postmodernity has not eliminated our need for God. It has magnified our need for Spirit. And it has changed how we deal with God and cope with each other. The new normal is that life is unpredictable, and God is uncontrollable. Life is well beyond our ability to manage it, and God is well outside the box in which we tried to contain "him" or "her." The difference between inertia and movement is accelerating:

- Religion to spirituality
- Christ to incarnational experience
- Certainty to mystery
- Truth to trueing
- Institutional church to *pilgrim band*

---

1. Wikipedia, "Postmodernity."

In short, the quest for meaning and purpose is no longer about finding firm ground on which to stand, but about guiding our kayak through the white waters of change.

Yet another implication of the transition from modernity to postmodernity is the shift in emphasis from *faith* to *faithfulness*. *Faith* is a subject to be studied, a set of doctrines to be affirmed, and a series of propositions to answer every question. But *faithfulness* is an activity to be pursued, an assortment of experiences to be interpreted, and an endless series of questions seeking answers. While the congregation used to recite creeds, the *pilgrim band* is more likely to sing songs. The songs might be in any musical genre, using many different metaphors, but the key themes might include:

- We believe in Spirit revealed in many ways, in many religions, and always a mystery.
- We believe Spirit is present in you and me and all of us, in everything and every event.
- We believe the Spirit embraces the best and worst of us, and in the best and worst of times.

"Faith" is about inertia. "Faithfulness" is about movement. The former gives us permission to *manage* meaning. We can drop in or drop out when life becomes too difficult, too tiring, too lonely, too expensive, or just plain *too much*. The latter imposes an unconditional urgency to find meaning and purpose regardless of what happens. Life is more complicated than we ever can realize. God is bigger than we can ever contain. Human life—and one's personal living—has more significance than we can imagine. *We* have a destiny. *I* have a destiny. We cannot be content for long. We are restless for more.

> As harts long for flowing streams, so does my heart long for Thee.
>
> My soul thirsts for God, for the living God.
>
> How long, Holy One, until I see you face to face?
>
> Deep calls to deep at the thunder of your cataracts; all your waves and billows have washed over me.
>
> And yet by day you command your steadfast love, and at night your song is within me . . .
>
> a constant prayer to the God of my life.

> Why are you cast down, O my soul, and why are you disquieted within me?
>
> Hope in the Holy One, and I shall again praise God who helps me.[2]

I think the best metaphor to describe the spiritual traveler is that he or she is *thirsty*. Their thirst is never quite quenched. They may travel through deserts, but they keep looking for an oasis. They never remain at an oasis, but they are compelled to follow the star.

Just as ancient travelers used the astrolabe and a compass, and modern travelers rely on global positioning satellites, so also spiritual travelers can navigate their journey through life. Mentors equip mentees to use these tools for navigation, and mentees will pass the art on to those who follow.

The greatest challenge for navigation historically has been the calculation of distance for east-west travel (longitude). Travelers could calculate the distance of north-south travel (latitude) using the stars. Navigation east-west was hazardous until the invention of accurate clocks. GPS is basically the synchronization to a millisecond of interconnected satellites orbiting the Earth that can not only observe the stars but pinpoint in minutes and seconds the exact east-west location of any traveler. Navigation is a combination of observing space and time.

In the same way, spiritual navigation is accomplished through observations across space and time. To be sure, this navigation is more *approximation* than *certainty*. Nevertheless, the mentoring relationship can offer the spiritual traveler a sense of *where* they are, and *when* they are, and *where* they are going during their quest for meaning and purpose. There are still going to be sidetracks (winds that blow you off course), roadblocks (reefs that lurk under water), and deadweights (anchors holding us back). And there are still going to be vicious cycles (cyclones?) interrupting and endangering progress. Yet through it all, the mentoring relationship can rely on certain tools for navigation to help the traveler know whether or not they are getting closer to, or farther away, from their destiny.

The diagram below is my best effort so far to illustrate this tool for navigation that helps travelers keep track of their walk and their work for meaning and purpose. Call it my "astrolabe" for the spiritual life.[3]

---

2. My paraphrase of Ps 42:1–11.

3. A similar alignment can be used to define the functions of non-profit organizations. Compare this to my book *Strategic Thinking*, 183–89.

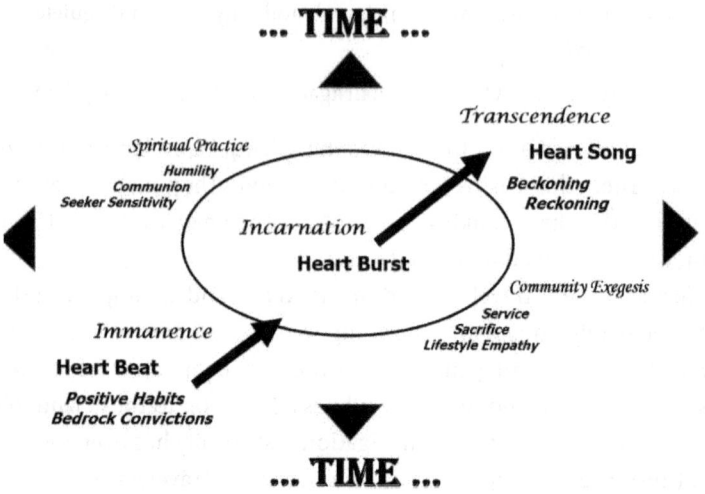

The spiritual journey is, theoretically, a straight line outward into the physical world, through culture, and onward toward God. Each traveler starts out in life with dispositions, habits, and attitudes. Each traveler progresses at different speeds, through ambiguous circumstances, shaped by multiple cultures. And as each traveler experiences incarnational events and discerns meaning, they gain a clearer sense of purpose and destiny that bring them closer to God. Spirit moves, influences, and breathes life into the entire process. The point of pilgrimage is to align one's soul to the nature of the divine. Life is most satisfying when there is an alignment between *heartbeat, heartburst,* and *heartsong.* The challenge of living is that this alignment is constantly going astray, and the role of the *pilgrim band* is to help us make navigational corrections and keep going.

Heartbeat

The beating heart is the *sign* of life, even though life itself is invisible. As travelers start their journey with the *pilgrim band*, God (or Spirit) is present for the spiritual traveler in two ways. I think of this as the spiritual "heartbeat" of an individual. It is, metaphorically speaking, the double rhythm that centers one's lifestyle. You take your pulse to discern your authentic self. This is not as easy as it sounds, for "heart rate" varies from individual to individual and changes from circumstance to circumstance. What is normative for one person may not be normative for another. The mentoring relationship helps a spiritual traveler discern his or her personal authenticity.

Blood pressure is measured using two numbers. *Systolic* measures the pressure on one's arteries at each beat. *Diastolic* measures the pressure between beats. Metaphorically, this is like the heartbeat of one's life. Authenticity is a dynamic that compares life under stress and life at rest. Together these are the signs of life. These are the reflections of the Power of Being and the Ground of Being. God is as close to us as our beating hearts.

One way to measure an individual's authenticity is to observe his or her "core values." These are the habits that are revealed in both conscious and unconscious behavior. I think of this as the "diastolic" measure of authenticity when life is observed "between beats." God's immanence is revealed in our moral attitudes and expectations and in our ethical behavior. Just as physical blood pressure can be altered by exercise, so also moral "blood pressure" can be altered by service and self-discipline.

Since I am a Christian, I will use St. Paul's description of the "fruits of the Spirit" as an example. The signs of an authentic Christian living in the immanence of God include behaving lovingly, joyously, peacefully, patiently, kindly, righteously, faithfully, gently, and respectfully. He contrasts this with negative habits of living spitefully, pessimistically, angrily, impatiently, cruelly, wrongfully, disloyally, meanly, divisively, etc.[4] (Similar contrasts in moral behavior can be found in all world religions.) Paul is aware that people always fall short of perfection, but the point is that a person can *exercise* (discipline themselves) to model one set of behavior patterns rather than another. When they fail, they can regret, be reassured of acceptance, and be helped to avoid making the same mistake again.

This, then, is the "diastolic" measure of the moral behavior of a spiritual traveler. It is the behavior they strive to model in daily living. They reveal their fundamental moral attitudes and strive to live up to ethical standards. Sometimes this is revealed in daring deeds. But more often this is revealed in the spontaneous behavior of everyday living. A life that reveals the "fruits of the Spirit" in daily living is the aspiration of the spiritual traveler, and a mentoring relationship helps one sustain moral discipline. It is one sign of the immanence of God.

A second way to measure an individual's authenticity is to observe his or her "bedrock beliefs." These are the deeply held convictions to which an individual automatically turns for strength in times of trouble.

---

4. My paraphrase of Gal 5:19–21.

I think of this as the "systolic" measure of authenticity when life is observed under stress. The heart beats faster when a person is in trouble, enduring adversity, facing some threat, struggling with some acute problem, or fighting some enemy. The person *automatically* (which is to say, unthinkingly, immediately, and urgently) turns to some conviction that gives them hope and courage.

This conviction may be expressed in words. Perhaps they recall a biblical or liturgical phrase; or a poem, song, or battle cry; or a name, prayer, or confession of faith. Perhaps they recall an image or heroic figure. Perhaps they hold a talisman, get a tattoo, or flee to some mental or physical refuge. These convictions are not abstract theological concepts or institutional dogmas, but ideas or symbols that are instinctively meaningful. They are convictions for which they make major sacrifices and which help them endure great suffering.

This, then, is the "systolic" measure of the faithfulness of a spiritual traveler. These become a kind of collage of faith that shapes relationships, careers, and other life choices. The convictions that inspire hope are often revealed in the décor in a person's home, or the jewelry that they wear, or icons and images used in technology. They are very personal, yet individuals are often unaware of their presence or power. The mentoring relationship helps the spiritual traveler uncover and understand what motivates their journey.

Motivation and *emotion* are associated with the "systolic" side of authentic heartbeat. They are critical in times of stress when the pressures of life seem overwhelming or when one lives on the edge of the unknown. The Power of Being inspires hope and instills courage. It stimulates persistence, perseverance, endurance, and determination. It inspires a "Can do!" attitude. Pilgrims are empowered to take risks, make great sacrifices, stake one's life for a moral principle or person in need.

Reflection and *reverie* are associated with the diastolic side of authentic heartbeat. They are critical in times of peace when life seems balanced or when one lives in relative serenity. "Reflection" does not just imply meditation but mirroring. The Ground of Being aligns thought and action to demonstrate or reveal God's immanence in everyday occurrences. Pilgrims see social and personal history in its "cinematographic" character as a flow of interrelated, significant events.[5]

---

5. Bergson, *Creative Evolution*, 322.

The "heartbeat" of the spiritual traveler is a tension between action and contemplation. It balances the stress of "life-on-the-edge" with the rest of "life-at-peace." This means that pilgrimage itself is an expression of "life-in-between." It is Spirit experienced under the conditions of existence characterized by ambiguity on the one hand and hope on the other.

Heartburst

The difference between immanence and incarnation is that the former is pure and the latter is paradoxical. The Power of Being is briefly visible in and through some cultural form (organic or inorganic). This person or object is more than a symbol that *reminds* us of the Holy, but it becomes a portal through which the infinite enters the finite to create a "sacred" space or Kairos moment in which the fullness of God is present to our sense of sight, sound, smell, taste, or touch.

Consider, for example, great portraiture. In late antiquity, portraits of an individual would be painted on a coffin at burial to recognize the *significance* of a loved one that endured after death. In the Renaissance, a painting by Rembrandt or sculpture by Michelangelo revealed the soul hidden behind the features of a person. In Eastern Orthodox iconography, the stylized image of Jesus funneled attention to the eyes that seemed to stare at an individual and lay bare their secrets.

When the disciples walked with Jesus, they felt that his physical presence revealed the fullness of God. This is epitomized in the story of the transfiguration of Jesus. His physical form is changed into a glorious light that transcends space and time. He is seen in the company of Moses and Elijah. But the moment the disciples suggest constructing booths to contain these revelations, the vision disappears. No cultural form can contain God's fullness for long. Jesus the Christ becomes a paradox, and for Christians, the paradigm of "God-with-Us."

There are two methods in a mentoring relationship that help spiritual travelers experience incarnation. These are methods that use cultural forms as portals to infinite meaning . . . or, perhaps better stated, these are methods used by God as portals to reveal infinite significance.

Although institutional religion and contemporary scholarship have tended to separate biblical exegesis from incarnational experience, ancient role models and contemporary spiritual travelers understand that biblical exegesis (or, indeed, the interpretation of all sacred texts) and community exegesis are two sides of the same coin. Just as the Spirit is revealed through the histories and writings of our spiritual ancestors, so also the Spirit is revealed through the stories and lifestyles of the publics living around us.

In an earlier chapter, I described the difference between demographic and lifestyle research. The former provides the bare bones of public trends but says little about how diverse people live their lives. The latter tracks the digital footprints of individual households and reveals their habits and attitudes. The more spiritual travelers empathize with diverse groups of people, the more they discern their hopes and fears and understand their religious practices and spiritual needs. The result is what I call a *heartburst*. At some point of deepening empathy, the traveler begins to laugh or weep alongside someone outside of their normal circle of friends. The traveler feels a surge of urgency to reach out and bless another human being. It is just this kind of *heartburst* that caused medieval pilgrims to pause their journeys to found hostels and hospitals.

Historians Philippe Aries and Georges Duby have done "community exegesis" in reference to the past. Their series of books entitled *A History of Private Life* traces lifestyle behavior from ancient to modern times.[6] Reading the table of contents is just like reading the behavioral traits tracked digitally today: intimacy and marriage, gender and sexuality, family and child-rearing, honor and secrecy, customs and traditions, civility and taste, work and leisure, pleasure and excess, liberty and slavery, prejudice and social class, private and public space, habitations and cohabitations, moral postures and religious practices, death and dying, and more.

Community exegesis is the study of the panorama of private life and what this can reveal about the human quest for meaning and purpose. It is rooted in observation, empathy, and intuition. It is "subjective" in the sense that all conclusions are tentative, but it is "objective" in the sense that insights are based on the collected evidence of behavior and the collective reflections of experienced and empathic observers. One pursues biblical exegesis that is rooted in the cumulative insights of respected observers from across religious traditions and cultures . . . in communion with Spirit. One pursues community exegesis that is rooted in the cumulative research of respected mentors from across religious traditions and public sectors . . . in communion with the Spirit.

Community exegesis brings the spiritual traveler face-to-face—and soul-to-soul—with the private lives of people they encounter along the

---

6. Aries and Duby, *History of Private Life*, 5 vols.

way. It is like a great portrait. Some of my favorite portraits are in the Art Institute of Chicago. For example, go and view:

- *Two Sisters (On the Terrace)* by Renoir
- *Beata Beatrix* by Rossetti
- *Beggar with a Duffle Coat* by Manet
- *The Captive Slave* by John Philip Simpson
- *Portrait of Madame Anne-Jeanne Cassanéa de Mondonville, née Boucon* by Latour
- *Max Herrmann-Neisse* by Ludwig Meidner

The artistic styles are different, but in each case a great portrait reveals the inner life of a stranger. You sense the reality of their lives. You glimpse their feelings of contentment or discontentment, joy or sorrow. Moreover, in a great portrait you see them "in situ" . . . in the context of their microculture. They are surrounded by cultural forms that mediate meaning and purpose to their lives. And your heart goes out to them.

The discovery (or recovery?) of mutual love is what the experience of *heartburst* is all about. The most profound empathy is a relationship in which the self is lost in concern for the other. Yet the most profound empathy is impossible for humans to achieve on their own.

- For one thing, *heartburst* (by definition) is specific and not universal. One does not have a *heartburst* for the world or for humankind in general. One has a *heartburst* in *this* situation for *this* individual or group, but not in *that* situation for *that* individual or group. That universal *heartburst* may be true for God, but we are not God. The human heart cannot burst for everything, for everyone, all the time. *Heartburst* is tied to the incarnation of "God-among-Us" here and now, but not necessarily over there and tomorrow. Metaphorically speaking, we must see Christ anew every day, in different situations, among different people. In a sense, the traveler connects with a stranger in mutual love one day at a time and one lifestyle group at a time.

- For another thing, there is always some residual instinct for self-preservation in even the most passionate *heartburst*. Humans are not really capable of *pure* philanthropy. If we are truly honest with ourselves, there is always some personal benefit to our generosity. Perhaps it is penance for previous indifference, or satisfaction in helping others, but the ego does *gain something* when the *heart bursts* for another. Indeed, the wisdom of counselors and philanthropists is that to wholly identify oneself with the other eventually defeats the purpose of mutual love. What starts out as service becomes self-centeredness all over again.

This is why incarnational experience (the experience of "God-among-Us") is so important to the spiritual journey. It is this divine immanence that elevates humans above finitude and beyond the limitations of history.

Among Christians, the cross is the primary symbol of sacrificial love, but the symbol can vary from religion to religion. (Consider, for example, the international symbols of hope and healing in the "Red Cross" and "Red Crescent.") While *heartburst* is the epitome of human agape, Jesus the Christ is the epitome of divine agape. The former is only fulfilled in the latter. Different lifestyle groups are driven by different existential anxieties in their quest for God, and different kinds of incarnational experiences are catalysts of hope. As human yearning reaches up, so also does divine grace reach down, to "join hands" or at least "touch fingertips" that connect the finite and the infinite, my history and God's purpose.

Sacrificial love is not only counter-cultural but also counter-contextual. It is counter-cultural because it transcends lifestyle. The empathy of mutual love occurs in a system of compatibilities. These compatibilities may or may not be obvious, but the connections of mutual love thrive by discovering bridges of shared behavior, attitude, need, and other cultural forms. Sacrificial love dispenses with compatibilities to embrace even the incompatibilities of a relationship. Sacrificial love is, therefore, counter-contextual. Friendship begins and ends within a given situation limited by space and time. Sacrificial love does not leave any relationship behind but carries it forward in the spiritual journey. Paradoxically, the mentoring relationship begins with a quest for self-fulfillment and ends with an attitude of self-forgetfulness.

Heartsong

The "straight line" from *heartbeat* to *heartburst* to *heartsong* is a trajectory of love that takes us out of ourselves, through history, and beyond history to the reunion of the loving soul with the loving God. The reality and hope of this trajectory is the transition from mutual love, through sacrificial love, to divine love. The goal of mentoring is to guide the spiritual traveler from self-interest, through self-sacrifice, to self-forgetfulness and by so doing transcend their own history into a legacy of grace.

The inner life of the spiritual traveler, and the outward journey of the pilgrim band, is a flow of experience across space and time that is driven by the vital force of Spirit. It flows from the immanence of God in the human soul that is intuited by the seeker or traveler. It enters personal and social history and the ever-changing cultural forms that symbolize or convey meaning and purpose. These are incarnational experiences in which the finite and infinite paradoxically intersect. But it also flows beyond history to envision or anticipate the reunion of the soul with God. This experience of transcendence may only be occasional and temporary, but the spiritual traveler can catch glimpses of personal destiny and even the destination of life itself.

In recent decades it has been trendy to talk about "vision" and "mission." People are encouraged to "get a vision" and write a personal mission statement. The assumption is that once a person has clarified their "vision" they can then lead a meaningful life. And once a person has clarified their personal mission, they can use that as a tool to make future choices. I think in practice the opposite is true.

- In my experience, vision emerges from the chaos and quest of living. It only emerges once you have greater clarity about your authentic self (accountable to ethical standards and reliant on bedrock convictions), followed by investment in diversity (lifestyle groups in proximate relationship).

- Similarly, a personal mission statement that seems quite clear today is reshaped tomorrow and evolves through the act of living. It does not emerge from a series of career moves or job changes, but through a changing network of positive or negative relationships in all aspects of life.

A vision for life and personal mission statement are valuable, provided one realizes that they are never complete. The images are reworked, and the words are revised. The import that lies behind the vision has facets yet to be revealed, and the meaning that lies behind the words have interpretations yet to be discovered. The Spirit is never done shaping your life.

We like to imagine that we can control, invent, create, or (in common church growth jargon), *cast* vision for the future. But a true artist will always say that authentic vision comes from beyond themselves. We do not *cast* vision. Vision is *cast at us*. Perhaps we picture ourselves as anglers casting a lure, attached to a fishing line, into a pond to attract a fish. The outcome depends on our skill and ingenuity. Yet the truth is that you and I are the fish, not the fisherman. God is casting the lure, attached to the line, and coaxing us to bite.

Now we see the limitation of the diagram I offered earlier as a kind of spiritual "astrolabe" to guide one's spiritual journey. The arrows point upward from lower left to upper right, as if we were in control of our inward and outward journeys. That makes sense if our point of view is from within history. Yet once we realize the quest for meaning and purpose leads us beyond history, our perception is reversed. The arrows should go the other way. For it is only because divine transcendence becomes divine immanence that we are compelled to start the spiritual journey in the first place. We thought we were pursuing God. In reality, God was pursuing us.

Although it is ultimately impossible to capture vision in words, doctrines, images, or any cultural form, we can describe the experience of vision in our lives in two ways.

First, vision is an experience of *beckoning*. It is the sense that something is waving to us from a distance, gesturing to attract our attention, calling to us to redirect the course of our lives. It calls us out of ourselves and connects us with something beyond ourselves. It arouses an interest that goes beyond curiosity to compulsion. It lures us and pulls us in. It is utterly beautiful to us, and in that beauty, we see both goodness and truth. In a sense, pursuing the lure of God is not rational, but it is reasonable. It is a fulfillment of our most profound desire.

Second, vision is an experience of *reckoning*. It is the revelation of the point, significance, or import of our existence on history (even if *my* history seems but a minor speck in world history). Vision is an experience of appraisal, a summation of our lives as they contribute to God's purpose. It is not a tool to judge or condemn, but rather to assess our worthiness of the beauty of God. Reckoning implies mercy. For in the end, we never deserve the vision, but the vision takes us in. We do not possess it. It takes possession of us.

Classical theologians might say that the *pilgrim band* has an "eschatological" focus. That is, they are interested in the destiny of the soul and humankind. They are not interested in the survival of the church and gaining universal religious agreement. As spiritual travelers, the *pilgrim band* journeys to a holy destination. This clear spiritual destination was objectified in ancient times as Jerusalem (or other shrines and places that were stepping stones, as it were, to get to Jerusalem). Yet it is clear from even the most ancient accounts that the outer or historical destination was only a sign of an *inner* destination beyond history. The goal of the *pilgrim band* is to be fully with God ... to experience unity with the divine ... to lose oneself in the greater mystery of Christ. This is the "New Jerusalem" that merges heaven and earth, where God is fully with the people, and tears shall be no more.[7]

Yet there is also something apocalyptic about the expectation of a *pilgrim band*. They may be journeying to a holy destination, but they also sense that the Holy is journeying toward them. Metaphorically, they not only believe that the finite can be reunited with the infinite but that the infinite can transform the finite. Heaven invades earth. The *pilgrim band* believes that incarnation is not just something of the past or the future, but of the present.

Our spiritual journeys started out by exploring what it meant to be human, but they soon transition into a search for what it means to become gods. We start with humanity, but we strain toward divinity. For some, this means the power to control, but for others it means the power to create. For some, this is an invitation to willfulness, but for others this means acceptance of radical responsibility. For some, the ultimate fulfillment of humanity is the demise of community. For others, the ultimate fulfillment of humanity is the realization of divinity. It is not the dissolution of culture, but the infusion of culture with Spirit.

In earliest Christian thought, the *divinization* of a human being was tied to incarnational theology. God is fully revealed in Christ so that, through participation in the experience of Christ, the soul might be reunited with God. "God-among-Us" elevates the spiritual nature of humanity. "Apotheosis" is the transforming effect of Spirit in human nature. Not surprisingly, it is impossible to describe this in words or imagine it in pictures because all our words and pictures are shaped by the cultures in which we live. The best way to personalize this abstract idea is to express it in music. It is what I mean by the *heartsong*, the culmination of that inward journey from the *heartbeat* of authentic self, through a *heartburst* for others.

The quest for meaning and purpose is carried out within history, but it is only fulfilled beyond history. There are no symbols to adequately express meaning and purpose that are not limited by history. Words are not enough. We may speak positively of "redemption," "reunion," "acceptance," "poverty,"

7. Rev 21.

"simplicity," or "salvation." Or we may choose a *via negativa* and speak of "selflessness," "non-desire," "non-self," or "renunciation." All these words try to express meaning and purpose that is beyond words. It is like artists trying to teach art, or lovers trying to define love. So, if it cannot be contained in words, perhaps it can be expressed in music. Hence, I use the term "heart-song" to best articulate the ultimate feeling of purposefulness.

Song has three elements: *rhythm*, *lyrics*, and *melody*. Altogether this composes a "song" that is unique to each person. It stays in the back of your mind. It plays in every activity and improvises in all creativity. It connects the rhythm (heartbeat) of living, with the lyric (passion) for life, to the melody (harmony) of the universe. It is always the same, but it is always adapting to every mood and every circumstance.

- It is motivational. It is like a marching song or rallying cry. Its rhythms stir your emotions. It may move you to tears of joy or sorrow. It moves you to initiate and sustain action. It encourages you to make moral choices and take personal risks.

- It is metaphorical. It raises to consciousness provocative images. It invokes imagination. The lyrics may describe any form. Ancient pilgrims imagined a "Promised Land" or a "New Jerusalem." Modern pilgrims might describe a vision of utopia. Metaphors help communicate hope but cannot contain reality.

- It is contemplative. It invokes awe. It strikes you dumb. It fills a pregnant silence. It causes you to reflect, critique, revise, and renew. It encourages you to doubt, confess, and affirm. It makes you think both strategically and entrepreneurially.

- It is harmonious. It is satisfying but makes you want more. It is fulfilling but encourages you to grow. It includes other people similar and dissimilar to you. It blends its unique beauty with the infinite beauty that is God. It is open to, and infused by, the Spirit.

When the spiritual traveler looks back on the journey from immanence to incarnation and to transcendence, there is often an awareness of music. The journey begins with a noise (jarring or joyous). It transitions into a ballad (saga or story). It ends in a chorus (paean or refrain). The alignment of *heartbeat*, *heartburst*, and *heartsong* is difficult to maintain in the chaos of life. And the *pilgrim band* can help the spiritual traveler maintain his or her course. But it is the vital forces of Spirit that moves you ever onward.

On the *Pilgrim Band*

RELIGION IS AN EXPRESSION of Spirit but cannot control Spirit. Similarly, the church is an instance of the Christian movement but cannot contain the Christian movement within its structures. Even as religion becomes more radical and rigid, and church institutions become more defensive and decline, Spirit spills over the rim and saturates culture. It bursts cultural forms and social norms, shapes new forms and norms, so that no religious institution or dogma endures forever unchanged.

The *pilgrim band* is the instrument of *regenerative* religion. It can be regenerative for any religious movement in the sense that it uncovers the origins of hope implicit in every religion. It is neither "traditional" nor "radical." Regenerative *Christianity* uncovers the origins of hope through incarnational experience. It is neither "progressive" nor "reactionary." It is profoundly relational. Meaning and purpose are restored through relationships of trust that are simultaneously transparent to the divine.

Mentoring. It seems so simple. Like many conversations, it just seems to happen. One moment you are sitting at a table or standing in a line, minding your own business, and the next minute you fall into a conversation. The primary reason the conversation goes deeper is that, in the beginning, it is anonymous. People are always more candid when they remain nameless. They can share intimate details . . . and then walk away. The conversation continues naturally, at least in the beginning. Then it becomes progressively more personal and profound.

Many modern people are desperate to find meaning and purpose in life, and when the opportunity to explore presents itself in a safe, non-judgmental situation they grasp it. They couldn't pursue it through public or even advanced education. Psychotherapy mainly solved problems rooted in the past but had little to say about destiny. Religion offered tradition, ritual, and dogma about the transcendent God(s), but only the clergy seemed to be "called" and most of them seem confused about it. The situation has only been exacerbated in the wireless world. It's just not possible to carry on deep conversation through instant messaging. It is even difficult today to carry on a deep conversation with someone you trust!

It seems so simple, and yet it has taken me over seventy thousand words to explain what happens. When you look back on the initial encounter, and reflect on the subsequent conversation, you realize that more was going on than you thought at the time. Mentors bring that intuition to consciousness.

- The encounter was not so accidental as we thought. It occurred in a context shaped by culture, and culture is an expression of Spirit. The conversation was only possible when a hundred "coincidences" came together.
- Listening reveals the hidden anxieties, needs, and hopes of another human being and stirs an empathy for another's spiritual quest. And we connect these with our own experiences of incarnation.
- Relationships uncover the roadblocks, sidetracks, and deadweights that hinder our way. Trust helps to free us from self-destructive habits to experience the immanence of God.
- Companionship encourages us to continue our search for meaning and purpose in good times and bad times, and we equip each other to see, know, and serve.

Once the mentoring process has been brought to consciousness, then we begin to look for it, anticipate it, recognize it, and seize upon the opportunity to help another find meaning and purpose . . . and realize that in doing so we are helping ourselves as well.

The *pilgrim band* also seems very simple. Isn't it just a small group of intimate friends, or an intentional internet network, a team, a task group, a service club, a study cohort? Do we not just naturally socialize and make friends? When the job is done or we move to another location, do we not just say goodbye and hello all over again? No, if anything our yearning for trusted relationships, deeper meaning, and purposefulness grows more urgent.

The recent pandemic has created a controversy over working in the office versus working at home, and businesses have surveyed the attitudes of generations. Everyone expected to see a trend away from physical presence to digital presence. The trend increased from Boomers to Busters through Millennials, but among Gen Z there was a surprising reaction. Gen Z wants to be *both* physical and digital. They want relationships to be "phygital."[1] Yet while they might return to the office, their expectation is for a new kind of office: more friendly, more casual, more fun, and more time for interpersonal relationships to deepen. The thing they missed most was the opportunity for mentoring.

When mutual mentoring emerges, a group is more than a group. It becomes so precious that we preserve the relationships, and continue the conversations, long after the group is done or the task is completed. Suddenly it spans space and time. It is pursued in every media and renewed in every reunion. We plan vacations together, and travel together, and (in the broadest and most profound sense of the word) pray together. The group goes "phygital." It becomes a *pilgrim band*.

The *pilgrim band* is a phenomenon. It is not a random occurrence. Neither is it an organization. It is not tied to any specific place like a church. It is not tied to any specific time like Sunday morning. It never has a membership. Its network is not limited to any specific media. It is sustainable in person or remotely because the relationships of the *pilgrim band* do not depend on being *there* but rather *being* there.

The *pilgrim band* is a timely confluence of lives. The best metaphor to understand the phenomenon is liquid rather than solid. The *pilgrim band* is like the merging and diverging of rivers (or many rivulets). The streaming of one life converges with another and for a time continues as one movement. Sooner or later, lives diverge again like water is diverted in different directions. It would be easy to say that confluence or divergence is simply determined by the contours of culture. This is often how it seems at the time. It is usually in retrospect that we realize the timeliness of these convergences and divergences in our relationships, although, the older we get and the more intuitive we become to discern meaning in coincidences, the more we discern hidden purpose behind comings and goings and life in between.

Meaning is shaped by form, content, and import or significance. For example, the meaning of my writing is shaped by the letters and words and grammatical requirements of prose, combined with the ideas that the words try to convey, but also by the purpose or point that I am trying to make. The meaning of religion is shaped by the structures and symbols of

---

1. Horwitz, "What Is Phygital?"

culture, combined with the thoughts and intentions of believers, but also by the significance or ultimate concern of faith. Yet the orderliness of this is deceiving. It might seem that, in the quest for meaning and purpose in life, we start by discovering meaning and eventually discern purpose. This is certainly the logic of the modern world.

The logic of the pre- and postmodern world, however, is the opposite. Perhaps the German language is more attuned to such logic because one doesn't know the verb or the action until one gets to the end of the sentence. We start with purpose and then work out the meaning. First there is the impact, import, significance of the divine. Then we try to form our ideas to interpret it. And finally, we express our ideas in words, institutions, ceremonies, and other cultural forms. By the time the purpose of life is filtered through our ideas and imaginations, and then through our words and structures, the mystery is fading, the *point* is obscured, and the *purpose* of life has been forgotten in the struggle to find meaning.

The *pilgrim band* is first and foremost about purpose. You are *compelled* to start a journey without a clear idea of the road to get there, or what you think or feel on the way, or how the mystery will be resolved at the end. The journey of one pilgrim converges and diverges with that of other pilgrims precisely because the journey is best undertaken through trusted relationships. We find meaning and purpose only by *helping each other*. The wisdom of those ahead of us is passed on to us, and our wisdom passed on to others.

The timely confluence of our lives is not just shaped by the contours of culture. Water may flow following the contours of the land, converging and diverging in many streams, but ultimately it reaches the ocean. The flow of water may seem arbitrary, yet it is always going downhill. It may be blocked. It may seem to stop and stagnate. But eventually blocks are eroded and pools are drained, and water flows again. A greater purposefulness motivates and guides the process. Spirit is the motivation and goal of the journey, but it is also the Power of Being hidden but suspected, tantalizing but unexplainable, behind every convergence and divergence in our relationships.

Perhaps this is why Christianity was originally described by the paradigmatic *pilgrim band* of apostles as "the Way." St. Paul is said to have defended Christianity as a sect called "the Way" before the Roman governor Felix, and Felix himself is said to have some experience with "the

Way."[2] The story of Phillip baptizing the Ethiopian diplomat is perhaps significant because it occurs early in the apostolic diaspora on the way to Gaza. "The Way" is tied to the immanent experience of God that cannot be contained in words or forms. It may be tied to Jesus' description of himself as "the way, the truth, and the life."[3]

The significance of incarnation was passed on through relationships with the apostles, and their disciples, and their disciples, and on and on. The Gospels described a true confluence of lives converging and diverging around this central experience of incarnation. People came and went. Some stayed longer than others. They came for healing, justice, acceptance, guidance, wisdom, transformation, hope, and more. Some stayed longer than others all the way to the cross. Some went in different directions, converging and diverging with other pilgrims.

Yet these convergences and divergences are not merely matters of chance. These relationships are influenced by Spirit. This is the movement that was later institutionalized using the concept of "apostolic succession." This "succession" is not an office or status passed down through the generations, but a great chain of spiritual movement that links pilgrims over time and space. We do not really know who has influenced our quest for meaning and purpose . . . and we do not really know who we influence in the same quest. Yet it is a timely confluence of lives.

The *pilgrim band* is the *movement* of religion, not a religious movement. It is a verb, not a noun. We tend to picture the *pilgrim band* as if it were some solid form of a small group or a structure of church, taking up space, stable, resident in culture. We think we can take a picture of it. *There it is here! There it is over there!* The truth is that if you attempted to take a picture of it all you would see is a blur. If you see it here or there, it is the same yet not the same. It has a cinematographic nature.

Time, not space, is the milieu of the *pilgrim band*. Therefore, the *pilgrim band* resists any form of idolatry. No specific form, structure, or space is sacred. What defines the *pilgrim band* is the trek itself and the evolving relationships of mutual mentoring on the journey. In the Middle Ages pilgrims received badges that certified the completion of a journey to, say, Santiago de Compostela. Yet the badge was but a symbol, a reminder, of the events and experiences that took place on the journey. The

---

2. Acts 22:4, 14.
3. John 14:6 NRSV.

companionship that shared such significance could never be contained, explained, or transferred.

Moreover, timeliness, not timetables, marks the progress of the *pilgrim band*. A trip may be measured in miles, but a *trek* is remembered through events. It is an unusual journey because it is not pursued chronologically but ecstatically. That is, pilgrimage is described or defined by experiences of the immanence of God. This is why, in the original Greek of the New Testament, time is described as "Kairos" rather than "Chronos." Pilgrims experience God "at the right time," in moments that are rich in content and significance.

> Time is an empty form only for abstract objective reflection, a form that can receive any kind of content; but to [those] who [are] conscious of an ongoing creative form of life it is laden with tensions, with possibilities and impossibilities, it is qualitative and full of significance.[4]

A pilgrimage is not a sequence of occurrences which, from the human perspective, are either fortunate or unfortunate. It is a lifestyle in which even minor occurrences can have spiritual significance. Spirit enables the human soul to transcend the passage of time. It is the ground for all hope.[5]

It helps to place the *pilgrim band* in the broader context of history and culture. The personalization of religion and the emergence of more sophisticated "bands" of mutual mentoring always emerge at a time of growing cultural diversity, technological innovation, and declining religious authority. These are times when culture becomes open to new meaning and people search for absolutes.

> The number of actively religious people can be greater in so-called "irreligious" than a religious period. But an age that is turned toward, and open to, the unconditional is one in which the consciousness of the presence of the unconditional permeates and guides all cultural functions and forms.[6]

In such a situation, all history becomes sacred history. Pilgrim bands travel in a "theonomous" reality, not in the sense of doctrinal obedience but in the sense of openness to Spirit. It is not a "heteronomous" reality in

---

4. Tillich, "Kairos," 33.

5. Tillich, "History and the Quest for the Kingdom of God," in *Systematic Theology* 3:300–303.

6. Tillich, "Kairos," 43.

which authorities dictate thought and behavior. Nor is it an "autonomous" reality in which individual egos think and behave however they choose. It is a "theonomous" reality in which power, justice, and love are held together. The fellowship of the *pilgrim band* parallels the greater consciousness of culture in embracing the paradox of Spirit. For, on the one hand, they proclaim that "the Realm of God is at hand." Yet, on the other hand, they acknowledge that "the Realm of God has yet to be fulfilled." It is recognized and yet unknown. Ambiguity persists. The journey (or better to say, the "trek") continues.

In practice, the *pilgrim band* is the enterprise of mutual mentoring. If life is constantly changing—and if the immanence of God can only be discerned intuitively and experienced ecstatically—then mutual mentoring is the best way for an individual to find meaning and purpose. It is not through scientific breakthroughs, economic prosperity, or political negotiation that we have a reason to hope. It is through trusted, deep, ongoing relationships that we help each other find meaning and purpose . . . and discover a good reason to resist despair and sustain hope.

Pilgrim bands thrive at the fringes of the modern institutional church in a manner like the monastic communities diverging from established Christendom. Churches will continue to be agents of social assimilation, but the *pilgrim band* is becoming the chief agent of social transformation. Their fellowship will be more intimate. Their individual and shared spiritual practices will be more intense. Their social service will be more urgent. Their advocacy for justice will be more passionate. *Pilgrim bands* require spiritual travelers to raise the stakes for spiritual living. The risk is not just an increase to percentage giving or unbalanced living, but the risk of martyrdom itself.

The "rules" of pilgrimage have changed and diversified over the centuries. In medieval times, a would-be pilgrim would be blessed by the bishop and confess their sins. He or she would don the "uniform" of a single coarse garment and a broad-brimmed hat, carrying a small purse and a multi-purpose staff that could serve as a tent pole or a weapon to defend against animals. They might carry a prayer book or portable altar. They would stop at monasteries or hospices along the way to rest, worship, and reflect . . . but did not tarry long.

Today, a would-be pilgrim might seek the blessing of their mentor, acknowledge their limitations, and imagine their hopes. They would simplify their lives. They might tear up their credit cards and resolve to be debt-free.

They might shed trendy clothes and wear all-weather coats and hiking boots. They might get a tattoo and carry a cell phone. They might stop at a local church, but more likely would seek out an outreach ministry or faith-based non-profit to rest, worship, and reflect . . . but would not tarry long.

The pilgrim will pass through all manner of experiences, adapt to many contexts, play many social roles, speak various languages, and even adopt many different lifestyles. In a sense, pilgrims seek instability over stability, because they are more likely to experience incarnation amid change. In ancient times, the pilgrim might be a scholar, diplomat, missionary, soldier, preacher, evangelist, hermit, abbot, or martyr. Today, the pilgrim might be an engineer, CEO, entrepreneur, janitor, soldier, politician, lawyer, social worker, priest, or refugee. The pilgrim will endure foul weather and fair, sickness and health, injuries and rescues, starvation and surplus, injustice and justice, persecution and rescue without losing their essential self. The giving and receiving of mentoring continue through it all. The thirst for God is the common thread aligning *heartbeat*, *heartburst*, and *heartsong*.

The goal of the trek is tied to the original motivation for the trek. Pilgrims long to experience the fullness of beauty, goodness, and truth; achieve their potential and experience new life; find healing and receive vindication; know authentic love in all its forms; and reunite their finite soul with infinite Spirit. But to do this, pilgrims must always be cognizant of the existential anxieties that prompted their journey in the first place.

I think this is why pilgrims from earliest times have customized special prayers that they can repeat to themselves or recite with their companions. They change and evolve over time. This is mine. You can find it on my websites where I have created a kind of digital "waystation" for pilgrims to rest, reflect, and renew.[7]

---

7. www.ThrivingChurch.com or www.SpiritualLeadershipWaystation.com

*God grant me the courage to overcome the anxieties of emptiness
 and meaninglessness,*
And the depression that lies beneath.
Let me experience your real presence as Teacher and Guide,
And give me the courage to participate.

God grant me the courage to overcome the anxieties of fate and death,
And the dread that lies beyond.
Let me experience your real presence as Promise Keeper and New Being.
And give me the courage to separate.

God grant me the courage to overcome the anxieties of guilt and shame,
And the anger that lies within.
Let me experience your real presence as Healer and Vindicator.
And give me the courage to accept acceptance.

God grant me the courage to overcome displacement and estrangement,
And the sense of abandonment that lies behind.
Let me experience your real presence as Rescuer and Gatherer.
And give me the courage to trust and be trusted.[8]

---

8. Bandy, "Prayer for Courage."

Bibliography

Anonymous. *The Way of a Pilgrim and The Pilgrim Continues on His Way*. Translated by Nina A. Toumanova. Mineola, NY: 2008.
Aries, Philippe, and Georges Duby. *A History of Private Life*. 5 vols. Cambridge: Harvard University Press, 1988.
Bandy, Thomas G. *Christian Mentoring*. Guelph, ON: BandyBooks, 2011. Independently published.
———. *Kicking Habits*. Toronto: United Church Publishing House, 1997.
———. *Mission Mover: Beyond Education for Church Leadership*. Nashville: Abingdon, 2004.
———. *Moving Off the Map*. Nashville: Abingdon, 1998.
———. "A Prayer for Courage." https://www.thrivingchurch.com/blog.
———. *Road Runner*. Nashville: Abingdon, 2002.
———. *Spirited Leadership: Empowering People to Do What Matters*. St. Louis: Chalice Press, 2007.
———. *Spiritual Leadership: Why Leaders Lead and Who Seekers Follow*. Nashville: Abingdon, 2016.
———. *Strategic Thinking*. Nashville: Abingdon, 2017.
———. *Talisman: Global Positioning for the Soul*. 1st ed. St. Louis: Chalice, 2006.
———. *Talisman: Global Positioning for the Soul*. 2nd ed. Eugene, OR: Wipf & Stock, 2017.
———. "Tillich and the Rise of Personal Religions." In *Why Tillich? Why Now?*, edited by Thomas G. Bandy, 145–62. Macon, GA: Mercer University Press, 2021.
———. *Why Should I Believe You?* Nashville: Abingdon, 2006.
Bandy, Thomas G., and Dwayne O. Ratzlaff. *Christian OptiMystics: Running the Rapids of the Spirit*. St. Louis: Chalice, 2006.
Bergson, Henri. *Creative Evolution*. Translated by Arthur Mitchell. London: Macmillan, 1911.
———. *An Introduction to Metaphysics,*. Translated by T. E. Hulme. New York: Putnam, 1912.
Cox, Harvey. *Fire from Heaven: The Rise of Pentecostal Spirituality and the Reshaping of Religion in the 21st Century*. Reading, MA: Addison-Wesley, 1995.
———. *The Secular City: Secularization and Urbanization in Theological Perspective*. Princeton: Princeton University Press, 2013.

Dante Alighieri. *The Divine Comedy.* 1 vol. Translated by Allen Mandelbaum. New York: Everyman, 1995.

Experian. *Mosaic USA E-Handbook.* Schaumberg, IL: 2023.

Hazelton, Roger. "The Devotional Life." In *A Companion to the Study of St. Augustine*, edited by Roy W. Battenhouse, 398–414. New York: Oxford University Press, 1969.

Horwitz, Lauren. "What Is Phygital?" *TechTarget*, June 2023. https://www.techtarget.com/searchcustomerexperience/definition/phygital#:~:text=Phygital.

Jung, Carl. *Memories, Dreams, Reflections.* New York: Vintage Random House, 1989.

LeClercq, Jean. *The Love of Learning and the Desire for God: A Study of Monastic Culture.* New York: Fordham University Press, 1974.

Meagher, John C. *The Truing of Christianity.* New York: Doubleday, 1990.

Schuster, John P. *Answering Your Call.* San Francisco: Berrett-Koehler, 2003.

Staniforth, Maxwell. *Marcus Aurelius Meditations.* Harmondsworth, GB: Penguin, 1964.

Strauss, William, and Neil Howe. *The Fourth Turning: An American Prophecy.* New York: Crown, 1997.

———. *Generations: History of America's Future.* New York: HarperCollins, 1991.

Sumption, Jonathan. *Pilgrimage: An Image of Medieval Religion.* Totowa, NJ: Rowman & Littlefield, 1975.

Tickle, Phyllis. *The Great Emergence: How Christianity Is Changing and Why.* Ada, MI: Baker, 2012.

Tillich, Paul. *The Courage to Be.* New Haven: Yale University Press, 2014.

———. "Kairos." In *The Protestant Era*, 32–51. Chicago: University of Chicago, 1966.

———. *Love, Power and Justice.* London: Oxford University Press, 1954.

———. *On the Boundary: An Autobiographical Sketch.* New York: Charles Scribner's Sons, 1966.

———. *The Religious Situation.* Translated by H. Richard Niebuhr. New York: Meridian, 1969.

———. *The Shaking of the Foundations.* New York: Pelican, 1962.

———. "The Significance of the History of Religions." In *The Future of Religions*, 80–94. New York: Harper and Row, 1966.

———. *Systematic Theology.* Three Volumes in One. Chicago: University of Chicago Press, 1971.

———. *Theology of Culture.* New York: Oxford University Press, 1959.

Torode, Sam. *The Meditations: An Emperor's Guide to Mastery.* Based on the 1862 translation by George Long. Ancient Renewal, 2017. Independently published.

Unamuno, Miguel de. *The Tragic Sense of Life.* Translated by J. E. Crawford Futch. New York: Dover, 1954.

Underhill, Evelyn. *Concerning the Inner Life with The House of the Soul.* London: Methuen & Co., 1956.

Wikipedia. "Postmodernity." https://en.wikipedia.org/wiki/Postmodernity.

www.ingramcontent.com/pod-product-compliance
Lightning Source LLC
Chambersburg PA
CBHW071437150426
43191CB00008B/1161